VAMPIRES TODAY

VAMPIRES TODAY

The Truth about
Modern Vampirism

JOSEPH LAYCOCK

PRAEGER

**Westport, Connecticut
London**

Library of Congress Cataloging-in-Publication Data

Laycock, Joseph, 1980–
    Vampires today : the truth about modern vampirism / Joseph Laycock.
        p. cm.
    Includes bibliographical references and index.
    ISBN 978–0–313–36472–3 (alk. paper)
1. Vampires—United States. I. Title.
BF1556.L39   2009
398'.45—dc22   2008051652

British Library Cataloguing in Publication Data is available.

Library of Congress Catalog Card Number: 2008051652
ISBN: 978–0–313–36472–3

First published in 2009

Praeger Publishers, 88 Post Road West, Westport, CT 06881
An imprint of Greenwood Publishing Group, Inc.
www.praeger.com

Printed in the United States of America

The paper used in this book complies with the
Permanent Paper Standard issued by the National
Information Standards Organization (Z39.48-1984).

10 9 8 7 6 5 4 3 2 1

Contents

Preface

One of the earliest books about vampires is *Dissertatio de Vampiris Serviensibus,* written in 1733 by John Heinrich Zopft. Zopft was a theological student in Leipzig, and his book was a serious academic dissertation on a vampire panic then occurring in Belgrade, Serbia.[1] Since Zopft, an ocean of ink has been spent writing about vampires, and it has become increasingly harder to discern books about actual vampires from works of fiction. There are novels and role-playing games in which vampires masquerade as humans and there are true-crime books in which humans act as vampires. When I tell colleagues that I "study vampires," they assume I am one of numerous scholars in the fields of English, folklore, and psychology analyzing the cultural implications of vampire fiction. When I say that I study "real vampires," this may imply that I am one of several specialists working to interpret historical accounts of vampires using modern forensics and medical knowledge. Among all of these assumptions, it is important to explain exactly what sort of book this is and why it was written. First, this book is not primarily concerned with the vampires of fiction and folklore. Compilations of vampire novels and movies have been written before and written well. There are also numerous other books that catalog the myriad vampire-like entities that appear in the folklore of almost every culture. Nor is this book primarily concerned with analyzing demented criminals who drink blood. When a criminal does something so heinous that the media labels him "a vampire," it is rare that the perpetrator actually embraces this label.

This book is about "real vampires" and the communities they have formed. Many people have a dim awareness that somewhere in the world there are people who consider themselves vampires. Beginning in the 1990s, several nonfiction books and documentaries appeared that featured interviews with real vampires. In 2008, the success of HBO's series *True Blood* and the film *Twilight,* both based on popular vampire novels, caused an intense media focus on this community. The History Channel show *Monsterquest* aired an episode entitled "Vampires in America," in which they exposed self-identified vampires to a gamut of scientific tests. Vampires also consented to appearances on *The Tyra Banks Show* and even *Sean Hannity's America.* The animated series *South Park* aired an episode called "The Ungroundable" in which children, under a spell of consumerism created by *Twilight* and the store Hot Topic, had begun to dress as the undead and call themselves vampires. Despite increased media attention, the vampire community remains poorly understood. Television interviews, often accompanied by ominous music, work to portray self-identified vampires as completely other. The reality is that vampires are all around us and that their subculture is a product of our mainstream culture. If we can look past the sensationalism, vampires pose compelling questions about how we define ourselves and the world around us in the twenty-first century. These are issues that cannot be explored without a deeper understanding of what real vampires are.

What exactly is a "real vampire"? A real vampire is first and foremost a self-designated label. This separates real vampires from the creatures of myth and folklore as well as from various criminals who have been labeled as vampires by the media. Monsters receive the vampire label from others; real vampires adopt it as an identity. Other than being self-designated, there is currently no universal definition of a "real vampire." Some drink blood to sustain their health and some do not. Some describe a sensitivity to sunlight while others enjoy the beach. Many compare vampirism to a medical condition with tangible health needs while others dissent. For some, vampirism is a religion or a spiritual path while others ascribe no religious meaning to it. It is amazing that a community has formed at all considering the many different ideas of what a vampire is.

The heterogeneous nature of vampire identity has led some outsiders to ignore the existence of the vampire community and instead study real vampires strictly on a case-by-case basis. This approach typically draws on psychoanalysis and often posits some event or pathology that caused the individual to identity as a vampire. An opposite approach has ignored the experience of individual vampires entirely and instead approached this community as a monolithic and sinister group. Dawn Perlmutter, director of the Institute for the Research of Organized and Ritual Violence has portrayed the vampire community as a network of cults that uses the Internet to "recruit lonely, alienated kids."[2] Both of these frameworks are inadequate: The former ignores wider cultural phenomena in the production of identity, while the later fails to consider the agency of individual vampires. Sociologist Nancy Ammerman describes identities as emerging, "at the everyday intersections of autobiographical and public narratives. We tell stories about ourselves (both literally and through our behavior) that signal both our uniqueness and our membership, that exhibit the consistent themes that characterize us and the unfolding improvisation of the given situation."[3] Vampires do not form their ideas about vampirism in a vacuum, nor are they ideological automatons that follow the doctrine of a particular vampire culture or sect. To understand modern vampires, it is necessary to consider both the experience of the individual vampire and the context of the larger vampire community.

Vampires arrive at their identities through two collective entities that are here termed "the vampire milieu" and "the vampire community." The vampire milieu is the sum total of ideas about vampires, real or fictional, that can be found throughout public discourse. The vampire community is an identity group consisting of the sum total of vampire institutions and social networks. For individual vampires, the vampire milieu determines what enters their concept of vampirism, while the vampire community informs how these elements are interpreted. The vampire milieu will be mapped out in detail in Chapter 3. It includes the vampire of folklore as well as over two centuries of literary and film vampires. But it also draws much of its substance from occult and Neopagan traditions, parapsychology, and complementary therapies such as qigong and reiki. Individual vampires as well as vampire groups may draw on any of this raw material to construct their own bricolage of vampirism. The vampire community, the subject of Chapter 5, does include formal vampire groups and even vampire religions. These institutions, however, are only a small portion of the community. More important are the networks by which various groups and individual vampires communicate ideas. These networks also provide the criteria by which ideas from the vampire milieu are either accepted or pushed to the periphery.

Many of the books currently available about real vampires rely almost entirely on interviews. Interviews can give insight into the experience of an individual vampire, but not the greater context of the community at large. Understanding the community as a whole requires observation. The most ambitious work of participant observation with vampires is Katherine Ramsland's *Piercing the Darkness: Undercover With Vampires in America Today*. To research this book, Ramsland donned prosthetic fangs and infiltrated the New York vampire scene as her alter-ego "Malefica." She describes having to decide whether to drink blood, offer her own blood, or use drugs in order find what she is looking for.[4] While this made for exciting reading, I am neither trained as a journalist nor a master of disguise. My training is in religious studies, and I negotiated entry into this community in the same way that I have contacted Muslim, Hindu, Buddhist, and Pagan groups in America: I tell them that I am a researcher and politely inquire if they are willing to speak to me. Typically some groups are eager to speak to me, others are more cautious, and a few tell me that they are not interested. It happened that the Atlanta Vampire Alliance (AVA) was willing to work with me.

For over a year I gathered ethnographic data with the AVA. I ate with them, I went to their business meetings, I attempted to manipulate subtle energy with them, I drove with them around Cleveland looking for a good Irish pub. I also conducted interviews and discussed the ways their community has been represented by academics and the media. I found that many of the problems described by vampires were the same issues I encountered while working with Atlanta's Muslim community—"The media portrays us as violent criminals" and "people judge us by the way we dress" were mutual complaints. The AVA introduced me to other vampires throughout the country and throughout the world. As word spread about my research, more vampires were willing to tell me their story.

Vampires are not just lurking in goth clubs in New York City; they are all around us. I have met vampires in the fields of social work, medicine, information technology, and law enforcement. Vampires cannot be studied as simply other than and isolated from society at large. To study real vampires is to study the state of the modern world. One of my goals in writing this book is to stimulate and inform a discussion of how groups like vampires may be understood by outsiders and by scholarship. Despite the public's fascination with vampires, the same two questions are repeated over and over: Are these people crazy and are they dangerous? (The answer to both these questions, for all intents and purposes, is a simple "no.") If we set these questions aside, the real vampire community challenges us with serious questions about identity, religion, and the search for meaning.

Sociologist Anthony Giddens has argued that "high modernity," a state in which social traditions have become disembedded and replaced with radical doubt, fosters and shapes emerging mechanisms of self-identity.[5] In premodern societies, most aspects of a person's daily life were determined by the culture in which the individual was born. Today, the individual is faced with an overabundance of options. Since the Enlightenment, we no longer have faith in experts who traditionally worked to restrain and limit these choices.[6] To adopt a narrative of identity prescribed to us by political leaders, family, or clergy may seem puerile or even irresponsible within a modern, Western culture. All of this produces a state of anxiety over essential questions such as "Who am I?" and "What should I do?" This anxiety compels us to create our own narrative of self in order to make sense of our world.[7]

The theory espoused in this book is that the vampire identity, as it appears at the dawn of the twenty-first century, is a particularly radical emerging mechanism of self-identity as described by Gibbons. The vampire identity is the product of a modern world in which even one's status as an ordinary member of the human species is subject to doubt.[8] By linking vampires to modernity, I do not mean to cast vampires as other or as "a horror of the modern world." Instead, I hope to emphasize that both vampires and non-vampires share the same modern anxiety and the same search for self. The vampire community and their quest for meaning reflects our quest for meaning. In short, by studying vampires, we study ourselves.

Acknowledgments

This book marks the end of three years working as an inner-city high school teacher by day and an independent scholar by night. Independent scholarship is a thankless task but a necessary one. Were it not for independent scholars there would be only dependent scholars whose research is beholden to the institutions that patronize them. Only those with nothing to lose are free to study whatever they want. Of course, no one is truly independent and this book could not have been produced without the aid of colleagues who smuggled resources to me from Emory University and Agnes Scott College. I extend a very special thanks to everyone who helped in this capacity, especially Kati Newburg.

I must also thank the vampires and vampirologists who provided materials and interviews without which this book would not have been possible: Merticus, Zero, Maloryn, Soulsplat, Eclecta, Kiera, Michelle Belanger, Father Sebastiaan, SphynxcatVP, Stephen O'Mallie, Daemonox, Lord Alistair, Nicholas, Vyrdolak, Lady CG, Martin Riccardo, Stephen Held, J. Gordon Melton, and others.

CHAPTER 1

What Is a Vampire? or, The Varieties of Vampiric Experience

Probably a crab would be filled with a sense of personal outrage if it could hear us class it without ado or apology as a crustacean, and thus dispose of it. "I am no such thing," it would say; "I am MYSELF, MYSELF alone."
          —*William James,* The Varieties of Religious Experience.

Jan L. Perkowski, in his treatise on Slavic vampirism, writes that the vampire's origins "are known to no one."[1] While belief in vampires can be traced to Eastern Europe, he suggests that the Slavs may have received the idea from the Middle East. Perkowski points to historical and philological evidence linking the vampire to a series of pre-Christian dualist cults that made their way into Europe from Iran. However, almost all cultures have stories of vampire-like creatures. The fear of the dead returning to life may have begun as soon as humans were able to comprehend death. In the summer of 2008, a "vampire grave" dating back to the early Bronze Age was discovered in the Czech Republic. The grave contained a 4,000-year-old skeleton pinned beneath two large stones: one on its head and one on its chest. Archaeologists believe this burial was intended to make sure the corpse remained in the grave.[2]

Vampirologist Eric Nuzum points out that although much of the folklore associated with vampires comes from Greece, Hungary, Turkey, and the Slavic countries, the term "vampire" does not originate in any of these places. The earliest recorded uses of the word appear in French, English, and German literature describing vampire panics in Eastern Europe. According to Nuzum, "The word seems to have just appeared."[3] Nuzum has admirably tracked down the first use of the word in the English language to Charles Foreman's *Observations on the Revolution in 1688,* a text that was written in that year but not published until 1741. Foreman was not describing the living dead but used the word as a metaphor. He referred to a group of unethical traders as "Vampires of the Publick and Riflers of the Kingdom."[4]

The word "vampire" continues to refer to anything that exists parasitically—especially economic systems. In 1867, Karl Marx wrote in *Das Kapital,* "Capital is dead labor, which, vampire-like, lives only by sucking living labor, and lives the more, the more labor it sucks." Bob Marley warned that the "Babylon system is the vampire." When Myanmar was devastated by a cyclone in May 2008, those accused of exploiting the tragedy for financial gain were called "vampire capitalists."[5] Even Liriel McMahon, a former practitioner of vampirism and founder the Vampirism Research Institute, suggested that Bill Gates and other corporate CEOs are "the real vampires."[6]

Manipulative or parasitic people are also referred to as vampires. When I taught secondary school, a colleague warned me not to be manipulated by the students, adding, "If you let them, they will drink every last drop of your blood." Dr. Jeanne Keyes Youngson, the founder of the Count Dracula Fan Club, received a letter from someone who described himself as a vampire by the sole criterion that he was a social parasite. He added, "Allow me to point out that I am no worse than the average man. I believe we are all vampires in one way or another. Show me the person who will really inconvenience himself to help a stranger, and I'll show you a non-vampire."[7] *New York Times* columnist Maureen Dowd resorted to similar vampiric imagery in a column about the 2008 Democratic primary:

> Maybe I've been reading too many stories about the fad of teenage vampire chick lit, worlds filled with parasitic aliens and demi-human creatures, but there's something eerie going on in this race. Hillary grows more and more glowy as Obama grows more and more wan. Is she draining him of his precious bodily fluids? Leeching his magic? Siphoning off his aura? It used to be that he was incandescent and she was merely inveterate. Now she's bristling with life force, and he looks like he wants to run away somewhere for three months by himself and smoke.[8]

It is interesting that in this attack on Senator Clinton, Dowd shows how knowledgeable she is of vampire lore. The suggestion that Clinton is siphoning Barack Obama's aura has its roots in nineteenth-century occult lore (see Chapter 3.) Dowd is also drawing on a tradition of self-help literature that uses the word "vampire" to describe those who drain our psychological and emotional reserves. Books like *Unholy Hungers: Encountering the Psychic Vampire in Ourselves and Others* by Barbara E. Hort, *Emotional Predators Who Want to Suck the Life out of You* by Daniel and Kathleen Rhodes, and *Emotional Vampires: Dealing with People Who Drain You Dry* by Albert J. Berstein use the word in this sense.

A peace protest in Budapest, Hungary, portrays George W. Bush as a vampire. (AP Photo)

Finally, the vampire has achieved cultural manifestations such as Sesame Street's The Count and General Mills' Count Chocula that signify nothing. Vampire fiction writer F. Paul Wilson expresses his disgust at this development, "We have lost the vampire; we've trivialized the vampire. I think it happened about the time 'Count Chocula' found its way to cereal boxes."[9] Wilson is correct: Count Chocula indicates that there is no longer a clear link between the sign of the vampire and a signified concept (assuming there ever was one). These modern cultural icons are imitations of vampires that are themselves imitations, compounded upon each other in what philosopher Jean Baudrillard called "the hyperreal." Count Chocula is an imitation of the actor Bela Lugosi. Lugosi's movies were adapted from Bram Stoker's *Dracula*, which was itself a departure from the vampire of folklore. Thus, we have a breakfast cereal based on an actor based on a book based on a myth.

"Vampire" is a term that comes from nowhere and can refer to almost anything. Accordingly, it is extremely difficult to interpret the statement, "I am a vampire." This has led both self-identified vampires and vampire researchers to devise taxonomies of vampires. The late Stephen Kaplan's Vampire Research Center divided its research between physical vampires, psychic vampires, psychological vampires, "vampiroids" (or vampire-like people), vampire cults, vampire tendencies, and vampire interested people (VIPs). Kaplan also added the category of "unsure and unknown types" to cover anything else.[10] Katherine Ramsland reports attending an online class run by Manhattan's Vampire Access Line with a different taxonomy: Class materials delineated six different "races" of vampires labeled Classicals, Inheriters, Nighttimers, Genetics, PsiVamps, and sexual vampires.[11] These vampire taxonomies are not only ephemeral, they are hopeless. Katherine Ramsland expresses her frustration with trying to circumscribe the modern vampire:

> Vampires today do not have to avoid the sun, kill anyone, or even drink blood. They can have families, get a tan, and drink wine. Anyone who wants to devise a definition of the vampire condition has the authority to do so . . . and plenty of people have stepped forward to do just that.[12]

Rather than attempting to present a systematic list of vampire types, this chapter provides some orientation by which the reader can contextualize the individuals who make up the vampire community. Toward this goal, there are three dimensions of vampire experience that are especially helpful. First, there is the distinction between "real vampires" and "lifestyle vampires." Second, there are different feeding methods. Finally, there are different models of how one arrives at a vampire identity that are here dubbed "awakening" and "initiation." These dimensions are not always mutually exclusive, and there are, no doubt, self-identified vampires who defy them entirely. However, they provide a foundation by which to understand the subsequent chapters.

Lifestyle Vampires versus Real Vampires

Much of a self-identified vampire's world is determined by whether or not the individual sees vampirism as a life-style or as an essential part of their nature.

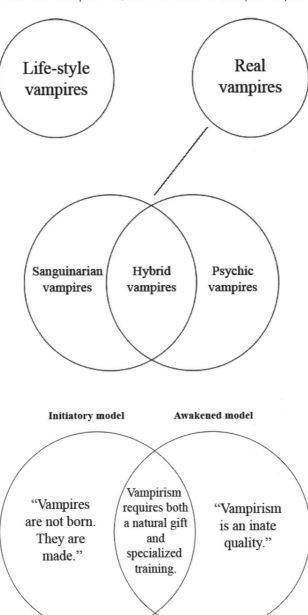

The three axes of vampire identity: lifestyle vs. real, sanguinarian vs. psychic, and initiatory vs. awakened.

Giddens suggests that "life-styles" have become so important to identity in part because modern society presents individuals with an overabundance of choices.[13] Thus, a vampire life-style represents a set of personal choices. "Real vampires" typically do not feel that they made a choice to become a vampire; it is simply part of their nature and cannot be changed.

Lifestyle vampires are fascinated by the vampire of film and literature and seek to emulate this archetype. They usually wear black clothing and may also sport makeup, prosthetic fangs, or special contact lenses. Vampire researcher Rosemary Ellen Guiley describes this appearance as "vampire drag." In 2000, *The New York Times* interviewed Ms. Saige, a self-described lifestyler:

> "I live the lifestyle," she says. "But I'm not a real vampire. Nobody can live forever." Ms. Saige estimates that there are 1,000 vampire lifestylists in New York City and thousands more worldwide. "There's a clan in Europe, one in California and a huge clan in Texas," she says. "We all know each other."[14]

Although lifestylers do not claim to be fundamentally different from non-vampires, many lifestylers still show profound dedication to their chosen identity. Journalists Jeff Guinn and Andy Grieser describe an interview in Indianapolis with a lifestyle vampire who sleeps in a coffin and has had resin fangs permanently installed. In the interview, Christine Darque describes learning to eat again after installing the fangs and having to sleep with a bit, lest they break off accidentally.[15]

For some, the vampire life-style also includes consuming blood. While lifestylers may enjoy consuming blood on a variety of levels, they do not need to feed to maintain their well-being in the way that real vampires do. Ramsland quotes an anonymous vampire on the desire for blood: "For me, being a vampire means fulfilling my needs through the willing sacrifice of others. I am offered blood, sex, and power over otherwise inert lives. . . . The ingestion of blood pleases me, it strengthens me, but it does not literally give me power."[16] Such a vampire would generally be considered a lifestyler by the community at large: They describe sexual and psychological gratification from consuming blood but not an actual health need.

Although many real vampires also participate in the vampire life-style, there is tension between the two types. Some lifestylers believe that there are no "real vampires" and that those who claim to be vampires are mentally ill. Conversely, many real vampires express irritation with lifestyle vampires. They feel that their use of the vampire label muddies the waters and makes it harder for real vampires to present themselves as having an actual condition. Real vampires use a number of pejorative labels for those preoccupied with the vampire life-style including "baby bats" and "kids in capes." Father Sebastiaan Tod van Houten, a leader in the New York vampire scene, said of the lifestyle/real vampire dichotomy:

What bugs me is most people who brought up the whole lifestyler are internet vamps and don't participate off their computers. It seems the people in the internet vamp scene, who labeled this lifestyler scene, think that vamps have to look un-kept, mullet-wearing and sloppy to qualify as a vampire. They scoff at dress codes and dressing up and having fun with it. Damn who doesn't think a decent looking girl wearing fangs, stiletto shoes and a corset is hot? And why would that disqualify her as being able to be a vamp.[17]

At any rate, real vampires are not *defined* by the way that they dress. Instead, they usually define themselves by their need to feed, either on blood or energy, in order to maintain their physical, mental, and spiritual well-being.[18] If a lifestyler claimed to require blood in order to be well, they would cease to be a lifestyler and instead would be characterized as a real vampire. By contrast, many real vampires have no association with gothic culture and some seem to view this association as a source of embarrassment. The Vampire and Energy Worker Research Survey (VEWRS) asked vampires, "Do you consider yourself Goth?" Sixty-four percent of respondents answered no.[19]

Many real vampires also believe that they have paranormal abilities similar to those reported by psychics. Suscitatio Enterprises, a research group created by real vampires, describes these abilities: "Vampires often display signs of empathy, sense emotions, perceive auras of other humans, and are generally psychically aware of the world around them."[20] Guinn and Grieser have interviewed vampires who describe abilities such as night vision, premonitions, and mind reading.[21] *The Psychic Vampire Codex* by Michelle Belanger describes numerous effects that can be accomplished by a vampire using psychic energy, such as healing injuries or increasing one's strength and stamina. Lady CG divides vampire abilities into the categories of charm, energy manipulation, empathy, strength, and night skills.[22] From my time in the vampire community, it seemed that virtually all real vampires accept that events defying any traditional scientific explanation happen on a regular basis. However, they were not uncritical, and more fantastic claims made by other vampires could become the subject of ridicule. One of my contacts in Atlanta described meeting a vampire who claimed that he could run up walls like a lizard. Sadly, when he made this boast at a party he added that he was too drunk to offer a demonstration.

Feeding: Sanguinary, Psychic, and Hybrid Vampires

While all real vampires must feed in order to be well, there are three subcategories, each with a different feeding method. "Sanguinarian" vampires consume small amounts of blood, typically human, while "psychic" vampires have the ability to draw subtle energy out of other people. This energy is often called "psi" and is considered to be the life force of the donor. There are also "hybrid" vampires who use both feeding techniques. Unlike the vampire taxonomies used by Kaplan and the Vampire Access Line, these feeding types have become a sort of *lingua franca* between different groups of vampires. A vampire interviewed for Copley News Service described the same fourfold taxonomy of sanguinarian vampires, psychic vampires, hybrid vampires, and lifestylers.[23]

Sanguinarian Vampires

Sanguinarian vampires are what most people think of when they hear the phrase "real vampire." Sanguinarian vampires (or "sangs") typically ingest small amounts of blood—in some cases only a few drops. Vampires may feed every few days or as infrequently as once a month. However, there are a wide variety of methods for obtaining blood from donors. This is partly because many individuals devise their own methods of consuming blood through private experimentation before they are able to make contacts with other vampires.

Biting to obtain blood is relatively rare as it is both painful and unsanitary. Biting is typically only done when there is a sexual relationship between vampire and donor. A more popular method of obtaining blood is to use lancets intended for diabetics to test their insulin levels.[24] For many vampires, the tiny drop of blood provided by this method is enough to sustain them. Those who need more use a variety of other techniques. Guinn and Grieser interviewed a vampire who used triangular shaped needles purchased from veterinarians.[25] Occasionally, vampires will cut their donor with a knife or a razor although this method can lead to scarring.

Sarah Dorrance is the founder of the Vampire/Donor Alliance community and e-mail list. She has written articles with a number of recommendations for safe feeding, including using mouth wash before biting someone to prevent infection and applying vitamin E lotion to prevent scarring. Dorrance has also suggested that making a "X" shaped cut can yield the most blood with the least scarring. She even addresses more unusual methods of obtaining human blood such as whipping (if the vampire has a sado-masochistic relationship with their donor) or consuming menstrual blood.[26] Lady CG's book *Practical Vampyrism for Real Vampyres* contains several tips for blood drinkers, including a recipe for creating and storing "blood wine."[27]

Question 827 of the VEWRS asked, "What is your preferred method of locating a potential donor? (Check all that apply)." Respondents could select from "bars or clubs," "classifieds," "direct referral," "friend or social group," "house et. al. sanctioned (indicating a vampire group)," "Internet or online forums," "romantic relationship," "sexual relationship," "word of mouth," "other," and "non applicable." The most common response was "friend or social group" with over 120 respondents indicating this as a preferred method. This was followed by "romantic relationship" with over 100 responses and "sexual relationship" with over 80.[28] These data suggest that vampires have many types of relationships with their donors and that the relationship is not necessarily sexual.

In addition to or in lieu of human donors, some sanguinarian vampires consume animal blood. Beef blood is preferred over pig blood, which may contain trichinosis. In the United Kingdom, many vampires describe eating blood pudding (also called black pudding).[29] Some vampires have described purchasing raw meat and licking trace amounts of blood from the bottom of the package.[30] Vampire Michelle Belanger stated that she found this practice repulsive and that most sanguinarians eventually find a better way to feed.[31] Dorrance advocates hunting as a more ethical way of obtaining animal blood.

In addition to animal blood, sanguinarian vampires consume a wide variety of foods and liquids to reduce cravings when human blood is not available. The VEWRS asked sanguinarian vampires to check their blood substitutes of choice. Curiously, chocolate was the most common after animal blood. Juice, herbal tea, and red wine were also popular.[32] Guiley describes a pair of vampires in London who required her to create a drink of ersatz blood out of orange and tomato juice that had been heated in the microwave.[33] At least one vampire has suggested that semen can serve as a substitute for blood because it also contains vital energy.[34]

Within the vampire community—defined as the networks and groups formed by self-identified vampires—it is almost unheard of for a vampire to take blood against the consent of the donor. Sanguinarian vampires often have a consensual relationship with a number of donors, which may even involve a written contract defining the rights of the donor. Many vampires also have their donor's blood tested for diseases. I do not know of a vampire acquiring the HIV virus through consuming blood, but Father Sebastiaan mentioned that several vampires in New York contracted hepatitis.[35] For many sanguinarian vampires, feeding is an erotic activity, while for others it is simply a necessary part of maintaining their health. There are a number of Internet forums and mailing lists for vampires and donors to find each other; however, it is still unclear what percentage of vampires are actually using these resources. Many vampires consume blood as a part of a romantic and/or sexual relationship. A hybrid vampire I interviewed in Atlanta described consuming blood from girlfriends. As his current girlfriend is not a donor, he has sustained himself through psychic energy rather than blood. Vlad, a sanguinarian vampire and rock musician, has suggested that blood drinking is not inherently sexual, but that a sexual encounter has traditionally been the most convenient way to obtain blood.[36]

Many vampires have found donors outside of an intimate relationship, although this may be easier for female vampires than for males. Norine Dresser interviewed Kristin, a vampire who described meeting donors in bowling alleys, arcades, parks, and libraries. Kristin would start by talking about movies (presumably vampire movies), then the occult, and finally her practice of consuming blood.[37] Curiously, Guinn and Grieser interviewed a female vampire named Cayne, who also described meeting donors at libraries.[38] One of the contacts interviewed for this book mentioned that some donors find blood drinking erotic even if the vampire does not. In this case, someone who enjoys having another person drink their blood may form a sort of symbiotic relationship with a sanguinarian vampire. Lady CG gives advice for forming a similar relationship with individuals who injure themselves, known as "cutters."[39]

While sanguinarian vampires may find it convenient to associate with people who are sexually stimulated by blood or who cut themselves, they see themselves as fundamentally different from these individuals. Sanguinarian vampires not only consume blood, but they identify themselves as someone who must consume blood in order to maintain their health. Conversely, those who consume blood for other reasons are usually not considered sanguinarian vampires. The defining question is not *if* they consume blood, but *why* they consume blood.

Anthropologists as well as laymen are quick to attribute the practice of consuming blood to a particular belief. For example, the practice of warriors drinking the blood of their enemies is attributed to their belief that this will give them their enemy's courage. The Hungarian countess Elizabeth Bathory (sometimes called "The Blood Countess") allegedly murdered young girls and bathed in their blood. Again, this behavior is usually attributed to her belief that bathing in blood would restore her youth.[40]

These explanations are an attempt to impose our own experience onto a perspective that outsiders cannot understand. We have no desire to drink blood and we assume that blood drinkers must be just like us but with a different set of premises informing their decisions. But sanguinarian vampires do not appear to be drawn to blood because of a belief. There is no organization or text within the vampire community that prescribes the drinking of blood or attributes special properties to this practice. Vlad actively discourages others from drinking blood, adding that, "I could be completely insane."[41] Instead, the pattern appears to be that individuals first begin craving blood and then must find a rational way to interpret this craving. In fact, several vampires report drinking their own blood from as early as four or five.[42] Interpreting these cravings becomes a self-narrative, as the individual searches for a category to explain them.

Sanguinarian vampires ascribe their cravings to a physiological need. Cayne, a vampire interviewed by Guinn and Grieser, claimed that she once became so starved for blood that she would have died had she not purchased a bloody steak.[43] We will, of course, never know if she actually would have died. However, this narrative to explain her action is what makes Cayne a sanguinarian vampire. Non-vampires may be drawn to blood as a source of psychological or sexual gratification rather than health. Ramsland describes a man who would make tea out of used tampons. This person was not a vampire, but a fetishist who received sexual gratification from drinking a woman's blood.[44] This sexual attraction to blood has been called "haemosexuality" and is more commonly referred to as "blood fetishism."[45]

Sanguinarian vampirism is frequently confused with a sexual fetish. This is partly because fetishists often use the term "vampire" themselves. For example, Leilah Wendell, the founder of the American Association of Necrophiliac Research and Enlightenment (an advocacy group for necrophiliacs) used the term "vampiristic romance" to describe drinking the blood from a fresh corpse as the climax to an act of necrophilia.[46] Wendell's use of the term "vampire" is totally different from that of sanguinarian vampires like Cayne. Furthermore, I have never heard a case of a sanguinarian vampire acquiring blood from a corpse—something that most vampires would find utterly repugnant.

However, even those who consume blood may express uncertainty regarding the best category for describing themselves. Guiley, for example, describes a rather troubled woman named Rose. Rose has been diagnosed with schizophrenia and is an outpatient at a mental hospital. She attributes her interest in drinking blood to her experience in a Catholic boarding school. Rose says that she equates blood with love in part because of the Catholic imagery of Christ and martyrs shedding their blood. After her mother died, Rose was raised by her grandparents, who physically abused her.[47] Rose thought of herself as a vampire and used several unusual methods to obtain blood. When she worked as a teacher, she would treat scrapes that children acquired during recess. Bloody cotton swabs would be saved to be "snacked on" later. Rose also had an interest in the occult and would cast spells for interested parties. Rather than charging money, clients would spill a few drops of blood onto paper which Rose would take home and consume. After sharing blood with Tanya, a self-described blood fetishist, Rose came to adopt this label rather than that of vampire.[48] Like Cayne, Rose's self-identity is dependent on the narrative she adopts to explain why she consumes blood.

Discourse about the two categories also influences which label will ultimately be adopted. Dresser describes Donna, another blood consumer vacillating between these two labels. Donna would drink beef blood, a practice she learned from her neighbor, a German-born butcher. Despite the fact that drinking beef blood is a common practice in some cultures, Donna describes herself as a vampire and not as a blood fetishist. Donna explains this decision: "A blood fetishist is somebody who is mentally sick and gets blood by illegal means. A vampire is somebody who likes to drink blood for reasons of his own. . . . I'm not too sure about these things, except that blood fetishist sounds like it has to be against the law."[49] Both Rose and Donna were consuming blood in the 1970s and 1980s when there was virtually no public information available about these practices. Today there is even a "Bleeding Ribbon Bloodplay Awareness Campaign," which was created to demystify blood fetishism.[50] As discourse of the varieties of blood drinking has spread on the Internet and in print, the distinction between vampires and fetishists have become more clear. Vlad told an interviewer, "Look, if you drink blood and it's a sex deal, don't call yourself a vampire. . . . You're a blood fetishist. Admit it, dig it, live it."[51]

Psychic Vampires

Psychic vampires do not have to worry about sanitation or whether or not their desire to feed is actually a fetish. In some cases, they do not even have to find donors. Instead of blood, psychic vampires feed on the subtle energy or "psi" of other people. In Ramsland's study of the vampire community in the mid-1990s, she found ten "psi vamps" for every blood drinker and was quite skeptical of their claims.[52] The idea of a vampire who drains energy rather than blood has existed since at least the start of the nineteenth century and was made famous in 1930 by Dion Fortune's occult classic *Psychic Self-Defense* (see Chapter 3). However, individuals did not identify with the label "psychic vampire" until the last decades of the twentieth century.

What exactly psychic vampires feed on is unclear. The term "psi" comes from parapsychologists who used the world "psi phenomena" to describe abilities like telekinesis and ESP. In 1967, a paper entitled "The feasibility of a physical theory of ESP" proposed the existence of particles known as "psitrons," emitted by the human brain.[53] Vampires often discuss psi as being synonymous with Asian concepts of vital energy such as chi and prana. However, Belanger commented that the word "energy" is used as a "place holder" for a concept that is not really understood.[54]

Psychic vampires are also interested in the emotional content of the energy they consume, and emotions are often discussed as being a source of energy unto themselves. Vampirologist Martin V. Riccardo cites the vampire Laila who writes, "For me at least, strong emotions sweeten the energy, and the only energy that surpasses fear or anger in strength is love/passion." Another vampire adds, "I do feed off the blood of others, but I much prefer to feed off the mental state of someone; their pain, anger, humiliation, sexual arousal, shock, happiness, and frustration."[55]

Like sanguinary vampires, psychic vampires feel that their health deteriorates if they do not acquire energy from other people. Belanger gives a compelling example of this deterioration that occurred when she was in college: In the fall of 1994, she attempted to prove to herself that she was not a vampire by ceasing to feed on energy. During this time, her health seriously declined. At the end of eight months without feeding, she collapsed during one of her classes and was hospitalized. Belanger was born with a heart defect and has a patch of GoreTex Teflon between her two ventricles. The doctors assumed her health condition was somehow related to the patch and began to discuss a heart transplant. Belanger checked herself out of the hospital and went to feed on her boyfriend. (Her college boyfriend was a consenting energy donor and had nicknamed her "Rogue" after the energy-draining superhero from Marvel Comics.) The next morning, Belanger woke up in fine health and began swimming laps in the college pool. Her boyfriend slept for about 15 hours.[56]

For other psychic vampires, the need to feed is not quite so dire. Kiera of the Atlanta Vampire Alliance (AVA) presents a counter example:

> Frankly, and this is an opinion that will probably ruffle some feathers, I don't think psi-vampires *must* have energy to survive. Due to a car accident, I spent the better part of eight months isolated from all people, alone 90 percent of the time. I do not wither up and die from lack of energy feeding. . . . Maybe we get a little distracted when we get low on energy. We may get a little grumpy, but we won't die.[57]

Regardless of severity, psychic vampirism is discussed first and foremost as a health issue. The model of psychic vampirism as a health condition represents a shift from older, more sinister descriptions of the psychic vampire as occult threat.

The most alarming aspect about the concept of psychic feeding is that, unlike consuming blood, it can be done subconsciously. We all know someone who seems to habitually "drain all the energy out of the room." For those who believe in psychic vampirism, this draining effect is more than metaphorical: Without realizing it, this person actually has siphoned energy out of you. Such a person may actually be a psychic vampire without even realizing it. The elderly are often accused of engaging in this sort of unconscious feeding. Consider the following description by occult writer Konstantinos of his encounter with a psychic vampire. He describes attending a party where he entered a light trance state and happened to look at an old woman sitting by herself:

> The lady looked like some kind of human spider! I knew that what I was seeing was not physical, but an astral vision as a result of my altered state. After the initial shock wore off, and I checked to see that no one was staring at me, I let my gaze fix on her once more. Again I saw the awful sight.
>
> She was surrounded by a dark purple aura that emanated about two feet from her body. Towards its edges, the aura seemed to darken so that it looked almost black, yet the darkened area did not prevent me from seeing through it to the purple area. From the dark edge of the aura, several thin, black tentacles were protruding and moving toward the group of people. . . . As I watched the tentacles continue their swarming, I realized she had no idea of what she was doing at the moment.[58]

This account is typical of occult texts as well as Neopagan literature that describe different methods of protection against psychic vampires. Konstantinos later said that this experience is what inspired him to write his book *Vampires: The Occult Truth*. This book was so popular that Konstantinos enjoyed a period of celebrity and appeared on the *Ricki Lake* show.[59]

One can imagine how someone who has just read the proceeding passage would react if you told them that you are a psychic vampire. Unlike the woman described by Konstantinos, those who identify as psychic vampires are aware of their feeding and often attempt to feed in an ethical manner. A number of psychic vampires want to reframe the concept altogether and adopt a new label such as "pranists" or "energy manipulators." These apologists point out that psychic vampires can feed on superfluous or negative energy, for example, stress energy. Kiera portrays psychic vampires not as parasites but as a natural part of a metaphysical order, absorbing and recycling stagnant energy.[60]

The "black tentacles" described by Konstantinos represent one form of energy feeding. *The Psychic Vampire Codex* describes a variety of techniques for absorbing psychic energy. These include ambient feeding, surface feeding, contact feeding, tantric exchange, deep feeding, and dreamwalking. Whereas feeding recommendations for sanguinarian vampires are primarily concerned with safety, Belanger's suggestions are primarily concerned with ethics. Interestingly, Belanger makes the distinction between feeding from a donor and feeding from a target. While a donor has consented to having their energy drained, a target is unaware of what is happening. There are also energy exchanges in which two individuals simultaneously draw energy from each other.

Ambient feeding entails taking tiny amounts of loose energy that are cast off from individuals, "as heat rises from a flame."[61] Because this energy is no longer connected to an individual, ambient feeding is believed to have no deleterious effects for anyone. Crowds are good places for ambient feedings, especially events like concerts where more energy is generated. Religious services are also charged with energy, although Belanger mentions that attending services only to feed is unethical.

Surface feeding occurs when a vampire visualizes a tendril of energy extending to another person and pulls some of that person's energy back to the vampire. This technique is called surface feeding because energy should only be drawn from "the outer layers of the target's energy body."[62] To probe the tendril deeper into the target would be considered a violent attack. Belanger also suggests creating several tendrils at once so that none of the targets will suffer the full draining effect. This, presumably, would create a feeding scenario similar to the one described by Konstantinos. The AVA's logo is designed to suggest this feeding pattern of energy tentacles. Belanger adds, "If you follow a strict code of ethics or have any personal qualms about these methods of feeding, you may wish to hone your skills at contact feeding and then only engage in this with donors who are both informed and consenting."[63]

Contact feeding entails physical contact between the vampire and the donor or target. Contact feeding may range from casually brushing a hand across the target or placing one's mouth directly onto a donor's neck. Tantric exchange is the exchange of energy during sexual contact. Belanger specifies that all sexual contact entails some energy exchange but cautions that not all sexual activity is a form of psychic feeding.[64] Deep feeding is described as drawing in "the utter essence of the other person."[65] Engaging in deep feeding is said to form a connection between the two partners that may continue into future incarnations. Finally, dreamwalking refers to the phenomenon of vampires' finding donors in their dreams and feeding from them remotely. Belanger suggests that this is

The sigil of the Atlanta Vampire Alliance. The radiating arms are meant to suggest the patterns of energy flow associated with psychic vampirism. (http://www.atlantavampirealliance.com/) (Merticus of Suscitatio Enterprises, LLC)

instinctive and that vampires may subconsciously feed this way in periods of dire need.

When the psychic vampire began to emerge as an identity, there was initially skepticism from the slightly more established community of sanguinarian vampires.[66] Some sanguinarian vampires declared "real vampires drink blood" and that those who fed on psychic energy were something else entirely. Some psychic vampires countered that consuming blood is only efficacious because blood serves as a medium for psi energy. Thus, sanguinarian vampires are mired in an outmoded and primitive method of feeding. This debate has since died down, although some in the Atlanta community have predicted that it will inevitably flare up in the future. Many vampires have considered that both sanguinarian and psychic vampires are engaged in the same process but through different means. This has led to the phenomenon of "hybrid" vampires who use both feeding techniques. One vampire compares this to the difference between drinking a cup of coffee or sucking on a coffee bean.[67] This idea is reflected in a T-shirt sold by the AVA. The shirt features a vampire holding a martini glass filled with blood. The caption reads, "How do you take your prana?"

Awakening versus Initiatory Models of Vampirism

A final dimension of the real vampire experience concerns whether one can become a vampire through initiation or whether some individuals possess an inherent vampire nature that may be "awakened." A vampire from the AVA explained that the community's sense of what vampires are is actually a fusion of two different schools of thought. An initiatory school of thought stemmed from early vampire groups modeled loosely after the Freemasons and other esoteric movements. These groups saw vampirism as a sort of ritual apotheosis. Vampires used rituals and magical techniques that were passed down as a tradition. In the initiatory model, anyone can become a vampire, although most people lack the discipline for such an undertaking. An alternate perspective drew on parapsychology and psychic research. In this school of thought, vampirism is a quality innate from birth and those who lack it can never acquire it. One cannot become a vampire, one can only "awaken" to what they truly are. Those who were not born vampires can at best only imitate the vampire's abilities through esoteric training.

Exactly how these two models of vampirism came together in unclear, although it is hardly surprising that different types of people calling themselves vampires eventually found one another. It was not until later that tension began to form between the awakened and initiatory models and arguments began over who the "real" vampires were. Today, the awakened model seems to be more popular and appeals to the radical individualism common to the vampire community. Awakened vampires sometimes label initiatory groups as "cults." Meanwhile, groups that practice vampire initiation tend to look down on awakened vampires, claiming that they are not gifted but rather suffer from a sort of paranormal defect.

The Awakened Model

A William Blake quote appears frequently on vampire Web sites and as an electronic signature for Internet communications. It reads, "Some are born to sweet

A T-shirt produced by the Atlanta Vampire Alliance references different modes of feeding. (http://atlantavampirealliance.com/) (Merticus of Suscitatio Enterprises, LLC)

delight, others born to endless night." For awakened vampires, this quote seems to reflect the idea that vampirism is an ontology—there is simply something essentially vampiric about them. This vampire nature can be ignored, but it cannot be changed. More scientifically minded vampires have suggested that this vampire nature may have a genetic component, while others posit a metaphysical cause. Belanger has proposed that actions in past lives may cause one to be reincarnated as a vampire.

Belanger and other researchers within the vampire community have found precedent for the awakened model in vampire folklore.[68] This may at first seem counterintuitive: Because vampires are commonly considered to be the living dead, it seems logical that no one can be born a vampire. However, folklorist Paul Barber shows that there is a tradition found throughout Russia, Poland, and Romania that some individuals are born predestined to rise as vampires. Babies born with teeth or a caul over their face may be future vampires, as well as individuals born with a split lip, a third nipple, or a tail.[69] Thus, the idea that special people are destined to be vampires is not a modern invention.

The awakened model claim that vampirism is an essentialist identity raises numerous concomitant issues that have thus far been overlooked by researchers. This is understandable as outsiders view the vampire identity as a purely cultural phenomenon. For example, an article entitled "Vampire Culture" appears in *The Encyclopedia of Religion and American Cultures.*[70] While there is undoubtedly such a thing as vampire culture, awakened vampires see vampirism as something completely independent of religion and culture. The awakened model is what cultural theorists call an "essentialist" model of identity.[71] One of my contacts, when describing elements associated with vampire culture such as role-playing games, BDSM,[72] and gothic music commented, "That's what we do, not who we are." Many real vampires feel that if they had never donned a black garment, read an Anne Rice novel, or even heard the word "vampire," they would still need to feed to maintain their health.

As an essentialist identity, the awakened model also produces the phenomenon of reluctant vampires. Belanger's failed attempt to disprove her vampiric nature has already been discussed. One of the first vampires interviewed in Atlanta for this book expressed that he would rather be normal than a vampire. He compared being a vampire to a mental illness such as manic-depression that can produce moments of brilliance followed by periods of misery. The VEWRS asked, "If you were given the means to permanently end your vampiric condition and could instead live a normal non-vampiric life would you eagerly pursue this opportunity?" The very question frames vampirism as a condition rather than a religion or culture. Sixty-two percent answered "No," 8 percent answered "Yes," 27 percent answered, "I'm not sure," and 2 percent gave no response.[73] These data indicate that while the majority of vampires enjoy their existence as vampires, a significant percentage is ambivalent.

As a discipline, religious studies is not well equipped to study essentialist identities. Religion scholars tend to classify vampires as a "new religious movement," but this category is not an ideal fit. Membership in a new religious movement can be refused or renounced, but many vampires see their condition as immutable. Perhaps the closest analog in the field of religion is the category of "shamanism." Like the word "vampire," "shamanism" is sometimes used as a catchall to include a wide variety of concepts. Religion scholar Mircea Eliade in his seminal book *Shamanism: Archaic Techniques of Ecstasy* notes that in some cultures one becomes a shaman through heredity as well as initiation. It is believed that the vocation of shamanism cannot be refused and that potential shamans will be tormented by ancestral spirits until they begin their training.[74] Not surprisingly, many vampires are interested in shamanism, and at least one of the members of the AVA was also a practicing shaman.

Vampires themselves often compare vampirism to discovering one's sexual orientation rather than finding a religion. They generally do not speak of vampirism "growing" as would a religious or cultural movement; instead more people have "awakened" to their identity as a vampire.[75] Because of this, I find that it is more productive to think of the vampire community *as a whole* as an informal identity group rather than a subculture or a new religious movement. Political theorist Amy Gutman gives the following definition of identity groups:

> Identity groups are politically significant associations of people who are identified by or identify with one or more shared social markers. Gender, race, class, ethnicity, nationality, religion, disability, and sexual orientation are among the most obvious examples of shared social markers around which informal and formal identity groups form.[76]

According to Gutman, identity groups will always exist as long as individuals are free to associate. There are two basic varieties of identity groups. Formal identity groups are formed by members who are both eligible for membership and choose to join voluntarily. The NAACP and the League of Women Voters are examples of formal identity groups. Informal identity groups consist of members who never asked to join the group—instead they are ascribed to that group based on social markers such as race or gender.

Awakened vampires see their place in the vampire community as ascribed rather than voluntary. In fact, Belanger has compared being a vampire to being born left-handed. She points out that many left-handed people purchase books, mugs, or T-shirts related to being left-handed, but this does not mean they chose their dominant hand.[77] This is not to say that there are no formal groups and religious organizations within the vampire community. But trying to understand the vampire community as a whole, simply by looking at the formal organizations, is analogous to studying African Americans solely by looking at the NAACP or women by looking only at the League of Women Voters.

The Initiatory Model

While many vampires see vampirism as something inherent to their nature, an alternative model is promoted by groups that see vampirism as a matter of knowledge, training, and initiation. Initiatory groups usually have an organizational hierarchy, texts describing their belief system, and other trappings associated with organized religion. Because of this, they are far more approachable to religion scholars who study new religious movements and have been the subject of several academic papers. The problem is that these groups are generally not representative of the vampire community as a whole, primarily because these groups understand vampirism as a chosen spiritual path rather than essentialist identity.

The idea that one may become a vampire through magical initiation also has a basis in folklore. Montague Summers wrote, "The vampire is believed to be one who has devoted himself during his life to the practice of Black Magic, and it is hardly to be supposed that such persons would rest undisturbed."[78] In Bram Stoker's *Dracula*, it is revealed that in life Dracula was a student of alchemy, necromancy, and other occult pursuits. Dr. Van Helsing tells the heroes that Dracula studied at a magical college known as the "Scholomance."[79] Stoker is drawing here on a Romanian legend, in which ten students would be admitted to the Scholomance to be tutored by the devil. At the end of their training, nine scholars would be allowed to leave while the tenth would be claimed as the devil's own. This unfortunate soul would ride a dragon known as an *ismeju* and assist the devil in creating thunderstorms.[80]

A modern formula for becoming a vampire through magic appeared in the late 1970s. Youngson of the Count Dracula Fan Club received a document entitled "How to Become a Vampire in Six Easy Steps." The document was mailed to her by a vampire known as Madeline X, who claims to have been a vampire for several years before falling in love with a mortal and renouncing vampirism. In 1985, Youngson published the pamphlet, which describes a six-day procedure involving an owl-figurine, a raw chicken liver, eggs inscribed with lightening bolts, vinegar, a black human hair, and a great deal of chanting and clapping. Nuzum, who accuses Youngson of writing the pamphlet herself, has written a hilarious article describing his misadventures conducting the six-day ritual.[81] Although Nuzum failed to turn himself into a vampire, he also discussed the ritual with his coworkers (who wanted to know why he was chanting over a piece of chicken liver). This violated the ritual, which demands that the operator maintain secrecy.[82] "How to Become a Vampire in Six Easy Steps" is usually regarded as a joke. Still, it is telling that vampire fans were interested in acquiring the formula.

Guiley's data gathered from vampires in the late 1980s and early 1990s describe more traditional methods of being initiated as a vampire—many of them sexual. One of her interviewees, Kevin, describes a drunken sexual encounter with a both a male and female acquaintance during which his male partner "sucked his blood." Afterward Kevin experienced a craving for human blood and sensitivity to sunlight. He described attempting to walk across a bridge and being unable to do so, due to intense anxiety. (This is the only story uncovered during research for this book of a self-identified vampire being unable to cross running water.) Judith, a vampire from Lancaster, England, describes being turned through an almost identical process.[83]

These narratives of being turned into a vampire as the result of a tryst smack heavily of contemporary vampire fiction; particularly the classical folkloric details in Kevin's story. Such narratives were probably more common when Guiley was preparing her book *Vampire Among Us,* which was before vampires were able to communicate on the Internet and the more integrated vampire community began to crystalize. Today, if someone were to post such a story on a real vampire Internet forum, they would undoubtedly become the subject of ridicule. Still, magical and even sexual forms of vampire initiation have survived in the vampire community.

The modern vampire community is now more self-aware and more interconnected than ever before. As forums and articles for real vampires become more readily available through the Internet and as vampire groups have begun to publish books, it is now quite easy for vampires to locate and contact one another. The result of this has been that different models of vampirism that were formed in relative isolation are now forced to confront one another. This has led to numerous arguments over who are "the real vampires" as well as to the production of endless subcategories of vampire to accommodate different perspectives. Despite this chaos, the community has endured and appears to be growing stronger rather than splitting apart. When the dust settles there will still be many ways to be a vampire.

CHAPTER 2

Why Vampires?

Almost as bizarre as vampires themselves is the principal theory with which scholars have attempted to explain the vampires.

—*Paul Barber,* Vampires, Burial, and Death

With so many diverse ideas about what it means to be a vampire, it becomes clear that the only factor the vampire community has in common is their self-identification with the vampire category. But how do individuals arrive at this identity? What factors lead someone to make the statement, "I am a vampire"? Within the awakened model of vampirism, being a vampire is not a choice. From this perspective, to ask *why* they are vampires would be like asking a lesbian why she is a homosexual or an autistic man why he has autism. As outsiders, vampire researchers from various disciplines have attempted to interpret vampirism as a medical condition, a psychological syndrome, or as a purely cultural phenomenon. In exploring these theories it is important to remember that vampires form their identities based on subjective experiences that researchers are not privy to. Nor can this obstacle be circumvented by dismissing these experiences as "psychosomatic." Regardless of why a self-identified vampire sees psychic energy moving through a room or experiences a craving for blood, these experiences still have a subjective reality that others can never fully understand. Responsible researchers should bear this in mind when considering why people identify as vampires.

Medical and Psychiatric Explanations of Vampirism

The most simplistic interpretation of vampirism is the thesis that vampirism is actually caused by porphyria. Although this theory is rarely applied to the modern vampire community, it received widespread media attention in the late 1980s, creating far more problems for porphyriacs than for vampires. Porphyria is a family of genetic disorders. Sufferers do not produce certain enzymes and this causes their body to compensate by releasing high quantities of porphyrin enzymes. Excess porphyrins are stored in different parts of the body leading to different forms of the disease. In the case of cutaneous porphyria, the skin is affected causing photosensitivity, itching, swelling, and necrosis of the skin and gums. In some cases, cutaneous porphyria can cause excessive hair growth on the forehead. The vampire theory of porphyria goes something like this—hairy, photosensitive porphyriacs with long teeth were skulking about at night craving blood to replace their depleted enzymes and ancient people interpreted these individuals as vampires (or perhaps werewolves).

The porphyria theory first appeared in 1964 in a paper published in *The Proceedings of the Royal Society of Medicine* entitled "On Porphyria and the Aetiology of Werewolves," but it received little attention. Then, in 1984, biochemist David Dolphin wrote a paper for the American Association for the Advancement of Science entitled, "Porphyria, Vampires, and Werewolves: The Aetiology of European Metamorphosis Legends." This time the porphyria theory received widespread media attention. In addition to coverage on network television and major newspapers, many local papers ran headlines such as, "The Vampire Disease." The story even appeared in the children's publication *Weekly Reader.* Folklorist Norine Dresser initially became involved with vampires because she was asked to comment on Dolphin's theory.[1] Following media coverage of Dolphin's paper, the American Porphyria Foundation reported that phone and mail contact had increased by 500 percent—much of it from angry porphyriacs. Several men considered divorcing their wives because they were porphyriacs. One woman became convinced that her porphyriac husband was sucking her blood in her sleep. She tried, unsuccessfully, to have a priest perform an exorcism on her husband.[2] (The fact that a medical paper inspired her to seek an exorcism is itself a fascinating comment on how the claims of religion and science are balanced in the popular imagination.)

Along with porphyria, rabies and even syphilis have been blamed for vampire legends.[3] These theories have a popular appeal because they bring "the color of science" to the vampire legend. In effect, the public never stopped believing in vampires; they simply changed their criteria for accepting their existence. It is telling that the porphyria theory did not interest the media until the 1980s. This same decade saw a surge of vampire films and novels known as "the vampire boom." Writers of the vampire boom had shifted from a supernatural understanding of vampires and were instead writing stories in which vampires were either infected with a virus or the product of a parallel course of human evolution. Dolphin's paper was given one year after David Bowie played a genetically altered vampire in the cult film *The Hunger.* The acceptance of the porphyria theory indicates the power of the vampire milieu. Even in the late twentieth century, the vampire milieu was not simply entertainment: Instead, it was formed in dialogue with the media, the medical establishment, and the very *zeitgeist* of the culture.

A more perennial theory is that vampirism is a disease of the mind. There is a significant body of psychiatric literature attempting to make sense of the parallels between the vampire of legend and certain patterns of pathological behavior (most often associated with schizophrenia) that involve drinking blood. These pathologies have come to be referred to informally as "vampiristic behavior" or "clinical vampirism."[4] Clinical psychologist Richard Noll popularized this diagnoses by giving it the more dramatic name, "Renfield's syndrome," after the mental patient who aids Dracula in Bram Stoker's novel. Psychiatrists have also coined the term "auto-vampirism," referring to people who drink their own blood. Philip D. Jaffe and Frank DiCataldo point out that while there are multiple and somewhat conflicting definitions of clinical vampirism, the pathologies associated with this term are exceedingly rare.[5] Nevertheless, the idea of vampirism as a mental illness has a certain appeal to the popular imagination, much as did Dolphin's theory of vampirism as a medical condition. The crime show *CSI* capitalized on this in an episode entitled "Committed," in which both the terms "clinical vampirism" and "Renfield's syndrome" were used.

This psychiatric literature is describing a phenomenon that is completely distinct from self-identified vampires. The majority of cases from which the concept of clinical vampirism has been constructed involve clinically insane individuals who did not describe themselves as vampires. Jaffe and DiCataldo comment, "One could argue, for instance, that the label 'vampire' is only a convenient metaphor for a form of mental pathology which includes the ingestion of blood."[6] Thus it is the psychiatrists themselves, rather than the patients, who associate these activities with vampires.

However, the idea of vampirism as a mental pathology does have social consequences for the vampire community. Although "clinical vampirism," "Renfield's syndrome," and "auto-vampirism" are not mental health conditions listed in the Diagnostic and Statistical Manual IV (DSM-IV), there are still attempts to "diagnose" real vampires.[7] A hybrid vampire told a story about a nurse he had once dated. He was not seeking a donor and had not told this woman he was a vampire. However, a third party referred to the vampire community in her presence, effectively "outing him" as a vampire. At first, the nurse assumed the reference to vampirism must be a joke, until he explained to her that this was not a joke and that he really did consume blood to maintain his health. The nurse, trying to help, consulted the DSM and diagnosed him with Pica.

Pica is characterized by eating substances that are not normally considered food, such as bags of flour, coal, paper, glass, or dirt. It is most commonly found in young children and pregnant women. To diagnose a self-identified vampire's desire for blood as Pica shows an almost stubborn refusal to listen to the vampire's own interpretation of his subjective experience. Psychiatric explanations of vampires hold the same appeal as the porphyria theory—a preoccupation with redefining the vampire as something on the periphery of science. The appeal of these theories is not that they make vampires less fantastic, but that they make a scientific world more fantastic for having vampires in it.

The "Escape Fantasy" Theory

Researchers who have contact with self-identified vampires often see vampirism as the symptom of a pathology rather than a pathology unto itself. Many researchers look to psychological profiles of self-identified vampires, attempting to isolate a cause or event that set them on the path of vampirism. Rosemary Ellen Guiley offers a concise outline of what might be called the "escape fantasy" theory of vampirism:

> Many of these living vampires feel they did not fit into mainstream society for any number of reasons. From early in childhood, they considered themselves to be outsiders. . . . The fictional vampire seemed to offer a way to escape to an exotic life or build self-image. Most immersed themselves in vampire fiction and films.
>
> Many of them say that they came from unhappy home environments, where they had suffered psychological abuse, sometimes sexual abuse, and sometimes physical abuse that may have made them taste their own blood at a very young age. It is possible that dissociation is a factor in at least some vampire escape fantasies.
>
> After someone decides he wants to be a vampire, he seeks out other living vampires, perhaps in a nightclub or at school. He is then made into a vampire in rituals involving a small exchange of blood and sometimes sex.
>
> After he is convinced he has become a vampire, the initiate undergoes some changes, which probably are really induced by auto-suggestion.[8]

It should also be noted that Guiley was writing in the early 1990s when the vampire community was less self-aware and the awakened model of vampirism had not yet established itself. In the twenty-first century, it is less likely that individuals will "decide to become a vampire" and then seek initiation. Instead of making a decision, they are more likely to "discover" that they are a vampire.

The escape fantasy theory is compelling but difficult to prove. Few vampire researchers are trained in psychological research, and, even if they were, getting an accurate sample of data from vampires is notoriously difficult. Guiley suggests that the vampire identity ultimately originates with abuse or feelings of isolation. There is some data to support this claim. Dr. Jeanne Keyes Youngson of the Count Dracula Fan Club has received a number of letters and phone calls from vampires who describe such a history. She is quoted, "Almost everyone I have talked to, with very few exceptions, has had a very unhappy childhood.

Rejection, being abused. Quite a few can pinpoint where they got their craving for blood from—they can pinpoint the exact circumstances. Sometimes there is a definite pivotal point, such as an accident or an incident of sexual abuse."[9] Youngson has been quoted elsewhere as saying that 75 percent of self-identified vampires were abused.[10] According to the VEWRS data, 54 percent of vampires reported being abused as a child—still a considerable percentage. Of these, 19 percent reported physical abuse, 12 percent reported sexual abuse, and 14 percent reported both sexual and physical abuse.[11] Even with proper data, it is difficult to demonstrate causation. For example, Lady CG believes that she was born a vampire and is also a survivor of abuse. Interestingly, she is trained as a social worker and uses her experience to help other survivors.[12] Her choice of vocation suggests that she is not pursuing an "escape mechanism" and calls for a more nuanced theory.

The Pathological Narcissism Theory

J. Gordon Melton in his work *The Vampire Book* makes some fascinating connections between the fictional vampire and self psychology. Specifically, he sees the vampire as a symbolic representation of narcissistic psychodrama. Although Melton makes these connections in order to explain the popular appeal of vampire fiction, self-identified vampires have also been explained as suffering from pathological narcissism.[13]

Melton begins with an overview of narcissistic personality disorder—a disorder that is listed in the DSM-IV. Those who suffer from the disorder have "a very inflated concept of themselves and an inordinate need for tribute from others." Melton cites Otto Kerberg's description of the disorder and notes that Kerberg could easily be describing vampires: "It is as if they feel they have the right to control and possess others and to exploit them without guilt feelings—and behind the surface, which very often is charming and engaging, one senses coldness and ruthlessness."[14]

According to self psychologists Heinz Kohut and Ernest S. Wolf, narcissistic pathologies are caused in childhood when an inadequate nurturing environment produces "narcissistic wounds." Neglect and other factors can cause a person to mature without a healthy sense of self. As a result they must constantly manipulate others in order to sustain their own self-esteem. Like the escape fantasy theory, pathological narcissism posits an origin with an unhappy childhood. However, narcissism may also have a much broader, cultural origin. Melton references cultural historian Christopher Lasch's book *The Culture of Narcissism*. This provocative book submits that cultural changes in postwar America have reached the point that pathological narcissism has now become the status quo. Melton suggests that if Lasch's thesis is correct, our culture is fascinated by vampires because they reflect our own narcissistic tendencies.[15]

Kohut and Wolf report that those who have been "preyed" on by the narcissist describe feeling "depressed, depleted, and drained of energy"—symptoms that Melton points out are attributed to the victims of vampires. Other symptoms associated with narcissistic wounds include antisocial activity, pathological lying, and being "hypochondriacally preoccupied with bodily states." Melton also sees a parallel between vampirism and what Kohut and Wolf label "mirror-hungry personality." He writes, "Because of their deep-felt lack of worth and self-esteem, these persons have a compulsive need to evoke the attention and energy of others."[16] When the mirror-hungry personality is not able to attract sufficient attention to maintain a sense of self, he or she initiates a "grandiose retreat," isolating him- or herself to shore up the self-image. Melton sees the castle of Count Dracula as the consummate representation of this grandiose retreat. If the vampires of fiction are actually a representation of pathological narcissism, it follows that when we call someone a "vampire," we are actually pointing out their narcissistic behavior. The various self-help books about "emotional vampires" use the word in this sense.

Real vampires differ from the emotional vampires because they have adopted the vampire identity as self-narrative, rather than being labeled a vampire by others. There are some cases where individuals appear to be drawn to the vampire narrative because they suffer from a poor self-image and a need for tribute. Katherine Ramsland interviewed an anonymous vampire who stated, "I am the master when I take their blood, the very life fluid of their existence, but my real power lies in owning control of their will. A person's will is more precious than their blood, the will being capable of summoning the heart, the emotions, and then . . . to any deed I desire."[17] The phrasing, "I am the master when I take their blood," implies that *without* taking from other people, this person is *not* "the master." In fact, without this sort of control over other people, this person probably has a very poor self-image. Here, vampirism has become a tool in the narcissist's arsenal.

In a similar case, Dresser describes Stefan, one of the first people to describe himself as a psychic vampire. Stefan reported childhood abuse, followed by auto-vampirism, and finally experiments with psychic vampirism. Stefan would use "ESP" to attack people he found napping in parks or on public buses. Unlike most psychic vampires, Stefan did not claim that he needed stolen energy for his personal well-being. Instead, he said he carried out these attacks because they made him feel superior.[18]

Observational research revealed some evidence to suggest that narcissistic pathology could be common in the vampire community. Most vampires characterized their community as one of radical individualists and some described this as a potential weakness.[19] Vampires complained to one another about antisocial behavior, individuals isolating themselves, and pathological lying. There were also certain individuals whom other vampires found irritating or melodramatic, or referred to as "flakes." However, there is currently no quantitative evidence that the vampire community has a higher percentage of such individuals than any other group.

While this might present an interesting area for future research, it is no more practical to assume that all vampires are pathological narcissists than to assume that they are all escape fantasists. It is likely that some narcissists *are* drawn to vampirism, but this does not at all mean that identifying as a vampire is inherently evidence of narcissism. Vyrdolak, a leader in the vampire community, responds to the connections between vampirism and narcissistic pathologies in an article entitled "Real Vampires Revisited." She points out that individuals suffering from personality disorders generally lack empathy for others. By contrast, many vampires feel they have an almost supernatural capacity for empathy.[20]

Finally, the fact that vampires have become organized is the greatest obstacle to a psychoanalytical theory of the vampire phenomenon. Ramsland's anonymous vampire quoted above added, "I am strongest when I am alone." However, the vampire community continues to become more interconnected and cooperative. Vampires who participate in groups or houses frequently describe a sense of family with the others in their group. A community cannot be formed from the voluntary participation of pathological narcissists. As the vampire community continues to become more self-aware, antisocial elements will continue to be pushed to the periphery. The more legitimate the vampire becomes as a category of person, the less appeal the vampire label will hold for escapist fantasists and narcissists.

Vampirism as a Technology of the Self

These psychological theories of the vampire and even the porphyria theory are all dependent on a cultural understanding of the word "vampire"—a category that is continually being redefined and gaining new meaning. Even if there is an empirical condition that vampires share—as is the hypothesis of many real vampires—only a discursive analysis can explain why the condition is called vampirism. Therefore, an explanation of why people call themselves vampires is first contingent on the cultural understanding of what a vampire is.

I understand the phenomenon of self-identified vampires as emerging through a four-stage process:

1. Discourse creates a category—the vampire.
2. Individuals come to identify themselves in the category
3. Individuals redefine the category and de-otherize it.
4. The category becomes a source of identity and a "technology of the self."

A vampire, whether understood as a supernatural revenant, a living person with psychic abilities, or someone suffering from a mental illness, is first and foremost a *category of person*. There is a theory of cultural discourse that categories of people function something like the movie *Field of Dreams*, in which the mere existence of a baseball field magically conjures baseball players. Philosopher Ian Hacking produced an essay entitled, "Making Up People," in which he argues that as new categories of people are defined, individuals will spontaneously come forth to fill them.[21] Thus, if the category of "vampire" appears in discourse, it is inevitable that someone will identify as a vampire.

Hacking's thesis can be applied even to categories of supernatural monsters. Montague Summers describes such a case in the Gascony region of France. In 1603, rumors began circulating that children were disappearing. At the height of these rumors, 13-year-old Marguerite Poirier claimed that she was attacked during a full moon by a beast resembling a wolf. Based on this evidence, French peasants naturally concluded that the children had been devoured by a werewolf. Strangely, Jean Grenier, a 13-year-old boy, confessed to being the werewolf. He stated that he had changed into a wolf and attacked Marguerite and that he had eaten all of the missing children. He was then tried and convicted of murder. Strangely, the chief justice did not believe in werewolves but still found Grenier guilty. It was concluded that Grenier was a mental deficient under the delusion that he had turned into a wolf. (His claim that he had eaten children was apparently not considered a delusion.) Deemed criminally insane, Grenier spent the rest of his life confined to a monastery in Bordeaux.[22]

Most people would agree that the werewolf is a fictitious category of person with no empirical basis. The case of Jean Grenier shows that even unhealthy, alien, or monstrous discursive categories will still draw people to identify with them. It should therefore not be surprising that with so much discourse about vampires, individuals will identify with this category. But the question remains: Why would someone identify as a vampire in the first place?

Some people apparently admire the predatory nature of vampires and werewolves and can consciously express their desire to become such a being. French folklore describes a variety of ways in which one can become a werewolf, and modern groups like the Temple of the Vampire will initiate those who desire to be ruthless vampires. However, the existence of such individuals cannot account for the awakened model of vampirism or the size of the vampire community. In fact, these self-described predators have been censured by the larger vampire community. *The Psychic Vampire Codex* states, "Do not be fooled by learned vampires. Many make a mockery of our need by engaging in feeding for pleasure or sport."[23]

Many vampires of the awakened model appear to define themselves as vampires because they have subjective and anomalous experiences that cannot be interpreted except through reference to the vampire milieu. Michelle Belanger says of her own identity as a vampire, "I came into it kicking and screaming because I was a skeptic with a rational approach to reality." She describes having anomalous experiences with no vocabulary or context to describe them until reading the description of vampires in Dion Fortune's *Psychic Self-Defense*. She stated, "I was kind of electrified with this notion that there might be a definition—a word—that other people recognized this." This quickly led Belanger through the entire vampire milieu including a study of yoga and Asian vital energies as well as Western concepts such as Mesmerism.[24] Belanger came to identify as a psychic vampire even though all of the descriptions she found of psychic vampires were completely negative.

The third stage is transformation of the category from within. Individuals identify as vampires and then attempt to re-frame the concept into a more positive narrative of self. The psychic vampire community has produced numerous "apologists" who have reframed vampires as part of a natural order—or even as energy healers—rather than a supernatural threat. Many awakened vampires have begun to reframe vampirism as essentially "symbiotic" rather than "parasitic." Early attempts at "de-otherizing the vampire" appear in Guiley's research from the early 1990s. Judith, who claims she was made a vampire through sexual initiation, states that she has the power to heal people by draining negative energy from them.[25]

Curiously, Fortune—the same woman who popularized the concept of the psychic vampire—also provides a model of a "symbiotic energy worker" very similar to modern de-otherized concepts of psychic vampirism. The protagonist of her novel *The Sea Priestess* (1938) is Lilith LeFay Morgan, a beautiful and mysterious magical adept. Although Lilith appears to be in her mid-to-late thirties, this is only due to regenerative magical energy. Her real age is closer to 120. She also routinely drains men of vital energy and is for all intents and purposes an energy vampire. Even her name references two occult villainesses, Lilith and Morgan LeFay. However, Fortune describes Lilith as a healer, not a vampire. Claire Fanger writes:

> Besides being older than most, this fatal woman has another unusual quality for the type: instead of destroying the men who fall in love with her (always at the point of meeting her they are sick, repressed, lonely, and near nervous collapse) she heals them. She does this not by satisfying their needs in any ordinary sexual way, but rather by inducing them to do magic with her. She uses the reflection their desiring admiration provides to build a magical body, a larger than life image of herself as Priestess of Isis, thus channeling all the stray libidinal forces in the men's lives into a massive cathexis of her own image, bringing down the goddess who (as it were) eats the surplus libido, and returns them to themselves refreshed and freed of their complexes. Lilith is thus not merely the ideal woman and ideal magician, she is also the ideal psychotherapist.[26]

This draining of stray libidinal energy is essentially the same process described by modern psychic vampire apologists. For Fortune, the difference between a negative and a positive drain of psychic energy seems to be that the former is labeled as vampirism while the latter is not. *The Sea Priestess* is significant because it indicates that the emerging concepts of psychic vampirism are utilizing concepts that have been in the milieu of Western occultism since the early twentieth century.

In the final stage, in which an individual has identified with the category of vampire and then de-otherized that category, vampirism becomes a tool for constructing and defining the self. "Technology of the self" is one of the many neologisms coined by Michel Foucault. Foucault used this term to describe practices that "permit individuals to effect by their own means or with the help of others a certain number of operations on their own local bodies and souls, thoughts, conduct, and way of being, so as to transform themselves in order to attain a certain state of happiness, purity, wisdom, perfection, or immortality."[27] Foucault framed his technologies of the self around Greco-Roman philosophy and health practices as well as the monastic practices of early Christians. However, later scholars have applied the concept to other phenomena. For example, David A. Palmer argues that qigong is a technology of the self.[28]

Real vampirism can be understood as a technology of the self in two ways. First, real vampires put a great deal of effort into maintaining their well-being. They must not only assess what type of nourishment is required (usually either blood or psychic energy) but also how much and how often they personally need to feed. Then they must find a way to feed—sanguinarian vampires must find donors and psychic vampires must weigh their feeding methods against their own sense of ethics. Most vampires are very sensitive to the energy of others, and this sensitivity must also be properly managed. Excess energy must be disposed of or "grounded" and they must use "shielding" techniques to protect themselves from unwanted energy. At the House Kheperu open house in 2007, there were continual references to the current state of the energy in the room and how each attendee was being affected by it. To me, the life of a vampire seemed exhausting—like a perpetual combination of dieting, yoga, and psychotherapy all at once. It is in many ways an ascetic life.

Second, real vampires seem to be on a perpetual quest of self-discovery. The identity as a vampire constantly acquires new and subtler layers of meaning. After discovering a vampire identity, the individual must discover his or her feeding typology: sanguinarian, psychic, or hybrid. Some vampire groups acknowledge different "castes" or roles among vampires, and these must be discovered too. Many vampires believe in reincarnation, and the discovery of past lives becomes yet another source of meaning. In fact, a number of vampires describe achieving immortality not through being undead, but through "serial immortality." In other words, their bodies will die, but as awakened beings they will retain more of their memories and metaphysical attributes in the future. In this way, the vampire community presents the individual with a variety of new mechanisms to define and construct a self-narrative.[29]

Vampires: The Way of the Future?

I argue that the vampire identity represents an adaptation to the conditions of modernity. The radical claims of vampirism as an essentialist identity can be understood as the next step in a series of changes in the construction of the self that has been underway in Western culture at least since the Enlightenment. Vampires frequently described their community as one of "radical individualism" and expressed concern whether any community composed of such individuals could endure.[30] The idea of "individualism" is regarded by many social theorists as a product of modernity. Modernity is often characterized by a shift from a group identity and hierarchy toward individuality and self-discovery. Furthermore, several theorist have suggested that, for better or worse, our culture has shifted toward a more "subjective" set of priorities. The weakening of mainline religious institutions in favor of a "spiritual marketplace," where individuals seek their own spiritual path, is one example of this subjective turn. Vampires have simply taken this subjective turn further, claiming the freedom not only to define their own spiritual path and to choose their own community but also to define their own ontological and metaphysical nature. Vampire identity represents a state of modernity in which even the individual's status as an ordinary member of the human species has become subjective.

Modernity is also frequently associated with the triumph of science over religion, secularization, and "the disenchantment" of the world. As vampires are normally thought of as supernatural creatures, an interest in vampires may strike someone as an anachronism rather than a phenomenon unique to the modern world. However, Christopher Partridge has argued that traditional religions have yielded, not to secularization, but rather to a host of new sources of sacred meaning. Partridge describes this process as "re-enchantment" and cites vampires among the many sources of newfound meaning. The vampire identity is uniquely adapted to these cultural changes, producing a new category of identity for a new subjective and re-enchanted world.

Melton cites Lasch's book *The Culture of Narcissism* in discussing how the appeal of the vampire in popular culture coincides with our culture's becoming more "self-centered." Lasch sees the culture of narcissism as a product of a gloomy view of the future, which has caused Americans to retreat inward. Interestingly, the same crisis of confidence cited by Lasch is also referenced by scholars of vampire fiction, author Anne Rice, and Belanger. This suggests that the rise of the vampire identity may be tied to broader historical processes and is part of a much larger trend in Western culture.

According to Lasch:

After the political turmoil of the sixties, Americans have retreated to purely personal preoccupations. Having no hope of improving their lives in any of the ways that matter, people have convinced themselves that what matters is psychic self-improvement: getting in touch with their feelings, eating health food, taking lessons in ballet or belly-dancing, immersing themselves in the wisdom of the East, jogging, learning how to "relate," overcoming the "fear of pleasure."[31]

Lasch's thesis is that narcissism originates from a sense of impending doom. The crisis of confidence experienced by Americans in the second half of the twentieth century has caused them to turn inward. (Note how Lasch's symptoms of narcissism resemble Foucault's technologies of the self.) The problem is not that Americans are now engaged in psychic self-improvement, but that this has been accompanied by a disengagement from civic duty, from political consciousness, and from history itself. He writes, "We are losing fast the sense of historical continuity."[32]

Lasch was writing in 1979, reflecting on a period that Stacey Abbot called "The Vampire Decade."[33] Interestingly, the historical events that Lasch cites as causing America's retreat into narcissism (The Vietnam War, Watergate, and other events of the era) are the same ones that Abbot cites as fueling a fascination with vampires. This is also the decade in which Rice wrote *Interview with the Vampire,* which she has since described as an expression of "post World War II nihilism."[34]

Lasch's thesis also resonates with a comment made by Belanger when discussing role-playing games. On her podcast *Shadowdance,* she described the appeal of *Vampire: The Masquerade* in the 1990s and why it is so much darker than the previous generation of Tolkien-inspired fantasy role-playing games characterized by *Dungeons and Dragons.* She commented:

> The people who were gaming at that time were . . . . We were not our parent's hippie generation who were trying to strive for a bright, shiny, sunshiny day. We weren't looking for a perfect world. We knew it was broken. It was probably broken beyond repair and mostly we were trying to just not be broken *by* it anymore than we already were.[35]

If an entire culture is attempting to disengage from history by withdrawing inward—to avoid "being broken by the world"—then the vampire identity may be uniquely adapted to this task. Not only is vampirism a form of "psychic self-development" *par excellence,* but the vampire allows for a more empowered and subjective approach to history. Partridge suggests that part of the appeal of the antiheroes of contemporary vampire fiction is their ability to move fluidly through history in pursuit of self-cultivation. Partridge writes of Lestat:

> He is free to roam history, to plunder societies and cultures in pursuit of gratification. Hence, for those, particularly young people, who feel disenfranchised, disempowered, subject to the forces of a history in which they did not ask to be born, the vampire represents a fascinating icon of empowered self-interest.

While self-identified vampires do not claim to be immortal, they are still able to "roam history" in order to define and construct their sense of self. This is achieved though the discussion of reincarnation, which is endemic to the vampire community. Question 119 of the VEWRS asked, "Do you believe your spirit has existed in a former lifetime?" Seventy-nine percent answered, "Yes." This belief exists independently of any religion, and one vampire referred to it by a term that reflects this: "reincarnationism."[36] Many vampires are interested in the meaning of their previous lives and frequently conclude that they have met other members of the vampire community in a past incarnation. At the House Kheperu open house, vampires mused about why so many of them had been murdered or met other grisly deaths in previous lives.

Reincarnationism—which is by no means unique to vampires—is also another form of psychic self-development. In 1990, a survey was conducted in Great Britain to measure how many people believed in reincarnation. After screening Hindus, Buddhists, and self-described "New Agers" from the sample, 24 percent still described a belief in reincarnation. The surveyors concluded, "We found a lot of thoroughly modern people accepting, playing with, or rejecting reincarnation in order to confirm or amplify their sense of self."[37]

Since Lasch, other theorists have noticed an increased interest in cultivating the self, but without the value judgment that this undermines society or constitutes "narcissism." Paul Heelas and Linda Woodhead's recent book *The Spiritual Revolution: Why Religion Is Giving Way to Spirituality* describes this cultural trend as "a subjective turn." They write, "It is a turn away from life lived in terms of external or 'objective' roles, duties, and obligations, and a turn towards life lived by reference to one's own subjective experiences (relational as much as individualistic.)"[38] Heelas and Woodhead argue that as a result of this turn, mainline religions with prescribed traditions and dogma are losing ground to new expressions of the sacred that appeal to subjective experiences—especially practices relating to holistic health such as therapy, yoga, and reiki.

Once again, vampires can be read as an extreme example of this trend. The "objective," traditional claim that vampires do not exist and that all human beings are ontologically the same is rejected. Instead, vampires draw authority almost entirely from their own subjective experiences. Understanding modern vampirism in light of this subjective turn serves to explain why the vampire community is so mistrustful of leadership or even an objective definition of vampirism. In fact, the AVA routinely denies the requests of individuals who contact them wanting to know if they are vampires. Their answer to such requests has been, "We do not diagnose. It is not our role to confirm or deny whether one is a vampire—that is something only the individual can come to know through serious introspection and experience." Again, this response can be read as a manifestation of the subjective turn.

In addition to being a technology for creating subjective narratives of self, the vampire identity is also a reaction to the disenchanted quality of modernity. Partridge, in his two-volume work *The Re-Enchantment of the West*, has suggested that as mainline religions have become weakened by secularization, other cultural elements have become "sacralized," gaining religious meaning. This process of "sacralization" has in a sense undone the Enlightenment project of "disenchanting" the world. Despite the triumph of science, the world has become re-enchanted. Partridge sees evidence of this re-enchantment in holistic health practices, Pagan and New Age spiritualities, belief in aliens and UFOs, and vampire spirituality.[39]

Many vampire groups (which are distinct from the vampire identity) can be understood as a place of resistance to the project of the Enlightenment and its concomitant state of disenchantment. A form of re-enchantment is achieved not only through group ritual and esoteric practices but also through the use of anachronistic customs such as courtly titles and dueling. (An overview of vampire groups and cultures is provided in Chapter 5.) During this research, I became struck by a connection between disenchantment and dueling societies. A contact in Atlanta showed me a document for a real vampire group from the 1980s. It described a number of traditions for the group including various methods of settling disputes through armed combat. Vampire duels, according to this document, could either continue until one duelist submits, until first blood is drawn, or until a duelist is killed. Probably no vampire duel was ever fought by this group and certainly not a lethal one. Why then, were these rules created?

Sociologist Max Weber (1864–1920) famously wrote, "There are no mysterious incalculable forces that come into play, but rather that one can, in principle, master all things by calculation. This means that the world is disenchanted."[40] Where Enlightenment thinkers celebrated "the triumph of reason," Weber questioned the value of a rationalized and bureaucratized modern world. As a teenager at The University of Heidelberg, he became very active in the University's dueling fraternities.[41] Daniel Martin and Gary Alan Fine have suggested that Weber's enthusiasm for dueling—despite the fact that he was otherwise unathletic as a teenager—was his form of rebellion against disenchantment.[42]

Many vampires appear to share Weber's pessimistic outlook for the future. This suggests that the function of dueling within this particular vampire group was not as a means for resolving disputes but rather as a rejection of an overly managed and banal society. Vampire groups represent a subjective alternative to a mediocre world that is seen as destructive and possibly doomed—a function that would be completely unnecessary in a premodern society. It is amusing to ponder whether Weber would have sought initiation into a vampire group if one had existed at Heidelberg.

CHAPTER 3

The Vampire Milieu

The reflexivity of fiction and fact have made it nearly impossible to separate the reality of the vampire from the archetype: One feeds into the other in a loop as complicated and infinite as the orobouros.

—*Michelle Belanger,* The Vampire Ritual Book

The phrase "vampire milieu" appears in the writings of Katherine Ramsland and others to describe our culture's ubiquitous and varied representations of vampires. However, as a religion scholar, I arrived at this term through a slightly different route. Sociologist Colin Campbell made an important contribution to the sociology of religion in 1972 when he introduced the concept of a "cultic milieu." Campbell points out that religious cults tend to be ephemeral and that studying them on a "cult by cult" basis is not very fruitful. However, cults tend to borrow ideas from each other openly, and new cults tend to recycle material from a common pool of ideas. He suggests that while cults come and go, this pool of ideas—the cultic milieu—is a permanent feature of our society. Furthermore, if a spiritual "seeker" enters this milieu at any point, they will rapidly be exposed to all of the various traditions and ideas within it.[1] Since 1972, many scholars have adapted Campbell's basic theory to explain related subcultural phenomena, including Massimo Introvigne's essay, "The Gothic Milieu: Black Metal, Satanism and Vampires."[2] Vampire groups, whether or not they are considered "cults" (see Chapter 6), tend to be short-lived. Furthermore, the majority of self-identified vampires function much like Campbell's "seeker," exploring different ideas to form a personal bricolage of vampirism. Therefore a study of modern vampires must focus on this underlying pool of evolving ideas about vampires—the vampire milieu.

In this book, references to the vampire milieu refer only to those ideas that appear to have influenced vampire identity. Many cultural references to vampires are not part of the vampire milieu because they have no significance for self-identified vampires. For instance, no self-identified vampire constructs their identity around *Bunnicula,* a children's novel about a vampire bunny. Also largely irrelevant is the Slavic blood-drinking revenant, the vampire of folklore. Father Sebastiaan Tod van Houten claims to have coined the term "vampyre," specifically to distinguish his culture from blood-drinking corpses.[3] Although these creatures are the "original vampires," they have been almost totally eclipsed by more modern concepts. Some vampire scholars have even used the term "ethnic vampirism" to differentiate the Slavic revenant from modern vampires. Paul Barber notes that horror writers have typically overlooked the more banal aspects of these creatures in favor of emphasizing their pale skin and sharp teeth. The teeth of Slavic vampires are rarely described, but their bodies are traditionally rather chubby in appearance and have a florid complexion.[4] Furthermore, ethnic vampires did not always drink blood and often resorted to other evil deeds such as eating flesh, frightening people to death, setting fires, or choking animals to death.[5] With a few rare exceptions (Viola Johnson has written that she cannot enter a house uninvited, for instance.), the vampire community borrows almost nothing from the folklore traditions of vampirism.[6] Indeed, the statement "I am a vampire," may have been largely meaningless in the medieval villages where the Slavic vampire originated.

This chapter focuses on five areas that have nurtured and helped to create the modern vampire milieu: (1) the fictional vampires of literature, television, and film, (2) explanations of vampirism put forth by occultism and parapsychology, (3) holistic health and accompanying notions of energy exchange, (4) vampire role-playing games, and (5) the work of "vampirologists" and contemporary vampire research. These categories function more like the threads of a tapestry than watertight compartments. However, dividing material into spheres allows for analysis of how different ideas have evolved along different routes, ultimately leading to a point where the statement "I am a vampire" is no longer meaningless.

Vampires and the Cultural "Tool Kit"

In the VEWRS, Suscitatio Enterprises asked vampires to rate their interest in both vampire folklore and vampire fiction on a scale of 1–10. The mode average for both questions was 10, indicating maximum interest in these subjects.[7] While it is hardly surprising that self-identified vampires would have an interest in the vampires of folklore and fiction, it remains unclear how exposure to this material has shaped their identities. Parallels between narratives of self and popular culture are a sensitive issue within the vampire community. It has been suggested that self-identified vampires have "fantasy-prone personalities" or else lack the ability to distinguish fantasy from reality.[8] In fact, much of the debate within the vampire community over who the "real" vampires are revolves around the accusation that a particular group has "lost touch with reality." Some lifestyle vampires claim that vampirism is only a life-style and that therefore anyone who calls themselves a "real vampires" has, *ipso facto,* lost touch with reality. Some real vampire groups, including the AVA, avoid all association with vampire role-playing groups because they fear being confused with role-players who have become unable to come out of their roles. Conversely, vampire role-players have tried to distance themselves from real vampires because they, too, fear the label that they have lost touch with reality. Furthermore, the idea that vampires are influenced by popular culture is seen as undermining the claims of many vampires that vampirism is an essentialist identity. Real vampires who follow the awakened model have objected to the idea that vampirism is culturally based rather than a condition inherent from birth.

By analyzing how vampire narratives of self are shaped by culture, I am not arguing that vampires somehow lack the capacity to distinguish between fiction and reality. Nor am I taking a position on the subjective experiences described by vampires. Instead, I am suggesting that vampire fiction and folklore as well as other cultural sources have provided the raw material with which vampires can interpret their experiences and construct narratives of self that appear meaningful and consistent. Sociologist Ann Swidler outlined a model of cultural studies in which culture (including art, belief, language, and stories) can be compared to a "tool kit" that is used to construct "strategies of action." The tool kit metaphor refers to the fact that any given culture contains prescribed modes of behavior that are diverse and conflicting rather than consistent. (For example, Swidler argues that the Bible can be used to justify almost any course of action.) This theory argues that we are often motivated not by a desire to achieve some culturally prescribed value but rather by a desire to produce a consistent pattern of decisions (a strategy of action) that is appropriate within a specific cultural context.[9] In line with this theory, if a culture is saturated with images of vampires, the vampire becomes a tool for making sense of the world and defining one's sense of self.

Norine Dresser does an excellent job of demonstrating how prevalent the vampire is in our culture, citing numerous pop cultural artifacts as well as commercials and jokes referencing vampires.[10] She cites mass media as the greatest promoter of vampiric knowledge and imagery but adds that these images are used commercially precisely because they evoke such a strong reaction from the general public.[11] Newspapers are a prime example of how mass media capitalizes on our preoccupation with vampires: Almost any person or thing can be labeled a "vampire" in order to create a more arresting headline. For example, the headline, "Slaying Vampire Energy Is Easy—Just Unplug Idle Appliances" uses the vampire to draw attention to a story about appliances that readers might otherwise ignore.[12] Crime stories are especially prone to incorporate the word "vampire" into the headline, even if the story has only tangential references to vampires, blood, or corpses. The earliest case of this may have been in 1849 when Sergeant Bertrand, a French soldier, was caught in an act of necrophilia. The Paris papers all ran the headline "Sergeant Bertrand the Vampire."[13] Apparently, Parisians found vampires even more scandalous than necrophilia.

In a culture that is so quick to label anything as a vampire, is it really surprising that some people would find this label useful for describing themselves? Anyone who feels compelled to consume blood would surely be labeled "a vampire" by the media. Is it reasonable to expect sanguinarian vampires to show more restraint than journalists? Similarly, psychic vampires have argued that vampirism is simply the most useful concept by which they can describe subjective experiences that might otherwise be ineffable. Belanger writes:

> For Westerners who have a fundamental and undeniable experience of vital energy, there is neither a language nor a context for them to put it in. . . . Along comes the vampire. As an undead being romanticized in fiction and film, the vampire really has very little in common with psychic vampires. Yet for those who encountered the archetype through books or movies, there was an obvious connection. The vampire feeds upon life. The need to take vital energy is typically the first and most undeniable quality awakening psychic vampires notice in themselves. Thus, even though they realized the term did not quite fit, there was enough of a resonance for these people to begin tentatively identifying themselves as vampires.[14]

To return to the tool kit metaphor, self-identified vampires should not be seen as motivated by a desire to conform to popular representations of vampirism. Rather, they are utilizing—often in a very conscious way—elements from the vampire milieu in order to make sense of their worlds and to construct a consistent narrative of self.

Vampires in Literature, Film, and Television

What might be called the "classical" vampire—a being that is aristocratic and has sex appeal—has its roots in Gothic literature. Gothic literature emerged in the eighteenth century combining elements of horror and romance. Ann Radcliffe (1764–1823) is often considered to be the first distinguished Gothic writer. The villain of her 1797 novel, *The Italian,* is a mad priest named Schedoni. For readers at the time, Schedoni embodied the Inquisition as well as the Reign of Terror in France. Roxana Stuart has argued that Schedoni is the prototype for a later Gothic villain—the vampire.[15] Consider the following description:

> His figure was striking, but not so from grace; it was tall, and, though extremely thin, his limbs were large and uncouth, and as he stalked along, wrapt in the black garments of his order, there was something terrible in its air; something almost super-human. His cowl, too, as it threw a shade over the livid paleness of his face, increased its severe character, and gave an effect to his large melancholy eye, which approached to horror.[16]

Schedoni's features, such as pale skin, dark clothing, and a penetrating stare have far more in common with modern notions of vampires than the Slavic revenant with its ruddy complexion. Stuart's interpretation suggests that the inspiration for the vampires' force of personality is actually the social gravitas associated with clergy and especially the Roman Catholic Church.

The first vampire antihero is considered to be Lord Ruthven, who appeared in Dr. John Polidori's short story "The Vampyre" in 1819. Ruthven is a British nobleman who becomes a vampire after being killed by brigands. As the undead, he maintains his aristocratic life, seducing virtuous women at London parties and becoming engaged to the protagonist's sister. The protagonist sees Ruthven for what he is but is too late to prevent their wedding, after which Ruthven drains his new bride of blood.[17] Ruthven seems to have eclipsed the Slavic revenant almost instantaneously, setting the stage for Dracula and especially Anne Rice's hypersexual vampire elite. Ruthven was a vampire with whom people could identify—who would not envy a wealthy playboy who was also an immortal?

Polidori was the personal physician of Lord Byron (1788–1824) and "The Vampyre" was based on one of Byron's unfinished works. When the story appeared in *New Monthly Magazine,* it was falsely credited to Byron.[18] (Indeed, Byron may have been the inspiration for Ruthven's high-society antics.) In 1820, "The Vampyre" was adapted into a Paris play. Lord Ruthven seems to have appealed to French xenophobia just as Dracula would later embody the Victorian fear of the foreigner.[19] It has also been suggested that the French saw Ruthven, as an undead aristocrat, as a symbol of the pre-Revolutionary nobility or even of the return of Napolean.[20]

Vampires gained in popularity throughout the nineteenth century. Alexander Dumas, Edgar Allan Poe, Nikolai Gogol, Leo Tolstoy, and Nathaniel Hawthorne all tried their hands at vampire stories. The "penny-dreadful" became another outlet for vampire fiction, and from 1845 to 1847 the exploits of "Varney the Vampire" were published in this format. Varney is something of a tragic figure and the series ends when the protagonist throws himself into Mount Vesuvius rather than continue his existence as a vampire.[21] Another interesting adaptation of the vampire myth was created by Texan writer, Charles W. Webber. Webber's 1853 book *Spiritual Vampirism* described a woman using mesmerism to steal vitality from her victims. This novel became an important precedent for the modern notion of psychic vampires and will be discussed in greater detail later in this chapter. In 1871, an article on vampire lore entitled "Vampires and Ghouls" appeared in the periodical *All the Year Round.* The editor at that time was Charles Dickens Jr.—who likely authored the article.[22]

In addition to the first vampire stories, the nineteenth century also saw the first vampire movie. Georges Melies's *Le Manoir du Diablo (The Devil's Castle)* was made in 1896. It is not only considered the first vampire movie but also the first horror movie. The vampire of the film is Mephistopheles, who shape-shifts into a bat. The film's hero, "the cavalier," must fight Mephistopheles armed with only a cross. When Mephistopheles is defeated, his body becomes a puff of smoke.[23] This became an important element for future scenes of vampire slayings.

A year later Irish author Bram Stoker published *Dracula.* Like Lord Ruthven, Stoker's vampire is also an aristocrat. However, Stoker did a great deal of research into history and folklore, restoring to the vampire elements of the Slavic revenant. (Stoker's Dracula has a number of unattractive features including pointy ears and hairy palms.) The early success of *Dracula* has been attributed to a state of "spiritual poverty" that affected Victorian England at the close of the nineteenth century.[24] Charles Darwin's *The Origin of The Species* appeared in 1859, and the concept of "Social Darwinism" had developed in England although without the negative connotation it would acquire later. As religious and moral traditions seemed to be yielding to secularization and science, an "occult revival" had begun in England.

Henry Steel Olcott and Madame Helena Blavatsky founded the esoteric Theosophical Society in 1875. In 1882, the Society for Psychical Research was founded by scholars from Cambridge University in London to investigate claims of the paranormal. In 1887, the Hermetic Order of the Golden Dawn was founded by William Wynn Westcott, a Rosicrucian Freemason. Stoker himself was rumored to be a member of the Golden Dawn, but this has never been sub-stantiated. What is more likely is that he had friends who were members or were otherwise part of the nineteenth-century occult revival. Thus, some of the super-natural details in *Dracula* also appear in occult writings from the time.[25] *Dracula* likely had the same appeal to Victorians as the occult revival—secularization had created a market for new ideas about the supernatural and new forms of religiosity.

As the nineteenth century saw the birth of the literary vampire, the twentieth century popularized the vampire on the silver screen. In 1922, German film-maker F. W. Murnau released the silent film *Nosferatu: A Symphony of Horror.* The film's plot was plagiarized from *Dracula,* replacing Count Dracula with Count Orlock. The film ends with Orlock being disintegrated by the rising sun. Many vampirologists cite this film as the origin of the vampire's weakness to sunlight. (On the other hand, it has also been pointed out that in folklore vampires never rose from their graves during daylight hours.)

Nosferatu was the first and last movie produced by the studio Prana Film. Prana's founder, Albin Grau, had no experience in filmmaking. However, he was an avid spiritualist and a member of Aleister Crowley's occult group the Ordo Templi Orientis.[26] The studio was to produce only occult and supernatural films but declared bankruptcy when Stoker's widow, Florence Stoker, sued for copyright infringement and won.[27] Interestingly, "prana" is a Sanskrit word meaning "breath." Modern psychic vampires often use this term to describe the subtle energy they take from other beings. After the demise of Prana Film, Murnau went on to produce another occult film, *Faust,* in 1926.

In 1931, Universal Studios produced the first film entitled *Dracula,* starring Bela Lugosi. Romanian-born Lugosi was chosen for his natural accent, his striking features, and his 6 feet 1 inch stature. There is disagreement whether Lugosi was considered to have sex appeal, or whether he was given the role because he was considered to have ugly, Slavic features and later became a sex symbol by accident. At any rate, *Dracula* was so popular that it spawned a franchise of Dracula movies including *Dracula's Daughter* (1936), *Son of Dracula* (1943), and *House of Dracula* (1945). It is from these films that the popular image of Dracula with a cape and a thick accent was formed. The 1950s saw a new generation of Dracula films produced by the Hammer studio and starring Christopher Lee.

While vampire movies were wildly popular in the twentieth century, they did not produce a mythos or a culture of vampire fans. The sort of "fandom" that now surrounds vampire series like *Buffy the Vampire Slayer* did not yet exist. This changed in the 1960s with a soap opera entitled *Dark Shadows. Dark Shadows* ran from 1966 to 1971, spanning 211 episodes.[28] (This is comparable to the combined 254 episodes of *Buffy the Vampire Slayer* and its spin-off series *Angel,* collectively known as "the Buffyverse.")[29] Set in the Gothic town of Collinsport,

Bela Lugosi as Dracula (1931). With his black cape and penetrating stare, Lugosi quickly became the most widely known image of the vampire. (AP Photo)

Maine, the show was originally intended as a soap opera with a Gothic setting. When the first season of the show received poor ratings, creator Dan Curtis introduced a ghost—a supernatural element that was unheard of for daytime television at the time. On April 18, 1967, the show's most famous character was introduced, a vampire named Barnabus Collins.[30] According to Dan Curtis, "Unless you count the ratings there was nothing particularly horrific about the old *Dark Shadows* during its first year." He said he introduced the character of Barnabus Collins because "I wanted to see exactly how much I could get away with."[31]

Collins was originally going to be a villain who would be staked after only a few episodes. However, the character was so wildly popular that a back story was added to make him a sympathetic character. It is revealed that Collins became a vampire through a witch's curse. Many of the show's plot arcs revolve around Collins attempting to cure himself of his vampire existence. In this way, Collins became the first "reluctant vampire" since Varney the Vampire, created over a hundred years earlier.

Belanger credits Collins with inspiring "a generation of vampire lovers"[32] This generation included Ramsland, who admits to watching *Dark Shadows*.[33] She describes Collins as the beginning of the vampire's transition from an "evil Other" to a "lonely misfit."[34] This exonerated vampire was appealing to a number of minority groups, especially gays and lesbians. Dresser, writing in 1989, mentions that four to six *Dark Shadows* conventions were being held every year.[35] *Dark Shadows* fans created networks that served as a sort of incubator for the real vampire community, allowing self-identified vampires and donors to find one another. Interestingly, William Patrick Day has argued that the direct descendent of Collins is actually "Blackula."[36] The 1972 blacksploitation film *Blackula* told the story of Mamuwalde, an African prince who journeyed to Europe seeking help in ending the slave trade. Sadly, his first stop in Europe was Transylvania where he was captured by Dracula and turned into a vampire. Like Varney the Vampire, Blackula commits suicide by walking into the sunlight.[37]

The twentieth century reimagined the vampire through print as well as film. Eminent religion scholar Mircea Eliade tried his hand at a vampire novella. He wrote *Domnisora Christina* in 1936, drawing on folk traditions from his native Romania.[38] The Cold War also affected the vampire genre. Richard Matheson's 1954 novel *I Am Legend* is set in the future where a Cold War virus has turned the earth's population into vampires. This appears to be the first attempt to explain vampires in terms of biology rather than the supernatural. However, the most important vampire writer of the twentieth century in undoubtedly Anne Rice. *Interview with the Vampire* was written in 1973 and published in 1976.

Several writers on vampire literature have commented that America in the 1970s was suffering from a "crisis of confidence."[39] Stacey Abbot, who character-ized the 1970s as "The Vampire Decade," writes, "In the 1970s, a decade of immense change in American history—marked by Vietnam, Watergate, the Kent state massacre, and the assassinations of Martin Luther King Jr., Malcolm X, and both John and Robert Kennedy—normality could no longer be restored: normality itself was deemed monstrous."[40] As *Dracula* had appealed to changes at the end of the nineteenth century, Rice's vampires appealed to social anxieties and a sense of alienation at the close of the twentieth century. Rice says of *Interview with the Vampire,* "This book reflects for me a protest against the post World War II nihilism to which I was exposed in college from 1960 through 1972. It is an expression of grief for a lost religious heritage that seemed at that time beyond recovery."[41]

Stuart credits Rice with making the vampire synonymous with the outcast rather than with terror.[42] In *Interview with the Vampire,* Armand tells Louis that he embodies the spirit of his age, to which Louis responds, "No, no . . . Don't you see? I'm not the spirt of any age. I'm at odds with everything and always have been! I have never belonged anywhere with anyone at any time!" Armand responds to this, "But Louis . . . This is the very spirit of your age. Don't you see that? Everyone else feels as you feel. Your fall from grace and faith has been the fall of a century!"[43] Rice capitalized on the elements that had made Barnabus Collins a successful vampire: Her vampires were sympathetic and often reluctant. Rice admits to being influenced by the story of Faust and reframed the vampiric condition as a "Dark Gift." Also, like the 211 episodes that make up the *Dark Shadows* series, Rice's Vampire Chronicles depict a large and detailed world that draws in readers and presents a sense of verisimilitude. Between 1988 and 1990, two women managed to find Anne Rice's unlisted number and asked whether vampires are real. When Rice told them they were not, they burst into tears.[44]

Rice may also have contributed to the modern vampire community's interest in shamanism. Rice created an origin story for vampires involving a shamanic relationship between humans and disembodied spirits. The first vampire is created when an Egyptian queen spiritually "fuses" with a wrathful spirit. Rice is also one of the first writers to describe the vampires' heightened sensory perceptions and states of consciousness. Interestingly, these new elements may be indebted to the influence of Carlos Casteneda's *The Teachings of Don Juan,* written in 1968. Casteneda claimed to have met with and been initiated by a Yaqui shaman named Don Juan. The book was initially praised as a significant work of anthropological research until it was debunked as fiction. According to Ramsland, "Rice reported being enthralled by the relationship between the teacher and student in this account, and used the vampire experience to describe an alternate path to enlightenment so many young people in the 1970s were seeking."[45]

In *The Teachings of Don Juan,* Don Juan tells Casteneda that he has "the energetic configuration" of a *nagual* or a spiritual visionary. Rice's vampires also appear to have an energetic makeup, and it is revealed that they are all energetically connected to Queen Akasha, the first vampire. The awakened model of vampirism believes that vampires are different from other people possibly because of unique qualities in their energy body, much like Casteneda's *nagual*. This suggests that the idea that vampirism is an essentialist identity may have been shaped by Casteneda by way of Rice.

One element of vampire culture that can be placed squarely on Rice is the significance of New Orleans. This connection does not appear to have existed before *Interview with the Vampire*. *Dark Shadows* was set in Maine because New England was at that time considered the most Gothic setting in America, having been home to horror writers such as H. P. Lovecraft and Edgar Allan Poe. Were it not for Rice, New England cities like Boston might have the significance now enjoyed by New Orleans.

The claim that Rice's books are the cause of the modern vampire community is overstated. The vampire community seems to have been forming in the 1970s before the publication of *Interview with the Vampire*. Still, Rice's creations have dramatically increased the popularity of vampires and had a profound influence not only on lifestyle vampires but on real vampires as well. Belanger's edited volume *Vampires: In Their Own Words* describes "Louis de Pointe du Lac syndrome." The term refers to the phenomenon of awakened vampires questioning whether being a vampire means that they are inherently evil or destructive, much like Rice's classic reluctant vampires. Belanger explains that the vampire community "cannot help but be influenced by portrayals of vampires in modern culture."[46]

The 1980s saw numerous literary vampires appearing in Rice's wake. Ramsland labeled this period "the vampire boom." She notes that vampires of the vampire boom enjoyed expanded powers including flight, heightened senses, telepathy and telekinesis, and speed-reading. By this point, they resembled superheroes more than the Slavic revenant. This period also saw more viral and genetic models of vampires in the spirit of *I Am Legend*. Ramsland also claims that the vampire boom opened up the vampire to "themes of feminism, gay rights, and experimental pornography."[47] These new elements of race, gender, and sexual orientation paved the way for the awakened model in which vampirism has become an identity group.

Suzy McKee Charnas's *The Vampire Tapestry* (1980) tells the story of the vampire Dr. Edward Lewis Weyland. Weyland is not a supernatural being but rather a separate species, a "perfectly evolved predator." The idea that vampires are the product of a parallel evolution is continued in Whitley Streiber's novel *The Hunger* (1981). Streiber's vampire Miriam Blaylock is an immortal and probably the last of her kind. She can turn humans into vampires but these hybrids live for only a few centuries before rapidly aging. Despite their age, they are unable to die and Blaylock has an attic full of the mummified but still conscious remains of her previous husbands.

In 1983, *The Hunger* was adapted into a movie starring David Bowie and Susan Sarandon. Although the movie received bad reviews it achieved a cult following among goths. The vampires of the film draw blood using bladed metal ankhs. The ankh has since become synonymous with vampires. Numerous vampire games as well as real vampire groups use different styles of ankhs as symbols of their groups. This also initiated a trend linking the origin of vampires to ancient Egypt rather than Eastern Europe. Rice's Egyptian vampire origin story would not appear until *Queen of the Damned* (1988).

Brian Lumley's Necroscope series presents vampires as aliens from another dimension. The series consists of five novels published from 1986 to 1991. Lumley's antagonists are a race known as "the wamphyri." On their own world, they not only hunt humans for food but construct buildings out of human bones and fabric from human skin. Throughout history, wamphyri have occasionally crossed into our world through a portal in Eastern Europe. A number of horror writers have wanted to reclaim the vampire as a demonic other and a force for evil, and Lumley's horrific vampires represent a backlash against Anne Rice and the sympathetic vampire. By portraying vampires as a separate species, the novels of "the vampire boom" period set the stage for an awakened model of vampirism. The vampiric condition could now be imagined as something you are born with rather than a curse or a transformation.

The greatest vampiric cultural event of the last few decades has been *Buffy the Vampire Slayer,* which aired from 1997 to 2003. Like *Dark Shadows* and The Vampire Chronicles, the series succeeds in creating a large world with its own supernatural laws and varieties of beings. Fans refer to this as "The Buffyverse" or sometimes "The Whedonverse" after the show's creator, Joss Whedon. The attention *Buffy* has received from scholars is phenomenal, with literally hundreds of books and articles dedicated to analysis and critique of the series.[48] As of this writing, "The Slayage Conference" for *Buffy* analysts has been meeting annually for the last three years, and in 2007 an international conference on *Buffy* was held in Istanbul, Turkey. At the last paper I gave on the vampire community, there was only time to take two questions, of which one was, "What do vampires think about *Buffy*?" Finally, a recent book review of Rob Latham's *Consuming Youth: Vampires, Cyborgs, and the Culture of Consumption* was rather critical and demanded to know, "Where the heck is Buffy?"[49]

Buffy has undoubtedly had a profound cultural influence, especially for adolescents and women. Lynn Schofield Clark indicates that *Buffy* contributed to young people's "swamping" The Pagan Federation with requests for information about witchcraft.[50] A forthcoming book by sociologist Kristin Aune is anticipated to link *Buffy* to the decline of female church attendance in the England. English women have been leaving Christian churches at the rate of 50,000 a year, and Buffy's portrayal of Wicca and empowered women is cited as a contributing factor.[51] However, there appears to be no evidence that *Buffy* has influenced the

Joss Whedon, creator of *Buffy The Vampire Slayer,* surrounded by vampire minions. Unlike Lugosi's suave portrayal of Dracula, Whedon's vampires are hideous. (AP Photo)

modern vampire community. During the research for this book, vampires never discussed *Buffy* or referenced the show in their online forums. Only when outsiders asked them what they thought of the show did vampires opine on *Buffy.* For example, an interviewer asked vampire Don Henrie, "Do you root for the bad guys on *Buffy?*" Henrie replied, "I root for both. We need all sorts in this world."[52] This was likely a purely political answer used by Henrie to divert this question into a larger issue of cultural pluralism.

It is obvious why no one watching *Buffy* would "root for the bad guys." The vampire antagonists of this show are physically hideous and literally soulless. The vampires' makeup is directly inspired by Quentin Tarantino's film *From Dusk Till Dawn* (1996). This film was itself part of the backlash against Rice's beautiful and tragic vampires and was panned in the vampire journal *Midnight Sun.*[53] With the exception of the Buffy's vampire paramours, Angel and Spike, the vampires and demons of this series represent cosmological evil. *Buffy* theorists such as Rhonda Wilcox and David Lavery point out that the monsters Buffy fights are typically metaphorical embodiments of problems faced by teenagers.[54] This leaves very little room for a sympathetic reading of these characters.

Buffy does feature several "redeemed" villains, but these have not enjoyed the same popularity as figures like Barnabus Collins and Lestat. Mary Alice Money describes a theme of "rehabilitation" throughout *Buffy* as several evil characters gradually gain depth and become protagonists. In the case of Spike, this redemption appears to be a plot device rather than the deliberate presentation of an anti-hero. Money quotes James Marsters as he explains why his character, Spike, was not sustainable as a villain, "At some point either the villain kills whoever he's wanting to kill or he gets killed and he hopes he has a good death. If neither of those two things happen, then the character gets bleached out and becomes a bumbling fool . . . I was just looking for a good body count and a good death."[55] This suggests that Spike's character evolved along a trajectory that parallels his predecessor, Barnabus Collins: A prolonged story line essentially demands that a vampiric antagonist is either killed or reformed.

The idea that vampires are "misunderstood" or that vampirism is desirable is explicitly attacked in an episode entitled "Lie to Me." In what appears to be a deliberate parody of lifestyle vampires, the plot of this episode involves an underground club of teenagers who are fascinated by the undead and see vampirism as a path to immortality and a higher state of consciousness. These would-be vampires are depicted as clueless losers next to Buffy and her friends who understand the grim reality of undeath. One character says of the vampire club, "These people are sheep. They want to be vampires because they're lonely, they're miserable, they're bored." The would-be vampires are, of course, horrified when they finally meet Sunnydale's actual vampires, who begin savagely devouring them until Buffy saves the day.

However, the primary complaint expressed by the vampire community about *Buffy* is not its portrayal of vampires, but the concern that the series has inspired self-styled vampire slayers. Tony Thorne quotes a vampire, "Did you know there is an actual fad for being a Vampire Slayer? This is dangerous stuff due to the TV show [*Buffy the Vampire Slayer*], there are people who think by hunting down a vampire and killing it, they will become the smart handsome/beautiful hero that they are so desperate to be."[56] Typically this "slayer-syndrome" manifests in the form of harassing e-mails and obnoxious posts on vampire Web sites, but there have been actual murders carried out by mentally ill people who believe they are destroying vampires (see Chapter 7).

Vampires in Occult Writing

The occult revival of the nineteenth century coincided with the rise of vampire literature. Various esoteric movements took interest in vampires and sought to explain these creatures in terms of occult science. Just as the writers of the vampire boom tried to make a more believable vampire by replacing the supernatural with viruses and parallel evolution, nineteenth-century occult writers tried to explain the vampire of folklore through fringe theories such as mesmerism and astral projection. These theories updated the vampire into a creature that seemed more believable by nineteenth-century standards. Occult writers like

Dion Fortune have profoundly influenced how the vampire community interprets their experiences. The concept of a "psychic vampire" could not have emerged had the vampire not been redefined by occult writers.

Writers in Western Europe first began to consider the reality of vampires in the eighteenth century. During this time there were widespread reports of vampire attacks in remote villages throughout East Prussia, Hungary, Austrian Serbia, Silesia, and Wallachia. While vampire panic was ensuing in Eastern Europe, the Enlightenment was underway in France. Several Enlightenment thinkers became interested in vampires, including Denis Diderot, Voltaire, and Jean-Jacques Rousseau.[57] Rousseau is famously quoted from one of his letters, "If there is in this world a well-attested account, it is that of the vampires. Nothing is lacking: official reports, affidavits of well-known people, of surgeons, of priests, of magistrates; the judicial proof is most complete. And with all that, who is there who believes in vampires?"[58]

The most famous vampire treatise from this time is *Dissertations sur les Apparitions des Anges, des Démons, et des Esprits et sur les Revenans et les Vampires de Hongrie, de Boheme, de Moravie, et de Silésie* (*Dissertation on the Apparitions of Angels, Demons, and Spirits and on the Revenants and Vampires of Hungary, Bohemia, Moravia, and Selesia*) written in 1746 by Antoine Augustine Calmet. Calmet (1672–1757) was a Benedictine monk and wrote several respected books of Biblical exegesis. Calmet investigated reports of vampires from Eastern Europe and concluded, on both theological and scientific grounds, that vampires probably do not exist. His treatise argues that only God has the power to raise bodies from the dead and suggests that exhumed bodies that appear fresh were buried alive or else are the result of other natural phenomena. He also points out that he has yet to hear a vampire story from a reliable witness and suggests that most of the deaths associated with vampire plagues were actually people who died of fright.[59] Most convincingly, he points out that if vampires did exist, it would be impossible for them to leave their graves and return to them without disturbing the soil.[60]

Interest in vampires was revived in the nineteenth century in part because of the spiritualist movement. Most historians place the birth of Spiritualism in 1848 in Hydesdale, New York, when Kate and Margaret Fox announced that they were in communication with the ghost of a peddler who had been murdered near their home. During séances, witnesses heard the spirit respond to questions through a series of raps. This started an American obsession with mediums and séances. The movement grew even faster after the carnage of the Civil War, as Americans sought to contact dead family members. The first national spiritualist meeting was held in 1864, by which time the movement had swelled to 11 million adherents.[61] The movement also spread to Europe, where it helped to spark the nineteenth century occult revival. In 1888, Margaret Fox confessed that she had been fabricating the knocks by using an apple tied to her toe. However, this confession did little to slow down the movement.[62]

One of the first occultists to begin redefining vampires was Alphonse Louis Constant (1810–1875), better known by his pseudonym, Eliphaz Levi. Levi was interested in revolutionary socialism as well as occultism and spent several years in jail for producing "seditious writing." Although Levi is often overlooked by modern vampirologists, he introduced early ideas that the modern vampire community might term "astral vampires" and "psychic vampires." Both are described as draining vitality, but the former was a disembodied entity while the later appeared human. These two basic types have been modified by occult theories ever since.

Levi believed that a magician could create "thought-forms" capable of attacking other people, and he referred to these thought-forms as vampires. He is quoted, "when one creates phantoms for oneself, one puts vampires into the world, and one must nourish these children of voluntary nightmare with one's blood, one's life, one's intelligence, and one's reason without ever satisfying them."[63] It is not clear here whether he means that vampires are *literally* non-corporeal spirits or if he is using the word "vampire" metaphorically, as did his contemporary, Marx. The idea that a vampire could be a non-corporeal spirit rather than a corpse would later come to be called "astral vampirism."

Levi describes a second type of vampire in his opus *Dogma et Ritual,* written in 1856:

> I must not conclude this chapter without mentioning the curious opinions of certain Kabalists, who distinguish between apparent and real death, holding that the two are seldom simultaneous. In their view, the majority of persons who are buried are still alive, while a number of others who are regarded as living are in reality dead. Incurable madness, for example, would be with them an incomplete but real death, leaving the earthly form under the purely instinctive control of the sidereal body. When the human soul suffers a greater strain than it can bear, it would thus become separated from the body, leaving the animal soul, or sidereal body, in its place, and these human remains would be less alive in a sense than a mere animal. Dead persons of this kind are said to be identified by the complete extinction of the moral and affectionate sense: they are neither bad nor good; they are dead. Such beings, who are poisonous fungi of the human race, absorb the life of living beings to their fullest possible extent, and this is why their proximity depletes the soul and chills the heart. If such corpse-like creatures really existed, they would stand for all that was recounted in former times about brucalaques and vampires.[64]

In this novel approach to the undead, Levi introduces several important concepts that are used by the twenty-first-century real vampire community. First, he introduces the concept of an astral body (Waite's translation of "sidereal body" uses a Greek root instead of a Latin one.) This astral body is a vital force and is distinct from the Judaeo-Christian concept of an immortal soul. Second, he does not describe the undead as consuming blood but rather as "absorbing life." Finally, unlike Calmet who was evaluating reports of vampires, Levi states that he is describing an entity that *would be labeled as* a vampire. This allows him to divorce his entity from the many folkloric traditions of vampires of which Calmet was so skeptical. The same distinction is made today by self-identified vampires.

Levi continues to give what appears to be an account of a psychic vampire:

> Now, are there not certain persons in whose presence one feels less intelligent, less good, sometimes even less honest? Are there not some whose vicinity extinguishes all faith and all enthusiasm, who draw you by your weaknesses, who govern you by your evil propensities, and make you die slowly to morality in a torment like that of Mezentius? These are dead people whom we mistake for living beings; these are vampires whom we regard as friends![65]

Levi rarely receives credit for his ideas about vampires—either from the occult community or the modern vampire community. Similar theories may have enjoyed more popularity because they were disseminated through the more popular spiritualist movement. A case in point is the French spiritualist Z. J. Piérart. Piérart was a professor at the College of Maubeuge and in 1848 founded a journal, *La Revue Spiritualiste*.[66] According to Piérart, vampire legends could be explained as a form of "bicorporeal existence."[67] According to this theory, the body—which is not completely dead—remains in the grave while its spirit detaches to drain the blood of the living. This astral vampire then deposits the stolen blood into the comatose body, maintaining a state of suspended animation. Piérart speculated that such an existence could be caused by the trauma of being buried alive. The theory was significant because it solved Calmet's objection that vampires could not physically move through the ground to emerge from the grave. Interestingly, Calmet mentions, "To say that the devil subtilizes or spiritiualizes their bodies, is an assertion entirely destitute of proof, and even probability."[68] Either Calmet anticipated Piérart's theory or he was responding to a similar one that existed in the eighteenth century.

Madame Helena Blavatsky (1831–1891), a founder of the Theosophical Society, promoted Piérart's astral vampire theory in *Isis Unveiled* (1877).[69] More than any other group, the Theosophical Society is responsible for disseminating ideas of psychic and astral vampires. Numerous Theosophical writers promoted and modified these ideas, making vampires part of the fabric of New Age spirituality.

In 1895, one of Blavatsky's students, Charles W. Leadbeater (1854–1934), explained in greater detail how it is possible for evil magicians to maintain an existence as astral vampires. His book *The Astral Plane: Its Scenery, Habits, and Phenomena* fused Piérart's theory with elements of Hinduism.[70] In an 1891 paper entitled "The Vampire," Henry Steel Olcott (1832–1907) links Piérart's theory to stories of yogis surviving for many weeks while buried alive. This same yogic practice is also referenced in a speech by Dr. Van Helsing in *Dracula,* suggesting that Stoker had read Olcott's paper. Olcott concludes his essay by arguing that all civilized people should practice cremation in order to prevent vampirism. Notable in this paper is Olcott's claim that the vampire draws not only blood but "nervous force."[71] This begins the vampire's shift from a diet of blood to a diet of energy. Franz Hartmann (1838–1912) was yet another Theosophist who modified Piérart's theory. Hartmann was obsessed with being buried alive and actually wrote a book on the subject. Hartmann's ideas about vampires were really a return to the work of Levi. He extended Piérart's theory, claiming that the astral body of a vampire could exist completely independent of a corpse as a free-floating non-corporal entity.[72]

At the same time that the Theosophists were developing theories of astral vampires, they were simultaneously describing a second type of living, psychic vampire. In an article on hypnotism written in 1890 for the Theosophical magazine *Lucifer,* Blavatsky describes vampirism as a loss of vitality through an "occult osmosis." Like modern psychic vampires, Blavatsky describes vampires as having a special faculty that allows them to siphon vital energy and adds that they are often not conscious of what they are doing. She writes, "Vampirism . . . is a blind mechanical process, generally produced without the knowledge of either the *absorber* or the vampirized party."[73] Similarly, Olcott's article on vampires describes a second type of "magnetic vampirism," which is seen as more natural than the undead astral vampire. He writes:

> This magnetic vampirism is practiced every day and hour in social, most especially in conjugal, intercourse: the weak absorb strength from the strong, the sickly from the robust, the aged from the young. One vampirizes by hand-shaking, by sitting close together, by sleeping in the same bed; the full brains of the clever are "sucked" by the spongy brains of the stupid. Throughout all these phases the law of natural equilibration asserts itself, as it does in the whole realm of physics.

He adds that great sages and mystics instinctively seek solitude so that their mental faculties will not be siphoned off by lesser minds.

Hartmann also believed in psychic vampires, which he called "psychic sponges." In 1896, he described such individuals in the occult periodical "Borderlands":

> They unconsciously vampirize every sensitive person with whom they come into contact, and they instinctively seek out such persons and invite them to stay at their houses. I know of an old lady, a vampire, who thus ruined the health of a lot of robust servant girls, whom she took into her service and made them sleep in her room. They were all in good health when they entered, but soon they began to sicken, they became emaciated and consumptive and had to leave the service.[74]

Hartmann's account goes a bit further than Blavatsky and Olcott in that he actually accuses an acquaintance of being a psychic vampire.

Possibly as a result of these writings, many elements of Theosophy still appear in the modern vampire community. Blavatsky derived her authority from her contact with "secret masters" in Tibet, much as vampire initiatory groups claim to have contact with disembodied vampiric entities. Ramsland describes chatting online with a individual named "NiteTrain," who claims his existence began 20,000 years ago on the lost continent of Atlantis, Atlantis having been a favorite topic of Blavatsky.[75] The vampire group Ordo Sekhemu lists Blavatsky among their recommended readings for vampires.[76]

The Hermetic Order of the Golden Dawn also took an interest in vampires, although not to the same extent as the Theosophists. From 1892 to 1894 the Golden Dawn produced a series of documents called the "Flying Rolls."[77] These documents would circulate in a chain being mailed from one member to another. Envelopes containing a flying roll were said to be unmarked with the postage stamp affixed upside down. Like Levi, these documents describe both living psychic vampires as well as disembodied astral vampires.

"Flying Roll no. V" was written Frater Resurgam, a pseudonym used by Dr. Edward Berridge (1843–1923). He accuses an old man of vampirism and prescribes a remedy for such people:

> A few years ago, I noticed that invariably after a prolonged interview with a certain person, I felt exhausted. At first, I thought it only the natural result of a long conversation with a prosy, fidgety, old gentleman; but later it dawned upon me, that being a man of exhausted nervous vitality, he was really preying upon me. I don't suppose that he was at all externally conscious that he possessed a vampire organisation, for he was a benevolent kind-hearted man, who would have shrunk in horror from such a suggestion. Nevertheless, he was, in his inner personality an intentional vampire, for he acknowledged that he was about to marry a young wife in order, if possible, to recuperate his exhausted system. The next time, therefore, that he was announced, I closed myself to him, before he was admitted. I imagined that I had formed myself a complete investiture of odic fluid, surrounding me on all sides, but not touching me, and impenetrable to any hostile currents. This magical process was immediately and permanently successful—I never had to repeat it.[78]

This passage was significant for Belanger, and she mentions it in *The Psychic Vampire Codex*.[79] Notably, Berridge's account of an unconscious vampire was written only two years after William James's *The Principles of Psychology*, which examines the use of the terms "subconscious" and "unconscious" in philosophical and psychological literature.[80] Berridge had attended The Homeopathic Medical College of Pennsylvania and was probably aware of psychiatric discussion of the subconscious.

"Flying Roll no. XXXIV" is entitled "an exorcism." The author is Frater Sub Spe, a Latin motto meaning "under hope." Frater Sub Spe is believed to have been John Williams Brodie-Innes (1848–1923), a lawyer and leading member of the Golden Dawn. He describes how his wife was suffering from influenza until both he and his wife reached a point of exhaustion. Brodie-Innes attributed this exhaustion to "a vampirising elemental." This would seem to be identical to the vampire thought-forms described by Eliphaz Levi. When he realizes this is the source of the trouble, a disembodied voice in his head begins describing an exorcism ritual. Brodie-Innes completes the ritual, banishes the vampire, and he and his wife make a full recovery. The document also contains commentary from Frater Resurgam (Berridge).[81]

Both stories contain similar elements: The occultist is suffering from a completely ordinary malady (fatigue or the flu), they attribute their health problems to a type of vampire, and they discover a solution to their problem. The turn of the century saw many similar occult theories in which vampirism posed a threat to one's vitality. More often, the vampire was conceived as a living person rather than the disembodied vampire described by Brodie-Innes.

Another unconscious living vampire appears in *Scientific Religion,* written in 1888 by Laurence Oliphant (1829–1888). Oliphant warns of what he calls "human vampire organisms." He writes, "for many persons are so constituted that they have, unconsciously to themselves, an extraordinary faculty of sucking the life-principal from others, who are constitutionally incapable of maintaining their vitality."[82] Like Berridge, Oliphant accuses the elderly of having this faculty. Interestingly, he goes on to describe how some people have this faculty in reverse, energizing those around them rather than depleting them. He also comments that married couples rarely have equal amounts of vitality and that one partner tends to drain the other.[83]

Occult theories of vampires continued in the twentieth century. In 1904, Albert Osman Eaves produced *Modern Vampirism: Its Dangers and How to Avoid Them.* Eaves combines descriptions of vampires by the various Theosophical writers along with the work of Oliphant and others. Like other occult models of vampirism, Eaves's descriptions are of living people who drain vitality as well as disembodied vampire spirits. Unlike most occult writers, Eaves also mentions "true vampires," which he believes may still exist in Eastern Europe. According to Eaves, true vampires are found in this part of the world because East Europeans still have "a strain of fourth race blood in them."[84] Modern humans, according to Eaves, are of the fifth race. It is only in populations that are evolutionarily inferior where true vampires may form.

Eaves's work was eclipsed by Montague Summers (1880–1948), who produced some of the most famous books of vampire lore: *The Vampire: His Kith and Kin* (1928) and *The Vampire in Europe* (1929). Summers had an interest in Gothic literature and was a friend of occultist Aleister Crowley. He converted to Catholicism and took the title "Reverend Alphonsus Joseph-Mary Augustus Montague Summers." Although he was not actually ordained, he modeled himself as a modern-day inquisitor. In 1928, he produced the first English translation of *The Malleus Maleficarium,* a fifteenth-century text used to detect witches. Summers writes approvingly of the disembodied vampire theories of Piérart and Hartmann. However, he objects to the terms "astral" and "ethereal" (possibly on theological grounds) and concludes that the vampire's subtle body must be made of ectoplasm.[85]

Aleister Crowley (1875–1947). A notorious British occultist, Crowley was briefly a member of the Golden Dawn and also studied yoga in India. His writings have had a profound influence on the left-hand path in modern Western esotericism. Crowley is also considered by some to have been a vampire himself. (AP Photo)

If there is one classical occult writer who has had the most influence on the modern vampire community, it is Dion Fortune (1890–1946.) Born Violet Firth, she joined the Alpha and Omega chapter of the Stella Matutina, an occult group affiliated with the Hermetic Order of the Golden Dawn. When she joined the order, she took the magical motto, "Deo Non Fortuna" (By God not luck), which was shortened into her public name, Dion Fortune.[86] In 1930, she published *Psychic Self-Defense,* which has been cited by Belanger and others in the vampire community. She also describes two types of vampire entities: an undead astral vampire and a living human vampire. Although Fortune does not actually use the phrase, "psychic vampire," she does speak of psychic energy. Fortune references Freud throughout her work, and her concept of psychic energy is heavily influenced by the Freudian notion of libido.

A chapter on vampirism relates the theory of an adept she calls "Z." Z, who may have been Brodie-Innes (also known as Frater Sub Spe), described vampires as the ghosts of evil adepts who have learned to survive by feeding on the life-force of others. Z theorized that vampires arrived in England during WWI, when dying occultists from Eastern Europe survived by latching astrally onto the bodies of British soldiers. Like Eaves, Z fuses fear of vampires with xenophobic attitudes toward East Europeans. Fortune adds to Z's theory a second type of vampire. She writes:

> Vampirism is contagious; the person who is vampirised, being depleted of vitality, is a psychic vacuum, himself absorbing from anyone he comes across in order to refill his depleted resources of vitality. He soon learns by experience the tricks of a vampire without realising their significance, and before he knows where he is, he is a full-blown vampire himself, vampirising others.[87]

Fortune is innovative in as much as her theory bridges these two types of vampires. Living psychic vampires are created after being "vampirized" by undead, astral vampires.

Psychic Self-Defense became a wildly popular book among modern New Agers and Pagans.[88] Konstantinos, Christopher Penczak, and others have modified Fortune's techniques for a new generation seeking to foil the attacks of astral and psychic vampires. As a result, Pagans have had a mistrust of self-described vampires that has only recently begun to abate. Belanger describes attending a panel on vampires at the Pagan "Northwest Con" in Seattle, Washington. To her disappointment, the panel discussed only protection techniques with no positive views of vampires expressed.[89] This led Belanger to describe enmity toward vampires as the only issue that Pagans and the religious right can agree on.[90]

In an interview with the magazine *Birth of Tragedy,* Anton LaVey claims to have coined the term "psychic vampirism."[91] *The Satanic Bible,* written in 1969, presents "Nine Satanic Statements," of which number six reads, "Satan represents responsibility for the responsible instead of concern for psychic vampires!"[92] LaVey's use of the term has led to a great deal of confusion. LaVey's "psychic vampires" are ordinary people who are simply unethical and have a gift for manipulation. The earliest use I have found of the phrase "psychic vampire," in the sense that vampire community uses it, appears in *Vampires Are* written by Stephen Kaplan in 1984.[93] Ramsland helpfully makes a distinction between "psychic vampirism," which is an occult theory, and "psychological vampirism," which is the ordinary manipulation described by LaVey.[94] (Of course, theoretically, one could be both a psychological vampire *and* a psychic vampire.)

In 2002, an article by Dr. Judith Orloff entitled "Energy Vampires" appeared on Oprah.com. The article begins by describing various sorts of manipulative people such as "the sob sister," "the charmer," and "the drama queen." However, Oprah's readers are advised to repel energy vampires by "using their own subtle energies" to create "an energy shield."[95] These are not psychological techniques but the occult methods offered by Fortune. This seems to be a continuation of the confusion between psychic and psychological vampires.

Metaphysical and Holistic Health

Catherine Albanese, in her book *A Republic of Mind and Spirit,* describes metaphysics as an "American religious mentality," which she sees as separate from occultism. Some the characteristics she ascribes to this tradition include a preoccupation with the mind and its powers, an emphasis on direct experience, an emphasis on movement and energy especially with respect toward healing, and a magical practice that brings about effects primarily through the use of will, imagination, and, most importantly, visualization, rather than through the use of magical artifacts and ritual.[96] Albanese could very easily be describing the energy paradigms of the vampire community. The idea of a vampire that drains vitality merged quickly with ideas of mesmerism, New Thought, osteopathy, and other metaphysical approaches to health and well-being that were spreading throughout the nineteenth century.

Although it is rarely considered, vampire slaying is essentially a technique of holistic health. Barber attributes belief in vampires primarily to a failure to understand disease.[97] In some cases, the vampire's heart or body was burnt and its ashes were made into medicine, which was administered to the afflicted. What is interesting is that many holistic health practices have since been reinterpreted as vampiric. Summers notes that in I Kings 1: 1–4, King David grows ill and a young woman is placed in his bed. David does not copulate with the woman, and it is assumed that by warming the bed with her body, her presence will help David recover. (Although any mammal could have provided heat as well as a young girl.) However, Summers interprets this practice as a kind of "spiritual vampirism" in which David is not only sharing the girl's body heat but actually draining her vitality.[98]

Holistic health practices are again interpreted as vampiric in Charles W. Webber's novel *Yieger's Cabinet: Spiritual Vampirism: The History of Etherial Softdown and her New Friends of the "Inner Light."* Originally from Kentucky, Webber went to Texas in 1838—when it was still fighting for independence— and had some affiliation with The Texas Rangers. He returned to Kentucky where he studied medicine before joining the Princeton Theological Seminary. Webber ultimately dropped out of seminary and moved to New York City, where he worked as a journalist and produced several novels—one of which was praised by Edgar Allan Poe.[99] During his time in New York, Webber has been described as an alcoholic and mentally ill.[100] He died in 1855 while fighting alongside the mercenary William Walker in the Nicaraguan Civil War. With such an adventurous life as well as a novel on vampirism, it is at least conceivable that Webber could be the basis for Quincey P. Morris, the Texan vampire hunter in Stoker's *Dracula.*

Webber is possibly the first writer of the nineteenth century to describe a psychic vampire, predating even Levi. Although *Spiritual Vampirism* is presented as a novel, the author never intended it as a work of fiction. Webber's vampiress,

Etherial Softdown, was actually early feminist and holistic healer Mary Grove Nichols. Nichols was a political radical who preached equality in marriage as well as the dangers of masturbation and corsets. She had an interest in spiritualism, mesmerism, and especially water-cure therapy. Nichols and Webber lived together in New York at a house on 261 Tenth Street along with other writers and radicals. Trouble started when Webber formed a passionate relationship with Nichols's daughter, Elma. Nichols sent Elma to live with a friend and Webber is believed to have written *Spiritual Vampirism* out of revenge.[101] Softdown is a medium and a mesmerist who is actually draining the vitality of those around her. Webber also goes to great lengths to describe how ugly and stupid Etherial is, adding that it is only through vampirism that she grows beautiful and intelligent. Nichols claims never to have read the book; however, she wrote an article defending herself in the September 1853 issue of her *Journal of Health, Water-Cure, and Human Progress.*[102]

Webber prefaces his book with a a treatise on mesmerism, explaining that this is the scientific basis of the vampire legend. Where Levi and Piérart would later attempt to explain vampires in terms of astral bodies, Webber uses the concept of "Odic force." Blavatsky and Berridge also cite Odic force in their descriptions of psychic vampires, and their ideas may be indebted to Webber. The theory of Odic force actually began with German scientist Franz Mesmer (1734–1815). Mesmer conducted experiments using magnets to heal illnesses. He believed that faith healing was possible not through divine intervention but through a vital force he called "animal magnetism." Several Enlightenment scientists, including Benjamin Franklin, investigated these claims and concluded that animal magnetism does not exist.[103] Regardless, a group of fringe scientists and healers continued the practice of "mesmerism" throughout the nineteenth century. In the mid-1840s, German chemist and metallurgist Baron Karl von Reichenbach (1788–1869) argued that mesmerism did utilize an unknown force, but one totally different from either magnetism or electricity. He named this phenomenon Odic or Odylic force. Spiritualists soon began incorporating Odic force into their explanations of spirit manifestations.[104]

Webber argued that prophets and holy men are the "positive poles" of Odic force while the "negative poles" are vampires. Furthermore, he states that mesmerism as well as clairvoyance and other abilities associated with spiritualism deplete the body's reserves of Odic force. Thus anyone who uses these techniques must drain vitality from others. He writes:

> They must have the Odic fluid restored and . . . in taking your "enough," they exhaust and undermine the holy purposes of your life to make up that deficit in their own . . . these human vampires or sponges may be, therefore, as well absorbents of the spiritual as animal vitality. Their parasitical roots may strike into the very centers of life, and their hungry seekers remorselessly draw away the virility of manhood, or spiritual strength.[105]

Webber's theory implies that most holistic healers—and certainly Mary Grove Nichols—are spiritual vampires. In fact, Webber begins his novel with the Shakespeare quote, "Be thou a spirit of health, or goblin damned?" Were it not for the thoroughly negative characterization of vampires, this model of energy is remarkably like the one described by Belanger in *The Psychic Vampire Codex,* in which vampires can use borrowed energy for a variety of healing abilities.

Twentieth-century holistic healers would also describe people as either emitting or absorbing vital energy, although without the negative connotations applied by Webber and other nineteenth-century writers. This can be seen in the practice of osteopathy as described by Robert C. Fulford (1905–1997). Fulford believed in channels of subtle energy flowing within the body and that their blockage could lead not only to physical maladies but also to mental and emotional stress. Fulford also seems to anticipate the vampire community's ideas about energy exchange. He confesses that he prefers to work with children rather than adults because adults "emit less energy" then children and take away his own energy during treatment, making him feel "depleted." By contrast, children are described as "more radiant" and absorb less energy.[106] For Fulford, this unconscious drain of energy is not pathological, but rather a natural part of the human condition. Not surprisingly, osteopathy has its roots in the nineteenth century, and its founder, Andrew Taylor Still, was heavily involved in the spiritualist movement.

By the late 1980s and early 1990s, the label "psychic vampire" was being applied to holistic health practices, usually in a pejorative sense. While writing *Vampires Among Us,* Rosemary Ellen Guiley received a letter from an occultist in California who described her neighbor as a psychic vampire. Pat, the alleged vampire, claimed that he never became sick and got whatever he wanted because he maintained a positive attitude. The belief that a positive attitude has material benefits is quite common among holistic health practitioners. This idea also has its roots in the nineteenth century, with an American movement known as New Thought. However, in this case, it was considered to be evidence that Pat was a psychic vampire. Pat also studied aikido and, because he had no interest in occultism, the letter speculated that his vampire abilities may be the result of "a perverted form of aikido."[107]

A lively dialogue was forming at this time between psychic vampirism, holistic health, and Asian metaphysics. Martial arts became an important vehicle through which these ideas were exchanged. Glenn Morris is an author, energy worker, and self-described "ninja master." He describes attending a seminar in 1990 entitled "The Healing Process: Exploring Body-Mind Integration." The seminar featured a medley of reiki practitioners, chiropractors, and other holistic healers. At the start of the conference, Morris introduced himself: "Dr. Morris, a fourth-degree black belt in Bujinkan Ninpo, and it is so nice to be a vampire here at play with all you nice people."[108] The other attendees looked shocked, which is no doubt what Morris intended. By 1990, the idea of an energy vampire would certainly have been familiar to those at the conference, but for someone to *admit* to energy vampirism would have been quite shocking. Morris's comment was an important moment in humanizing the psychic vampire. It may represent the first case of a holistic health practice that was perceived as vampirism and yet still presented as positive.

As other Asian practices including yoga, qigong, and reiki became incorporated into the milieu of Western holistic health, many vampires have turned to these traditions to explain their experiences. These came to replace the Western concepts that had shaped the idea of a psychic vampire such as mesmerism, Odic force, and libidinal energy. Nineteenth-century writers knew very little of Asian concepts of energy, and their ideas are based on studies of the nervous system as well as emerging theories of electromagnetism. But in the late twentieth century, one was far more likely to know someone who practiced yoga or tai-chi than a mesmerist. Accordingly, vampires now typically explain subtle energy by borrowing Asian terms for vitality such as the Chinese word "*qi*" and, especially, the Sanskrit word "*prana.*"

Interestingly, the first mention of vampires feeding on prana is found in an article entitled "Real Vampires" that appeared in the Pagan publication *Fireheart* in 1987. Inanna Arthen describes being part of the Aquarian movement of the 1970s, which led her to join the EarthSpirit Community, a Pagan network based in Boston. The community was aware that Arthen was a vampire and asked her to write the article. When asked about her use of the word "prana," she commented that she never converted to an Eastern religion but that she incorporated yoga and Chinese holistic medicine into her larger spiritual practice.[109] Although *Fireheart*'s circulation was quite small, the vampire article was found by vampirologists and cited in several books. As a result, "prana" is now the most common term for energy used by vampires, with the possible exception of "psi."

Today the dialogue between psychic vampirism and Eastern healing techniques has led to some interesting exchanges and collaborations. I observed one meeting of the Atlanta Vampire Alliance that was attended by a reiki practitioner. Although he was not a vampire, other members commented that they enjoyed his presence, describing him as "our battery." (This recalls Webber's discussion of positive and negative Odic poles.) Belanger describes meeting "Casey," a Chinese-American holistic healer, at an energy conference in Modesto, California, in 1995. Casey assessed Belanger's energy and was shocked by what he found. Belanger explained that she was a vampire and that there was nothing "broken" with her energy body. This led to an experiment in which Casey emitted energy at Belanger to see how much she could absorb. This lasted several hours before the contest was declared a draw. Casey's interpretation of Belanger's vampirism was that she was missing a major energy center known as the *hara*. Casey and Belanger maintained contact after the conference and Casey became interested in "curing" Belanger by constructing a new *hara* (Belanger, however, has no interest in such a cure).[110]

Vampire Role-Playing Games

When describing their methodology for surveying the real vampire community, a researcher from Suscitatio Enterprises commented, "We avoid role-players like the plague." The real vampire community is often confused with the role-players, to the irritation of both groups. However, these two groups have emerged together and each has been influenced by the other. The vampire culture that formed in New York was certainly indebted to role-playing games. However, it has also been suggested that the vampire role-playing games based the culture of their fictional vampires on a previously existing real vampire community.

The first vampire role-playing games were noncommercial and began to form online. Players would assume the roles of Anne Rice's vampires and interact with each other in a free-form conversation.[111] However, this role-playing paled in comparison to the first commercial game inspired by Rice's vampires, *Vampire: The Masquerade*. *Vampire* was published in 1991 by White Wolf Games. At the time, White Wolf was a tiny company located in Stone Mountain, Georgia, a suburb of Atlanta. That same year the game received an award for having the best rules of a role-playing game. Players take the role of vampires and must navigate the often deadly politics of vampire society. Where previous role-playing games had primarily emphasized combat, *Vampire* emphasized political intrigue, storytelling, and dynamic characters. *Vampire* was the consummation of the literary "vampire hero." As vampires, characters must struggle to maintain their humanity, otherwise they succumb to their inner beast and are reduced to raving, bloodthirsty monsters. The characters are neither good nor bad, they are simply "protagonists."

Interestingly, Atlanta has been home to a club called "Masquerade" since 1989. Although Masquerade has branched out into a wider variety of acts, it has traditionally been a goth club. Masquerade is actually a converted turn-of-the-century mill and the bare stone walls have an obvious gothic appeal. There are a number of rumors about the connection between a game entitled *Vampire: The Masquerade* and the nearby goth club. One is that goths had invented a game played at Masquerade in which they pretended to be vampires and this became the basis for White Wolf's game. An alternate rumor is that the real vampire community had a presence in Masquerade or even that the club's owners were involved in the real vampire community. One contact suggested, "Masquerade was a vampire club posing as a goth club posing as a vampire club."

I contacted Sam Chupp, one of White Wolf's game designers and an Atlanta native. He said that there was no direct connection save for the title and the fact that some of the game designers were patrons of the club. He writes, "When doing initial brainstorming for *Vampire* with Mark Rein-Hagen, they threw it out there as a cool place and Mark seized on it as an idea—the central idea of a 'Masquerade' becoming central to the whole rationale behind Vampires having power but hiding in plain sight." Chupp added that the fictional "Succubus Club" featured in the games is actually an homage to Masquerade.

The success of *Vampire* was followed with a series of related games including *Werewolf: The Apocalypse, Mage: The Ascension, Changeling: The Dreaming,* and *Wraith: The Oblivion.* Collectively, these games all occurred in a fictional earth known as "The World of Darkness." White Wolf produced dozens of books describing the different creatures, political structures, and alternative histories of the World of Darkness.[112] *Vampire* was originally a tabletop game played by rolling dice. However, in 1993, White Wolf made an alternate version of their games known as The Mind's Eye Theatre. The Mind's Eye Theatre version of *Vampire* was a live action role-play (LARP).[113] LARPs involve dressing as vampires and interacting with other players "in character," often in a public place.

The World of Darkness games had a high degree of verisimilitude, complete with their own lexicons of vampiric terms. In fact, they were so realistic that real vampires were sometimes confused when they read White Wolf's books. Belanger mentioned that she encountered White Wolf books while researching vampires. Apparently other real vampires had this experience and mistook the game books for actual vampire lore. The vampire journal *The Midnight Sun* features an article by a Frater Shinobi who cites *The Book of the Damned,* a game book. He writes that, "Principally, I relate to the sect known as Gangrel, with a string of Malkavian, destined to become Inconnu."[114] All of these terms were created by White Wolf and have no basis in vampire lore. Shinobi states in a follow up article, "I was made aware . . . the book I made some references from, *The Book of the Damned,* was part of a role-playing game. I was not aware of this."[115]

A vampire interviewed by Thorne also describes being confused by the role-players themselves:

> The first time I had access to the Internet, I immediately entered "Vampire" into the search engine. For the following few months I was fooled into believing a group of LARP gamers, and though their claims were not wild, they convinced me that I was human and they were not. When I finally realized that these people had spend [sic] the entirely of our correspondence in fantasy I felt more betrayed than I can put into words.[116]

This experience was common and led a real vampire to publish an article in the *Journal of the Dark* on how identify role-player vampires online. Warning signs include an overemphasis of the word "mortal," references to "Elders," and "gratuitous substitution of i with y."[117]

However, many real vampires were not opposed to the growing LARP sensation. People interested in vampirism might drive from several states away to attend a LARP. This created opportunities for the real vampire community to become more organized and more self-aware. Father Sebastiaan made a name for himself in the emerging vampire community as a "fangsmith." Sebastiaan was trained as a dental assistant and his company, Sabretooth, made custom fangs as well as contact lenses. There were not enough lifestyle vampires to support such an enterprise, but that changed with the advent of the *Vampire* LARP. Exactly how many LARPers were around in the late 1990s is unclear. The Camarilla, the game's official fan club, boasted around 3000 members at this time. However, the number of people playing LARPs who were not members may have been two to three times this number—enough to keep a fangsmith in business for a long time. In fact, the first commercial fangsmiths seem to have appeared in Seattle, which at the time was the headquarters of the Camarilla.[118] Johnson also mentions Seattle as a city where fangs can be acquired in *Dhampir: Child of the Blood.*[119] In addition to supplying LARPers with fangs, Sebastiaan was also heavily involved in organizing games in New York through his group Syn Factory/New York by Night.[120] This put Sebastiaan in a place of leadership to begin further projects with the vampire community including The Sanguinarium and Ordo Strigoi Vii.

Belanger was also interested in LARPs and would run games at national conventions. Where Sebastiaan saw LARPs as a way to begin organizing the vampire community, Belanger saw it as an opportunity to create a network of like-minded vampires and metaphysicians. This actually led to the creation of House Kheperu. She writes:

> While the game itself as based upon fiction and heavily influenced by the novels of Anne Rice, it still attracted many isolated psychic vampires. The live-action version provided them with a social outlet where they could openly adopt the identity of a vampire, even if this was only within the context of a game. More helpful than being able to play at being what they already were, was a the fact that vampirism became an acceptable topic of conversation among players who met socially outside the game. . . . During the game, I would study the players, noting who wore jewelry or other symbols typically associated with occult practices and getting a feel for these people's energy. I learned to identify certain types of people by "feel" alone, and once the game was over, I would approach them and invite them to a closed-door discussion on beliefs, practices, and experiences. . . . It was through these closed-door discussions after games that my group was born.[121]

As the vampire community became more self-aware and more organized, several traditions were brought from the game into actual vampire culture. This naturally led people to assume that real vampire groups were also playing a game, creating further confusion. This is especially prominent in Johnson's book. Johnson describes the Biblical character Cain as the founder of a clan of vampires—distinct from the author's clan, The Clan of Lilith. The idea that Cain was the first vampire, and that vampires are divided into clans, comes directly from *Vampire: The Masquerade.* Johnson's lexicon of vampire terminology includes "the beast," another term taken from the game.[122] Interestingly, Johnson claims that the role-playing game has stolen authentic vampire traditions rather than the other way around. She writes, "Imitators and game players are simulating our ways and traditions often to unsafe ends. It is no longer easy to distinguish a true blood drinker from someone who emulates us because we are today's craze."[123]

Father Sebastiaan used material from *Vampire* in a similar way to create traditions for his own group, The Sanguinarium. Sebastiaan created a code of ethics for vampires to follow known as the Black Veil. (Its name was derived from The Long Black Veil, a Goth night at the New York club Mother.) As it was originally conceived, the Black Veil was almost identical to the "Traditions of the Masquerade"—the seven rules of vampire society from White Wolf's game. The Black Veil 2.0 was created, with the help of Belanger, primarily to make it distinct from the role-playing game.[124]

Borrowing between these two groups was not one-sided, and role-players clearly had an interest in real vampires and magical practices. In 2007, Belanger was invited to speak at "DragonCon," a large convention held in Atlanta for role-playing games as well as science fiction and fantasy enthusiasts. Belanger stated that she *really* was a vampire and that this was not a role-playing game, but this made her no less interesting to those at DragonCon. She read a paper on horror writer H. P. Lovecraft to an audience that was standing room only. Similarly, several of the designers for White Wolf practice Pagan religions and have an interest in metaphysics. Chupp described a ritual held in a White Wolf warehouse intended to aid the design of White Wolf's game *Mage: The Ascension:*

> Although it was not an official White Wolf function, it involved many of the WW employees after work hours. The ceremony was held on Brigid's Night, February 2nd, to both mark and celebrate the start of work on the Mage: The Ascension rules design.
>
> I am reminded of the Shinto ceremonies Japanese companies conduct at the start of new endeavors.
>
> Lindy McKeeman and myself put it together. We built an altar of book boxes starting with the oldest books we had on hand and going until we got to the latest release, and put the design notes made for Mage so far in the middle of the altar as a focus for the energy. It was a neat thing, very appropriate for Mage, although whether or not it was efficacious I leave as an exercise for the observant. I do think that the Fundamentalist Christian church down the road a bit would have swallowed their gum had they known what we were doing![125]

The greatest strain on the relationship between role-players and the real vampire community came with Roderick Ferrell's murder trial in 1996. Ferrell claimed to be a vampire and the gang of teenagers who followed him came to be known as "the vampire clan." Ferrell had played *Vampire: The Masquerade* prior to committing a double homicide, and it was simple for the media to conclude that Ferrell had "lost touch with reality" and committed murder as a result of his involvement with the game. A *National Examiner* article with the headline "Your Kid Could be Next!" claimed, "The five teens graduated from sitting around the table throwing dice to masquerading as vampires and DRINKING BLOOD."[126] Public universities across America began banning the LARP.[127]

Ferrell's ties to both the real vampire community and role-playing seem to have been tenuous at best. However, media coverage of the murder created a new category of person—the dangerously confused role-player. As a result, both role-players and real vampires began taking steps to avoid being placed in this category. White Wolf began putting material in its books reminding players that vampires do not exist. Real vampires began distancing themselves from role-players because they, too, did not want to be seen as role-players who had become lost in their roles.

Vampirology and Vampire Research

The vampire milieu found a new tributary in the late twentieth century when various groups became interested in gathering data on vampires. A number of information clearing houses appeared, and various parties began attempting to survey the vampire community. One of the first modern vampirologists was Dr. Jeanne Keyes Youngson, who started the Count Dracula Fan Club in the late 1960s.[128] This organization still exists today and is known as the Vampire Empire. Although not the original purpose of the organization, the Dracula Fan Club has received and collected numerous letters and phone calls from real vampires. Before the vampire community had a presence on the Internet, many vampires may have seen vampirologists as the only ones who would understand them. Guiley has commented that many of these letters seem to have a "confessional" quality to them.[129] Youngson's collection of vampire letters became an important "first stop" for various writers researching the vampire community in the 1990s.

In 1977, Martin V. Riccardo of Chicago began The Vampire Studies Society, now known simply as Vampire Studies. The group published the *Journal of Vampirism* for several years and now acts as a communication network and an information clearing house for all aspects of vampire lore. In 1978, Eric Held and Dorothy Nixon started the Vampire Information Exchange (VIE) in Brooklyn. Like The Dracula Fan Club, this group was originally intended to study literary vampires, but began receiving mail from real vampires. John L. Velluntini of San Francisco published the *Journal of Vampirology* from 1984 to 1990.[130] He too, received mail from self-identified vampires.

In 1972, Kaplan started the Vampire Research Center in Elmhurst, New York. Where most vampirologists were interested primarily in literature and folklore, Kaplan actively sought self-identified vampires. Kaplan's center, which advertised itself in *Playboy* magazine, engaged in a wide variety of bizarre activity in the name of research. He describes visiting one "vampire" at his home and found him to be a BDSM enthusiast who invited Kaplan to join his circle. At one point, Kaplan (a married man) and a female research assistant bit each other on the neck in order to determine if this was an erotic act. (Their conclusion was that being bitten on the neck is very painful and in no way erotic.[131]) Kaplan had plans for another experiment in which lab rats would be fed with the blood of other rats. These "vampire rats" would then be studied to see if they lived longer or acquired any vampiric powers.

Kaplan is best remembered for conducting a "census" of vampires. The census form consisted of a 99-item questionnaire sent to everyone who had contacted the Research Center. A census was run in 1980–81, 1982–83, and 1988–89 receiving 21, 35, and 25 responses, respectively.[132] From this scant data, Kaplan concluded that there are 50–60 vampires in America and 500 worldwide.[133] Brian Frost gives the following synopsis of his research:

> If one pools the findings of Kaplan with those of other contemporary American vampir- ologists, the following description of the average male "genetic" vampire emerges: he has blonde hair and blue eyes, is 5 ft 10 in. tall, and weighs around 150 pounds. Distinguish- ing features include very pale skin, fang-like teeth, and an absence of facial hair. He also has a highly developed sense of smell, but less sense of taste than a normal person; and, besides being incredibly strong, is double-jointed and can run very fast. His genito- urinary system is similar to that of a human being, but the semen is pink and the urine has a reddish hue. Life expectancy is between 400 and 500 years.[134]

Although this model of the vampire claims to draw on scientific authority, it is far sillier and less cogent than the astral vampires described by nineteenth-century occultists. Kaplan's only criterion for controlling the "sample" for his census data was whether the survey subject had contacted the Vampire Research Center, and it is likely that the majority of calls to the center were made in jest. Conversely, it is difficult to imagine how Kaplan could have done a proper survey in the 1980s. The vampire community at that time was not self-aware, and there were few networks by which large numbers of vampires could be reached.

Vampirologists Youngson, Riccardo, and Jerome Miller also conducted a survey. Their data are now available in the book *The Vampire in Contemporary Society Via a World Wide Census,* which can be purchased from the Vampire Empire Web site.[135] Although these researchers had a better sample than Kaplan, their survey has received little attention. In the 1990s, vampire researchers, such as Guiley and Konstantinos, solicited letters from vampires but did not attempt quantitative analysis through a survey. By this point, data from self-identified vampires, rather than vampire fiction, had become an important part of the vam- pire milieu. Guiley's *Vampires Among Us* seems to have had an especially wide audience among real vampires.

The next step was for the vampire community to begin producing its own data through introspective surveys. In fact, there seems to be no other group that is so preoccupied with surveying itself. By the 1990s the vampire community had more established networks. Unlike Kaplan, researchers familiar with these networks could reach a wide number of vampires while reducing the number of false responses. Liriel McMahon of Seattle, who then identified as a vampire, began the Vampirism Research Institute in 1991 and conducted a series of surveys.[136] The vampire publication *The Dark Rose Journal* began soliciting surveys as did *The Midnight Sun.*

All of these surveys paled in comparison to the work of the AVA. In 2006, AVA members launched the previously mentioned "Vampire and Energy Work Research Survey: An Introspective Examination of the Real Vampire Community" (VEWRS), a global survey aimed at reaching as many vampires as possible. Subjects were asked to complete a basic survey featuring 379 questions, followed by an advanced survey with an additional 608 questions. The survey addressed everything from income and education level, medical history, spiritual beliefs and philosophical attitudes, and feeding habits, to psychic abilities and theories about vampirism. Despite the incredible length of the survey, there were 650 responses before the project was concluded on October 31 2007.[137] While various parties have wanted to do such a project for the last 20 years, the means and the resources were not available until the twenty-first century.

It is difficult to convey how ambitious a project the survey is compared to the size and resources of the AVA. A limited liability company, Suscitatio Enterprises, was created to oversee the project. Paper copies of the survey had to be mailed to vampires who did not have Internet access or did not wish to submit their responses in digital form. Surveys were translated into French, Spanish, German, and Russian. At the time of this writing, promotion, distribution, and analysis has already cost over $4,850 with a total estimated post-analysis of $7,500–$10,000. AVA members stated that they anticipated their methodology to be attacked and endeavored to make their study as professional as possible. Several textbooks in survey design were consulted before a methodology was chosen.[138]

The survey's title states that it is an introspective examination of the "real vampire community." Although the modifier "real" is not always used in the survey's literature, the methodology was designed to discourage responses from lifestyle vampires and role-players. In promoting the survey, Web sites and groups frequented by lifestyle vampires or role-players were avoided as much as possible. These elements were typically referred to as "flaky," as in one member's statement, "Those people are flakier than a croissant factory." Additionally, Suscitatio Enterprises offers their operational definition of a vampire on their Web site:

> A vampire is essentially a blood drinker or an energy feeder that may display various levels of psychic ability. The vampires that are the focus of this study are individuals who cannot adequately sustain their own physical, mental, or spiritual well-being without the taking of blood or vital life force energy from other sources; often human. Without feeding (whether by a regular or infrequent schedule) the vampire will become lethargic, sickly, and often go through physical suffering or discomfort. Vampires often display signs of empathy, sense emotions, perceive auras of other humans, and are generally psychically aware of the world around them.[139]

Although respondents included vampires from the initiatory model such as the Temple of the Vampire and the Order of the Vampyre, this operational definition represents the awakened model in which vampirism is an essentialist identity.

In addition to employing strategies for soliciting the surveys and presenting an operational definition to respondents, the survey contains a built-in mechanism to determine how conversant respondents are in the vampire community and how their ideas about vampirism were shaped. A section within the basic survey labeled "Knowledge" is essentially a multiple-choice quiz to see if the respondent can distinguish different paradigms of vampirism from with the vampire milieu. For example, question 207 presents the terms: KINDRED / MASQUERADE / EMBRACE / CAIN / BOOK OF NOD. The respondent must then select with which group this lexicon is associated: life-style vampires, role-playing games, occultism, etc. (All of the terms in question 207 are taken from *Vampire: The Masquerade* and are not widely used in the vampire community. Thus, if a respondent answered question 207 incorrectly, this would suggest that they have confused role-playing games with real vampirism or that they are not conversant in the vampire community.) Additionally, the knowledge section also asks respondents to indicate on a checklist which books they have read regarding vampire fiction, folklore, and real vampirism.

When asked if they simply throw out responses from vampires who answered incorrectly on the knowledge section or made fantastical claims about their experiences with vampirism, an AVA member responded, "No. We *can't.*" Instead, the data are tracked and correlated to look for differences between vampires with more accurate or accepted knowledge and those with less exposure to the vampire community. In time, analysis of the knowledge section may produce, for example, different trends among vampires who have read Anne Rice versus those who have not.

What can be made of surveys like the VEWRS? For one thing, they show that this is a community concerned with evidence. Guiley writes of self-identified vampires, "Not surprisingly, they do not seek out or agree to medical exams for proof. Most likely, they don't want their fantasy to burst."[140] (I cannot imagine what sort of medical exam would prove that someone is a vampire.) "Fantasy," in this case, is used pejoratively to refer to a personal idea someone expresses but which they know will not stand up to reason. At a paper I was giving on vampires, I was asked, "These vampires . . . isn't it all just a fantasy?" For some individuals vampirism may be a fantasy, but for the AVA it is not. No one would dedicate thousands of dollars and countless hours of work to prove the existence of their fantasy. The survey shows that vampirism is not a fantasy but a theory.

More importantly, I believe that the VEWRS could potentially redefine the category of vampire, just as the nineteenth-century writers redefined the vampire tradition of folklore. The AVA has stated that they are not trying to present an overarching definition of vampirism. However, they don't need to: The survey data will do that on its own. This chapter began with a theory of how categories are created and defined by culture. Critical theorists argue that even seemingly "objective" categories may in fact be constructed by culture. Statistical analysis, especially, has been a powerful tool for creating these categories. Michel Foucault and others have argued that categories like "homosexual" as well as a wide variety of "mental conditions" simply did not exist before the nineteenth century.[141] It took the work of researchers to invent these labels as valid categories of people. Similarly, social scientists have observed how the category of "young people," which seems to have an objective reality, was given new meaning due to social changes in the 1960s.[142]

The vampire is a category of person with which real vampires identify. So far, that category has been defined from the outside by authors, filmmakers, role-players, and occultists. Now, we see that vampires have begun to take ownership of the category, redefining it from the inside. Under this new definition, "vampire" is becoming a valid category of person. In the eighteenth century, the statement "I am a vampire" would have been incomprehensible. In the twentieth century such a statement would usually be considered a sign of madness. However, in the twenty-first century, "I am a vampire" may simply indicate one more category with which someone identifies.

CHAPTER 4

Initiatory Vampire Groups: Vampirism as Apotheosis

Every church is a stone on the grave of a god-man: it does not want him to rise up again under any circumstances.

—*Friedrich Nietzche*

Although the majority of vampires are not part of any formal group, a handful of initiatory groups tend to gain the most publicity. Vampire occult groups like the Order of the Vampyre, the Temple of the Vampire, and Ordo Strigoi Vii, although they represent a minority of the vampire community, have the resources to publish more books, create more ambitious Web sites, and have their representatives appear on talk shows and documentaries. The publicity of these groups has led scholars to make over-generalizations of the vampire community, namely that vampirism is a religion and that it is associated with Satanism.

These groups share five characteristics: First, they have at least a philosophical association with Satanism and locate themselves within an occult philosophy known as "the left-hand path." Second, they derive authority through revelation given to them by some sort of disembodied vampiric beings. Third, they tend to exist as networks facilitated by the Internet, meeting face to face only occasionally. This is reflected in the frequent use of acronyms to describe these groups, for example, ToV for Temple of the Vampire. Fourth, they typically condemn the practice of consuming blood, which is generally tolerated by the vampire community at large. Finally, these groups all express antipathy to the awakened model of vampirism, especially psychic vampirism.

These similarities are not coincidental. In researching this book several former and current members of these groups were contacted. There is evidence that many of the various vampire religious movements are actually the product of reiterating, repackaging, and in some cases plagiarizing the same ideas. This process began when a Satanic group known as the Order of the Vampyre set the precedent for a vampiric religious movement. They presented vampirism as a sort of apotheosis achieved through occult knowledge and willpower. This became the prototype that has been imitated and modified as various leaders step forward to try their hand at running a vampire religious group. Some have met with success while other initiatory vampire groups are still struggling to establish themselves.

The Left-Hand Path

To understand the idea of a vampiric apotheosis, it is first necessary to know something about the school of thought known as the left-hand path. The distinction of left-hand path versus right-hand path originates in the Tantric practices of Buddhism and Hinduism.[1] The Sanskrit terms *dakshinachara* and *vamachara,* translated as right-hand (*daksina*) path and left-hand (*vama*) path, refer to two different types of aesthetic practices. The word "*achara*" is typically translated as "spiritual attainment."[2] *Dakshinachara* refers to techniques such as fasting and meditation that are generally condoned by Buddhists and Hindus. *Vamachara* refers to practices that incorporate elements normally condemned as immoral. For example, the Aghari are considered a left-hand sect and have been known to frequent graveyards, steal human skulls, and even consume the flesh of corpses.[3] Practitioners of *vamachara* do not see these practices as immoral but rather invoke a nondualistic perspective of morality, which Indologist Georg Feuerstein describes as "antinomian."[4] For example, although the Tantric exercise of having sexual intercourse in a graveyard defies traditional morality, it is not done out of lust. Instead, the Tantra attempts to emulate the god Shiva by maintaining a state of utter dispassion, throughout the exercise.[5] The point of the exercise is not to enjoy sex but rather to train oneself not to enjoy it. The Tantra transcends the dichotomy between lust and restraint.

It was Western occultists who assigned new meaning to the idea of the left-hand path. The occult Theosophical Society, founded by Madame Helena Blavatsky and Henry Steel Olcott, moved its headquarters to Adyar, India, in 1882. Blavatsky seems to have modified the idea of *vamachara* and used the term "left-hand path" to describe occult traditions that she considered immoral. As a result, the idea of the left-hand path has a different connotation in Western occultism than in Tantra.[6]

In modern occultism, so-called right-hand path traditions draw from esoteric religious movements such as Gnosticism, Kabbalah, and Rosicrucianism. These traditions emphasize secret knowledge with the aim of mystical union with divinity. Left-hand path traditions, drawing on Social Darwinism and the philosophy of Friedrich Nietzche, emphasize using magic for the apotheosis of the self as well as material goals. Richard Sutcliffe writes, "Left-hand path magick is characterized by an attempt to engage in magickal praxis which does not accept externally imposed limitations, but rather to celebrate the totality of human experience in all of its folly and grandeur."[7] This Western concept of the left-hand path has been developed by the occultist Aleister Crowley as well as Anton LaVey, the founder of the Church of Satan. Vampire groups associated with the left-hand path tend to emphasize the vampire as a predator that is superior to humans.

Modern Satanic Movements and the Order of the Vampyre

The Church of Satan (CoS) was founded by Anton Szandor LaVey in San Francisco in 1966. Lavey chose April 30th, the Pagan festival of Walpurgisnacht, for the official beginning of his church. His philosophy, as espoused in *The Satanic Bible* and other writings, does not actually involve the worship of the devil. Instead, it has been described as "an atheistic, self-centric philosophy."[8] LaVey preached the cultivation of the self and a rejection of traditional Christian values in favor of a brutal form of Social Darwinism. LaVey's "nine Satanic sins" are stupidity, pretentiousness, solipsism, self-deceit, herd conformity, lack of perspective, forgetfulness of past orthodoxies, counterproductive pride, and lack of aesthetics. LaVey's church received wide media attention throughout the 1960s and 1970s. This made LaVey a minor celebrity, which seemed to have been his goal at the time. At the height of his career, LaVey even appeared alongside Johnny Carson on the *Tonight Show.*[9] Church of Satan covens or "grottos" began forming in major cities, of which one of the most successful was "The Lilith Grotto" in New York City. The Lilith Grotto was founded by Lilith Aquino and at the time of this writing is still a registered church.

In 1975, there was a schism within the Church of Satan. LaVey made the decision to sell priesthoods for cash, alienating many Satanists.[10] This led Lilith and Michael Aquino to form their own Satanic organization, the Temple of Set. Like the Church of Satan, the Temple of Set is antiauthoritarian and emphasizes self-actualization. The Temple derives its name from the Egyptian god Set, who murdered his older brother, the benevolent Osiris. Aquino believes that the Judaeo-Christian concept of Satan is actually derived from the earlier deity Set. Where LaVey saw Satan as merely a symbol for strength and rebellion, the Temple of Set regards Set as a literal deity. However, they claim that instead of worshipping Set, they honor him for his act of rebellion in pursuit of personal gain. Setians seek to emulate Set's will to power through a process of radical self-actualization. They refer to this process by the Egyptian word *xeper,* which they translate as "becoming."

It was Lilith Aquino, along with William T. Butch, who founded the Order of the Vampyre as a group within the Temple of Set. Setians belonging to the Order of the Vampyre specifically emulate the vampire as a glamorous and superhuman being. Thus, the *xeper* of becoming the vampire represents an apotheosis. In 1988, Lilith and Michael Aquino appeared on the Oprah Winfrey show, where they described both the Temple of Set and the Order of the Vampyre. Some of the techniques described to emulate the vampire include use of cosmetics, learning to use the voice in order to influence others, and cultivating a powerful gaze.[11]

The Aquinos do not claim to have simply invented the Temple of Set or the Order of the Vampyre. Michael Aquino claims to have written the Temple's sacred text *The Book of Coming Forth by Night* with the help of Set.[12] Similarly, the Order of the Vampyre attributes its techniques to contact with vampiric entities. According to their Web site, "The Order's founders undertook research that brought them into a 'dialogue' with, and the acquaintance of, existing Vampyric characteristics and Archetypal Forces."[13] This set an important precedent that has been emulated by other groups such as the Temple of the Vampire and the Ordo Strigoi Vii: All of these groups cite their techniques as coming from a sort of vampiric divine revelation.

Another important innovation used by the Order of the Vampyre was to organize its members as a loose network using annual meetings and a newsletter. This was an adaption of the Temple of Set's existing organizational structure. Order of the Vampyre initiates meet during the Temple of Set's International Conclave and receive the newsletters *Nightwing* and *The Vampyre Papers*.[14] Norine Dresser points out that aside from an annual meeting, members of the Order of the Vampyre never congregate on a regular basis. She writes, "They claim that their deliberately individualistic atmosphere is not easily conducive to group activities on a routine or programmed basis and point out that they are not a congregation of docile followers—only cooperative philosophers and magicians."[15]

The Order of the Vampyre forbids illegal activity as well as consuming blood. This has been implemented by most other initiatory vampire groups. The Order of the Vampyre declares, "A true Vampyre knows that he does not achieve the Posture of Effortless Power through the mundane act of physical blood drinking. In fact to pursue such acts would mean that he did not understand his own condition, let alone Vampyric Black Magic."[16] The emphasis on being law-abiding is actually common to left-hand path organizations and can be traced back to LaVey. This is an apparent contradiction of the antiauthoritarian rhetoric espoused by groups like the Church of Satan. It is likely that these groups publicly advocate obedience to the law precisely because they are under closer scrutiny by law enforcement.

Recently, the Order of the Vampyre has begun to denounce the awakened model, especially those who claim they were born psychic vampires. The Order of the Vampyre states:

It should be readily understood by all who seek admission to our Order, that we are unique, and separate from the various Right-Hand Path driven "on-line vampire community" groups, and "houses" that have sprung up over the past few years. Such groups promote a weak and powerless version of the Vampyric Archetype, among a myriad of fuzzy New Age ideas, such as missing chakras, "other-kin," and a need for blood drinking. We do not tolerate such in our ranks.[17]

It is interesting that the vampire community is described here as a right-hand path even though few vampires see themselves as part of the left-hand/right-hand dichotomy. Driving this perspective of psychic vampires is a Darwinian rhetoric common to left-hand path movements. Christopher Partridge characterizes LaVey's Social Darwinism as "brutal," promoting survival of the fittest as the principal law by which everyone should live life.[18] In light of this Darwinian perspective, the awakened model of vampirism is interpreted as a weakness and a defect and therefore something to be scorned.

The Order of the Vampyre is still in existence although they seem to have been less active in the last two decades. Contacts in the vampire community interviewed for this book were aware of the group, but the Order never came up in conversation. However, the significance of this group was profound. The Order displayed all the elements needed for a successful vampire religion and became a prototype that was emulated by other left-hand path vampire groups.

The Temple of the Vampire

The Temple of the Vampire is probably the most active, secretive, and controversial of the left-hand path vampire groups. The Temple became a registered church in 1989 under the leadership of its founder, Lucas Martel.[19] The Temple regularly calls itself "The one true vampire religion" and publishes a document entitled *The Vampire Bible*. Like the Order of the Vampyre, members pursue vampirism as an apotheosis, learning to take vital energy from others in order to become a consummate predator. The "vampire creed" states:

I am a vampire, I worship my ego and my life, for I am the only God that is. I am proud that I am a predatory animal and honor my animal instincts. I exalt my rational mind and hold no belief that is in truth a fantasy. I acknowledge the Powers of Darkness to be hidden natural laws though which I work my magic. I realize there is no heaven as there is no hell, and I view death as the destroyer of life. Therefore I will make the most of life here and now. I am a Vampire, bow down before me.[20]

The vampire creed's stark worldview, emphasizing the ego and survival of the fittest, is clearly in the tradition of the left-hand path and the Church of Satan.

The Vampire Bible describes an apocalyptic "final harvest of humankind" in which "undead gods" will take their rightful place as rulers of the world.[21] Only those who have sided with the Temple will survive the coming catastrophe. The undead gods are a source of divine revelation that provides the Temple with its authority. They serve much the same purpose as the "archetypal forces" cited by the Order of the Vampyre. Initiation as a vampire occurs by offering one's life force to these undead gods.

Like the Church of Satan and the Order of the Vampyre, the Temple also forbids illegal activities and drinking blood. In a rare interview, Martel said of blood drinking:

> Real Vampires don't drink blood. That is a myth that has been perpetuated to hide the truth from the mundane masses. We take the excess Lifeforce radiated from human beings and, in turn, give this Lifeforce to the more advanced Members of our Family, who then, also in turn, return this Energy for Vampiric Metamorphosis. This completed "circuit" of Energy exchange is known as Communion and is the fundamental process required for the practice of true Vampirism.[22]

However, despite its ban on unlawful activity, the Temple has nevertheless tried to cultivate a sinister image. In 1994, the Temple published a highly critical letter from an outsider in their newsletter. The Temple's response mocked the author of the letter and added, "This Temple disclaims any responsibility for the writer's recent death. . . . The writer sent this letter unsigned assuming this would shield his identity. The Temple sends its condolences to his survivors." Jeff Guinn and Andy Grieser contacted the Lacey Police Department, who confirmed that there had never been a murder investigation involving the Temple.[23]

More than any other group, the Temple of the Vampire is antagonistic to the awakened model of vampirism. The Temple declares prominently on its Web site, "Vampires are not born, they are made." Belanger describes contacting the Temple in the 1990s and receiving a letter that she found condescending and offensive.[24] In a phone interview, Belanger was extremely critical of the Temple of the Vampire, stating, "I don't throw this term around lightly, but they are a cult." She went on to describe doing a book signing only to find that cards for the Temple of the Vampire had been inserted into all of her books. Belanger also told me that any Temple member who contacted her would be immediately excommunicated. In one case, membership was revoked for leaving a comment on Belanger's Livejournal Web page.[25]

An Internet archive contains an e-mail exchange from August 8, 1996, between a Temple priest and a psychic vampire. The priest, who signs his e-mail, "Radu V. Priest, ToV" is excoriating a psychic vampire for uploading a copy of *The Vampire Bible* onto the Internet. The exchange is typical of the antagonism between the awakened model of vampirism and the Temple. Radu informs the psychic vampire, "You are just another 'tragic hero' type who cannot stand those more succesful [*sic*] than you. You feed out of a need for abject survival, ToV members feed conciously [*sic*] to fuel and improve themselves—to make themselves 'more.' You cannot learn to be something so you punish and attack those who do." The psychic vampire responds, "Indeed not. I violated copyright laws because I wanted people so see the truth of the pathetic temple. ... Shortcomings? I was born a psivamp, not like the *humans* like yourself the temple teach to become energy-leaches."[26] Note that the psychic vampire sees the Temple as humans engaged in magical practices that he or she considers to be unethical. By contrast, Radu speaks in terms of self-improvement and emphasizes personal responsibility, both of which are considered virtues in the left-hand path.

The Temple of the Vampire also holds other vampire groups in disdain, claiming, "They are quite ignorant. Most of them practice being victims and eschew immortality in favor of what is usually a neogothic aesthetic that romanticizes death as somehow desirable. None of them understand the truth we offer."[27] The Temple holds special contempt for psychic vampires, possibly because their feeding methods are so similar to the magical techniques taught by the Temple. They state that, "Self proclaimed 'psi vamps' or 'psychic vampires' are almost universally deluding themselves. Those rare few who touch real power remain ignorant of what to do with it and therefore will still die someday. By way of contrast, we fully understand what we are doing and why."[28]

Like the Order of the Vampyre, the Temple functions through a network. Although the group is headquartered in Lacey, Washington, there is no physical Temple in Lacey, only a post office box. Guinn and Grieser went to great lengths trying to find the Temple, even contacting the Lacey chamber of commerce. No one had heard of it.[29] The Temple's current leader is referred to as "Nemo," a Latin term meaning "no one." It is widely assumed that Martel and Nemo are one and the same, although it is also possible that various leaders alternate being Nemo. Instead of meeting face to face, members engage in correspondence across the country and across the world. Members receive the Temple's newsletter, *Lifeforce,* and as they are initiated deeper into temple mysteries, they are allowed to purchase *The Vampire Predator Bible, The Vampire Priesthood Bible, The Vampire Sorcery Bible,* and *The Vampire Adept Bible.*[30]

While researching this book, I received an e-mail from a man named Nicholas, whom other contacts confirmed had been a member of the Temple for over a decade. Nicholas described how within a few years, he had achieved the highest degree offered by the Temple—apparently without ever having met Lucas Martel or other Temple members face to face. His entire involvement was through correspondence. Nicholas ran an occult bookstore in Venice Beach and when Martel learned of this, he asked Nicholas to use his store as a "recruitment center" for the Temple. Nicholas also had connections in Hollywood and agreed to promote the Temple though giving television interviews on CNN and A&E as well as being quoted in several books and articles about modern vampires. When Temple members complained about the television appearances, Nicholas's status with the Temple was suspended and he was made to issue a formal apology in the group's newsletter.

Nicholas's relationship with the Temple ended in 2001. He writes:

It was a couple of years later that something happened at the TOV in Washington (I don't know what—perhaps Mr. Martel made some new friends—but everything changed.) They put up a forum online and I noticed many new names listed as supposed "authorized officers of the TOV" such as the new forum administrator "Nemo"—when I contacted them via the forum—I was summarily told that I had been excommunicated—that was my last dealing with them.

So, as you can see, there really never was a true organization—we never held meetings—we never even spoke on the phone—we only had to buy their products (which I have witnessed changing much over the years)—obey their "commands" and other such nonsense—and continue to pay them money to be a member. I cannot support an organization that treats its members in this fashion—and arbitrarily abandons them when they do as they are asked (as in my case)—so yes, there is "bad blood" between us. I don't know who these people are (never have)—but they appear to be members of the COS by the propaganda they are spreading.[31]

Belanger and several others share Nicholas's suspicion that the Temple of the Vampire is actually a front for the Church of Satan. She believes the Temple was created as a direct response to the Church's rival, the Temple of Set and their vampire organization. She also believes that the primary purpose of the Temple of the Vampire is to generate revenue through the sale of memberships, dues for gaining ranks, religious books, and vampiric jewelry, revenue that is then passed on to the Church of Satan.

One rumor circulating on the Internet suggests that "Lucas Martel" is actually an alias used by an unknown member of the Church of Satan. The alias allowed Martel to form the Temple of the Vampire without the consent of LaVey and the Church of Satan. According to this rumor, Martel held a secret meeting in 1988 with other leaders of the Church of Satan including Peter Gilmore (now the high priest of the Church of Satan) and Diabolus Rex (a Portland artist famous for having two rows of Teflon balls inserted under his forehead to resemble horns.) A deal was allegedly struck in which leaders of the Church of Satan were given free membership in the Temple of the Vampire, in exchange for helping to recruit other members from the Church of Satan. Some of my contacts even suggested that the Temple of the Vampire is now in position to take over leadership of the Church of Satan.

Although it is difficult to prove such claims, there is evidence to support such a connection. Martel is indeed a registered member of the Church of Satan.[32] Diabolus Rex is both a leader in the Church of Satan and a Temple of the Vampire adept. Finally, the Church of Satan, headed by Peter Gilmore, has served as an advocate for the Temple of the Vampire. The Church of Satan's Web site features a link to the Temple of the Vampire. Furthermore, The Church has promoted the Temple of the Vampire in their newsletter *Not Like Most* and the Temple of the Vampire has reciprocated in their newsletter *Lifeforce.* Despite this evidence, Nemo has denied any connection between the two groups. He explained in an interview with Corvis Nocturnum, "The Temple is not a subset of Satanism and while we enjoy the presence of many members of the Church of Satan, and also have great respect for the Church of Satan, the vast majority of our members never were Satanists."[33]

The goals of the Temple seem to have shifted in the last few years. The vampire apocalypse is no longer described on the Temple's Web site.[34] Instead, the Temple has taken a new direction emphasizing physical immortality. Their Web site now describes the work of gerontologist Aubrey de Gray of The Methuselah Foundation and his promotion of radical life-extension technology. Vampirism is seen as a technique to live long enough and to have enough wealth to take advantage of these coming technological innovations.[35] Presumably, de Gray's vision of ordinary people living for hundreds of years would be at odds with a "vampire apocalypse." The Temple's new agenda may reflect a changing market in new religious movements: Immortality sells better than being on the winning side of a bloody apocalypse.

Ordo Strigoi Vii

Just as the Temple of the Vampire borrowed from the Order of the Vampyre, its ideas were in turn borrowed and modified to create the Ordo Strigoi Vii. "Strigoi vii" is a Romanian term, which is translated as "vampire witch" in the group's literature. (Romanian oral tradition contains terms for numerous subspecies of vampires, many of which have been borrowed from neighboring languages.)[36] Unlike the undead strigoi mort, the strigoi vii is a human born with supernatural powers. Upon death, the strigoi vii may rise again as a vampire.[37] The concept of the strigoi vii is significant to the vampire community who see themselves as gifted rather than undead. The term seems to have first caught the interest of the community in 1995 through an article by Belanger that appeared in her journal *Midnight Sun*.[38]

The Ordo Strigoi Vii was founded by a New York vampire known as Father Sebastiaan Tod van Houten. Born Aaron Todd Hoyt, Sebastiaan has become something of a celebrity in the vampire community, appearing in numerous television interviews. In 1997, Sebastiaan organized an entity known was The Sanguinarium as an umbrella organization for a number of other vampire groups. Each member group of The Sanguinarium, known as a "house," was expected to create a name as well as a unique symbol.[39] The Sanguinarium originally served primarily as a social entity and helped to organize a number of vampire gatherings and events. Ordo Strigoi Vii evolved out of The Sanguinarium as an initiatory group.

While researching this book, I was lucky enough to do a telephone interview with Father Sebastiaan, who currently lives in Paris. His account of how Ordo Strigoi Vii was formed was quite different from the story commonly told by the larger vampire community. Sebastiaan told me that he first learned about occult forms of vampirism in the mid-1990s through a Romanian man called Dmitri—a figure that my other contacts had never heard of. Sebastiaan worked at the New York Renaissance Faire where Dmitri also worked as a leather-smith and sported a Scottish claymore. Sebastiaan described him as 6 feet 4 inches tall, burly, and bearded, adding, "He basically looked like Little John from Robin Hood." Dmitri also ran a small coven of vampires who called themselves strigoi vii.

The story implied that Dmitri was privy to occult vampire lore that may date back to Romania. He gave Sebastiaan a copy of *The Vampire Bible* and other Temple of the Vampire resources and told him that the Temple's methods were the closest thing in print to the secret techniques of his coven. However, (in the opinion of Dmitri, not Father Sebastiaan), the Temple of the Vampire is a fascist and Satanic organization: While their occult practices are effective, their organizational structure is too draconian. Dmitri and most of his coven disappeared in 1996. When Sebastiaan heard that Dmitri had died, he took this as a sign to implement Dmitri's teachings into a new group, the Ordo Strigoi Vii.

The Dmitri story explains the similarities between the Temple of the Vampire and the Ordo Strigoi Vii. Of course, some vampires have expressed skepticism that Dmitri ever existed. When I interviewed Belanger, she suggested that Sebastiaan simply plagiarizes the Temple of the Vampire to produce new litera-ture for his organization. If Dmitri was invented, this would hardly be new in the history of religious revelations. In Tibetan Buddhism, monks periodically produce writings known as *terma* or "treasure texts" that were either written through communion with deities and legendary masters of the past, or else were "found" buried in secret locations where they had been placed "until the world was ready for their secrets to be revealed." In America, Joseph Smith wrote the Book of Mormon by translating golden plates that he allegedly found buried in Manchester, New York. For religion scholars, the origin of these texts is not as important as the tradition that has formed around them.

Sebastiaan explained to me that the Temple of the Vampire had been very successful in creating what he called "a university of vampires." He praised the Temple adepts for their progress and efficiency but said that they acted like "little workers bees" and hoarded their knowledge from everyone else. By con-trast, he described the Ordo Strigoi Vii as being more open and "a lot more fun." He said that he never wanted to encourage "cult-like behavior" and repeat-edly described his organization as "a think tank." Sebastiaan's Livejournal page uses similar academic terminology. In 2005, Sebastiaan organized a series of summer seminars called "University Vampyricus" to discuss vampirism and metaphysics. Another post informing readers that he will be taking a leave of absence from the community refers to this leave as "going on sabbatical."[40]

Like the Temple of the Vampire, Ordo Strigoi Vii is a network facilitated by the Internet. Members can purchase a variety of jewelry as well as a series of books. The Ordo Strigoi Vii is especially interested in developing its own vernacular of vampire terms and phrases. The group has even made its own alphabet of 28 glyphs. The group's literature also openly borrows from many occult and religious traditions. Belanger claims to have done most of the research into occult traditions and folklore that appears in these materials. As of 2005, she has since stated that she will no longer work with Father Sebastiaan and has threatened him with prosecution for plagiarism.[41]

Like other left-hand path groups, the Ordo Strigoi Vii are interested in human potential and personal evolution. They have borrowed the term *xeper* from the Temple of Set, which they render as "Zhep'r." Strigoi Vii literature also describes cultivating "the dragon," a term that refers to one's highest potential. Also like the Order of the Vampyre and the Temple of the Vampire, Ordo Strigoi Vii members are in contact with disembodied entities. The strigoi morte are referred to as "our sorors and fraters on the Otherside" and are equated with the undead gods of the Temple of the Vampire.[42] I asked Sebastiaan what exactly the strigoi morte are. He used several analogies such as cloning and supercomputers to explain how human consciousness can continue to affect the world after death. The strigoi morte did not seem to be ghosts in the traditional sense (they are more like thought-forms than disembodied souls), but they had definitely once been human.

In addition to the strigoi morte, the Ordo Strigoi Vii also work with a "collective thought-form" called Elorath. Sebastiaan writes, "Elorath is not a god or deity! It is an Egregore, or the result and current of the collective will, soul, and dharma of The Family."[43] The word "egregore" was originally a Greek word meaning "watchers." This term appears in Greek translations of the Hebrew Bible where it is used to describe a type of fallen angel. However, in the late 1980s, the word "egregore" gained an entirely new meaning in occult circles. The word is now commonly used to define an entity created by the collective effort and will of a group of people. Many modern occultists believe that if enough thought and energy is directed to an idea, the idea takes on a kind of sentience with its own occult abilities. According to Belanger, who has helped Sebastiaan in ritual workings to strengthen Elorath, Elorath is actually an acronym for Eternal Lord Our Regent: Aaron Todd Hoyt.

Like other initiatory vampire groups, Ordo Strigoi Vii has expressed contempt for the awakened model of psychic vampirism and a desire to remain separate from the vampire community at large. According to the organization's literature:

> Traditional psychic vampires, which We of the Family call *asarai,* are those individuals in this world who truly drain you of your emotional energy. They are clearly defined in Dion Fortune's book *Psychic Self Defense* and Anton LaVey's 1969 magnum opus *The Satanic Bible.* ... Those asarai who have come in to the sphere of Our Family are truly

weak and pathetic beings who have tried to attach themselves to Our movement. We are a traditional and rational Family and have no interest in re-defining terms such as "psychic vampire" to accommodate social trends of people who do not remember or respect the old ways as properly defined by notable logicians such as Dion Fortune and Aleister Crowley.[44]

At the same time, the Ordo Strigoi Vii still harbors elements of the awakened model. After all, the strigoi vii of Romanian folklore were born, not trained. Potential members must have a certain quality that Sebastiaan has compared to a genetic marker.[45] In the phone interview, Sebastiaan stated that as a few as one in one hundred applicants are granted admission into Ordo Strigoi Vii. When I asked Sebastiaan what he thought about psychic vampires, he said, "people are sick of feeling depressed." He seemed to feel that an initiatory approach to vampires was more fulfilling and more fun than comparing vampirism to a medical condition.

Other Left-Hand Path Groups

Several new groups have attempted to establish themselves following a similar prototype to the Order of the Vampyre, the Temple of the Vampire, and the Ordo Strigoi Vii. One such group is the Aset-ka, based out of Portugal. Like the Temple of the Vampire, they promote vampirism as "a dark and predatory spirituality."[46] Like the Temple of Set, the group derives its name from Egyptian mythology. The group also produces a text called the Asetian Bible.

All of the vampires contacted for this book had an extremely negative view of Aset-ka and believed they were actually a group of computer hackers rather than sincere vampires. They apparently contacted Sebastiaan who described the Asetian Bible as "Harry Potter meets the Scorpion King." Sebastiaan said that almost all of the ideas in their Bible were plagiarized from the Temple of the Vampire and Belanger. He added that he was a little offended that his own writings had not been plagiarized.

Another group has formed in the United Kingdom that is known as Countess Elizabeth's Vampire Coven (CEVC). This group admits to borrowing ideas from Belanger and the Ordo Strigoi Vii and is also clearly influenced by the Temple of the Vampire. Members pay 15 pounds a month for which they receive a coffin shaped medallion, a subscription to a weekly newsletter, special access to bars and clubs, and a T-shirt. Members may not attend special events unless they are wearing their coffin medallions. The CEVC also has its own Bible known as the Blood Bible. What sets this group apart from other left-hand path vampire groups is that members apparently do drink blood, which all of the preceding groups have expressly forbidden.[47]

The group's membership is divided into 13 clans. New members are directed to a clan based on their strengths and weakness. Like many esoteric groups, the

CEVC does not claim to have invented their tradition but rather to have redis-
covered an ancient mystery. In their case, they claim that their rituals are taken
from a secret society of Victorian aristocrats known as the Order of the Blood
Adepti that died out in 1876.[48] The Order of the Blood Adepti are almost
certainly invented, although they are said to have been associated with the hellfire
clubs that did exist in the eighteenth century. A product of the Enlightenment,
hellfire clubs were gatherings in which wealthy intellectuals came together to sati-
rize religion. These groups were not actually engaged in any sort of Satanic
worship, although this was rumored. The hellfire clubs served as the inspiration
for The Order of the Blood Adepti and the dark, Victorian aesthetic of
the CEVC.

Although these initiatory groups have a tremendous capacity to generate secret
knowledge, mystery, and intrigue, they are not representative of the vampire
community as a whole. The VEWRS indicated that 74 percent of vampires have
no affiliation with any sort of group or institution, suggesting that most vampires
view vampirism as a matter of personal identity rather than membership in a
group.[49] In an interview with Belanger, she described her sense that these
vampire religions are dying out and that the American vampire community has
become "inoculated" to them. (However, she indicated that Ordo Strigoi Vii is
gaining members in France.) The fact that vampires are so leery of these left-
hand path groups points to the vampire phenomenon's origins in modernity.
Despite the overt religiosity of America's social and political culture, Americans
also have a long history of mistrusting religious authority. Thomas Jefferson once
declared, "I am a sect myself," and his contemporary Thomas Payne stated,
"My mind is my church."[50] Robert Bellah has referred to this tradition as
"radical religious individualism" and suggested that the highest goal of this tradition is "self-realization"[51] American vampires who see their identity as religious
are not pursuing membership in an institution but rather this self-realization
described by Bellah.

CHAPTER 5

The Vampire Community

Ours is the lonely path.

—*Michelle Belanger,* The Psychic Vampire Codex

But thou, false Infidel! shalt writhe
Beneath avenging Monkir's scythe;
And from its torment 'scape alone
To wander round lost Eblis' throne;
And fire unquench'd, unquenchable,
Around, within, thy heart shall dwell;
Nor ear can hear nor tongue can tell
The tortures of that inward hell!
But first, on earth as Vampire sent,
Thy corpse shall from its tomb be rent:
Then ghastly haunt thy native place,
And suck the blood of all thy race;
There from thy daughter, sister, wife,
At midnight drain the stream of life;
Yet loathe the banquet which perforce
Must feed thy livid living corse:
Thy victims ere they yet expire
Shall know the demon for their sire,
As cursing thee, thou cursing them,
Thy flowers are wither'd on the stem.
But one that for thy crime must fall,
The youngest, most beloved of all,
Shall bless thee with a father's name—
That word shall wrap thy heart in flame!
Yet must thou end thy task, and mark
Her cheek's last tinge, her eye's last spark,
And the last glassy glance must view
Which freezes o'er its lifeless blue;
Then with unhallow'd hand shalt tear
The tresses of her yellow hair,
Of which in life a lock when shorn,
Affection's fondest pledge was worn,
But now is borne away by thee,
Memorial of thine agony!
Wet with thine own best blood shall drip
Thy gnashing tooth and haggard lip;
Then stalking to thy sullen grave,
Go—and with gouls and Afrits rave;
Till these in horror shrink away
From spectre more accursed than they!

—Lord Byron, *The Giaour,* 1813

Loneliness has been a theme of the vampire milieu for the last two hundred years—from the poetry of Lord Byron to the angst-ridden vampires of

Anne Rice. Vampirologist Martin V. Riccardo once said that loneliness is the single unifying pattern of vampires.[1] While there is now an international community of vampires, it has taken decades for this community to become self-aware and to develop channels of communication. Michelle Belanger has attributed this slow progress to a mistrust of organization that has discouraged both cohesion and cooperation.[2]

The AVA has compiled a list of 250 different vampire groups that have come and gone in the last few decades. Most of these groups are ephemeral, lasting only a few years. Catherine Albanese, in her work on the history of American metaphysics, indicates that all metaphysical communities have been prone to fragmentation due to a mistrust of authoritarian voices. As a result, her historical approach has focused more on "networks" created between individuals rather than an endless series of ephemeral groups and organizations. A similar approach is necessary to study the vampire community. According to the VEWRS, 74 percent of vampires have no affiliation with a vampire group. Some self-identified vampires are largely ignorant of the community at large. Others are aware of the community but choose not to affiliate with a group. In the New York vampire scene, such individuals began referring to themselves as "ronin," a Japanese word that originally referred to a masterless samurai.

The community continues to evolve and to change shape. An influx of young vampires searching for answers, new innovations in Internet technology, the rise and fall of charismatic leaders, and newfound media attention have all worked to accelerate changes, not only to the structure and culture of the community but to the very criteria for defining a real vampire. Describing the vampire community is a bit like trying to paint a cloud that is perpetually changing shape. By the time this book has been published, some of this information will already be out of date. Nevertheless, this chapter will attempt to accomplish three things: first, to give a brief history of this community and to shed light on its emergence from other subcultures; second, to make some broad characterizations about vampire culture and how vampires see the world; and, finally, to offer an overview of the current incarnation of the vampire community.

Womb Communities: The Genesis of Vampire Culture

The vampire community did not begin on its own from whole cloth. Instead it was woven together from a number of different subcultures: horror film fans, role-playing games, fetish clubs, left-hand path magical groups, and others. Belanger has referred to these elements as "womb communities." Until relatively recently, it was quite difficult for vampires to locate one another. In large cities, vampires could begin their search in goth clubs or through esoteric groups. In rural communities, role-playing games and networks dedicated to horror movies offered a similar opportunity. The womb communities provided networks though which individuals interested in vampires could arrange to meet face to face. These meetings led to the rise of new networks and groups entirely devoted to vampirism. Although the vampire community has become an autonomous entity today, Belanger points out that it still bears traces of the various womb communities.[3] Father Sebastiaan Tod van Houten, who was active in organizing the New York scene, described the vampire community as "a place where the gothic movement, vampire archetypes and aesthetics, horror, occult and fetish/BDSM could come together in one package."[4]

One of the earliest of these womb communities was the subculture that formed around the television series *Dark Shadows*. *Dark Shadows* conventions brought together significant numbers of vampire fans, some of whom were self-identified vampires and donors. One of Carol Page's contacts, an attention-seeking vampire named Misty, attended a *Dark Shadows* convention, announced that she was a vampiress, and offered to bite anyone who came to her hotel room. This apparently resulted in a line of two hundred people outside her door. (Misty later stated that the number was closer to 20 and that most of her bites did not break the skin.)[5] Riccardo also describes "a bite line" at a *Dark Shadows* convention in New Jersey in 1984.[6] It is likely that Page and Riccardo are describing the same incident. Misty later went on to form an early vampire group known as the

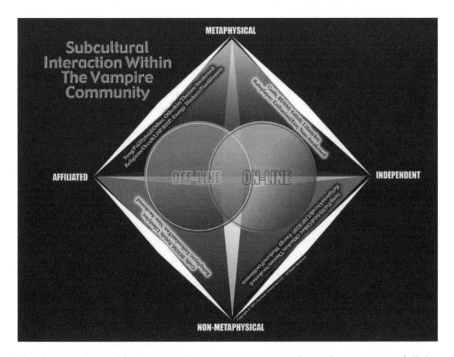

This diagram, designed by Suscitatio Enterprises, attempts to depict the interaction of all the subcultures, traditions, and orientations within the vampire community. (Merticus of Suscitatio Enterprises, LLC)

Lost Shadows Gang, which regularly met to drink blood. The gang was formed by correspondence through horror fan publications. Norine Dresser also encountered vampires and donors who had found each other through horror fandom. She interviewed a vampire named Pam who met her donor, Brad, in 1984 through a network of *Dark Shadows* fans. *Dark Shadows* has since been largely eclipsed by Anne Rice's Vampire Chronicles. The Anne Rice Vampire Lestat Fan Club may have also served as a womb community. The group holds an annual Gathering of the Coven Halloween party every year in New Orleans.[7] The Endless Night Festival, the largest vampire gathering in America, coincides with the Anne Rice festival. In 2008, the two festivals began cross-promotion so that vampire enthusiasts can attend both events at a discounted rate.

In addition to live action role-play games (see Chapter 3), Renaissance festivals also served as another way for vampires to network. Neil Steinberg of *The Chicago Sun-Times* comments, "If theme parks with their pasteboard main streets, reek of a bland, safe, homogenized, whitebread America, the Renaissance Faire is at the other end of the social spectrum, a whiff of the occult, a flash of danger and a hint of the erotic. Here, they let you throw axes. Here are more beer and bosoms than you'll find in all of Disney World."[8] From this description one can imagine why Renaissance festivals appealed to vampires. Father Sebastiaan got his start as a fang-smith in a New York Renaissance festival. "Lord," "Lady," and other feudal titles are frequently used by the vampire community to denote status, a practice that was likely derived from Renaissance festivals.

Finally, we should add to this list the New York fetish scene, which Belanger cites as another important womb community.[9] Many vampire groups incorporate elements of BDSM into their traditions. Viola Johnson's *Dhampir: Child of the Blood* contains numerous photographs of vampires tormenting scantily clad women locked in cages. Restraints and flagellation are incorporated into the rituals of several vampire groups, including Ordo Strigoi Vii. Belanger has commented that there are forms of energy exchange inherent to sadomasochism, making it a form of psychic feeding. There are also some sanguinarian vampires who draw blood from donors through flagellation or other BDSM practices.

The line between blood fetishism and vampires interested in BDSM can become quite blurred. Proponents of the awakened model of vampirism argue that there is no inherent connection between the two: BDSM is a product of culture and vampirism is a product of nature. One vampire said of her involvement with BDSM, "That's what we do, not who we are." By contrast, Dawn Perlmutter has interpreted both BDSM and vampirism as part of a subculture of ritual violence. Perlmutter's sensationalistic thesis is that fetish clubs are a gateway leading to vampirism and ultimately to acts of murder. She writes:

> Unfortunately, the violence that occurs in these clubs will only continue to escalate until ritual meaning is restored. The logical resolution of the sacrificial crisis as manifested in the various "Scenes" is the sacrifice of an original victim in order to reestablish

meaning to future surrogate victims. It is at this point that the line of demarcation between performance and reality collapses and ritual violence erupts into what is designated occult murder.[10]

Needless to say, Perlmutter's writings are not popular in the vampire community.

I submit that there is a connection between BDSM and vampirism, but that it has little to do with a culture of violence. Rather, BDSM and vampirism are both technologies of the self. Philosopher Sylvere Lotringer has suggested that BDSM is not really about one person dominating another, but rather two individuals cultivating and perfecting their roles and their sense of self. He writes, "The bottom doesn't compete with his master; he manages with his help to challenge his own limits. The two configurations overlap, both struggle to achieve separately, their own singularity."[11] Thus, developing one's role in a BDSM context serves a similar function to defining one's relationship with psychic energy or discovering past lives: It is another tool for constructing and enhancing a self-narrative.

The relationship between the vampires and BDSM raises an important point about womb communities: The fact that the vampire community emerged out of various subcultures does not mean that the vampire community is somehow an "extreme" form of a larger subculture, as has been argued by Perlmutter and others. In the eighteenth century, French revolutionaries were networked primarily through cafés. At Café Foy in Paris, the bourgeoisie debated issues such as what color the flag of the revolution should be. However, it does not follow that the French Revolution was somehow an *extreme* form of café culture or that there is a fundamental link between revolutions and cafés. Cafés were merely the medium by which like-minded people were able to meet each other and exchange ideas. The emergence of the vampire community from womb communities should be understood in the same way.

A Speculative History of the Vampire Community

There are several obstacles to uncovering a history of the vampire community. First, the vampire community is still largely underground and secretive. Those rare individuals who were active in the community in the 1980s have largely withdrawn from the community and are reluctant to speak about their experiences. Second, most of the history is not recorded. From the late 1980s to the early 1990s, small vampire groups seem to have used a form of oral tradition. As the community became more self-aware, they communicated primarily through electronic means, which usually leaves no record. It is rumored that certain vampire groups possess books and binders known as "grimoires" that contain carefully guarded histories. Needless to say, no one invited me to see these alleged documents. I have seen transcripts of conversations held via electronic instant messaging from the mid 1990s, however, these may have been altered and cannot be considered a reliable source.

Third, there appears to have been more than one "vampire community." Multiple communities, each with their own culture and traditions, seem to have mimicked each other and become confounded together as new forms of communication emerged. The distinction between awakened and initiatory communities of vampires has been especially confusing. Initiatory groups generally pay more attention to traditions and the lineage by which those traditions were transmitted. By contrast, awakened vampires often assume that all vampires are more or less like them.

Fourth, there is a problem of revisionist history. Many leaders in the vampire community describe having mentors that no one has ever met. This has led other vampires to conclude that these mentor figures never existed. According to one contact, it is fairly common for vampires to lie about how long they have been part of the vampire community. Status is primarily bestowed by how long one has been involved with the community. Many vampire organizations bestow titles such as "elder" upon senior members. Father Sebastiaan's *Vampyre Alamanac* uses the special term "Azralim" to refer to "legendary" senior vampires.[12] The easiest way to progress from a neophyte to an elder is simply to exaggerate how long one has been involved with vampire culture. The same individuals who will exaggerate how long they have been in the community are also likely to make false histories or to present rumors as fact. As a result of all of these factors, the history of the community is highly speculative, even to vampires themselves.

The London Vampire Cult

Because the history of the vampire community is already a speculative project, there is little harm in beginning with a potentially apocryphal source. An article in *The Occult Review* from 1934 by Elliott O'Donnell describes a vampire cult in London.[13] O'Donnell produced both occult writing and fiction with occult themes. He did believe in vampires and defined them as "an elemental that under certain conditions inhabits a dead body, whether human or otherwise, and thus incarcerated comes out of the grave at night to suck the blood of a living person."[14] However, the vampires described in the article are not animated corpses but what today would be described as psychic vampires.

According to the article, O'Donnell met the vampire cult in a basement decorated with red walls and a red floor. There he met eleven women, each wearing blood red dresses and matching nail polish. He adds that one of these girls was only 18 or 19 years old. O'Donnell was first asked to tell the cult some news he has heard of vampires. He had traveled in America and pleased his hosts with an American ghost story involving a vampiress who exsanguinated people with her long fingernails.[15]

After preliminaries, the "president" of the cult arrived, a man who is described as ugly and accompanied by two equally ugly lieutenants. O'Donnell implies throughout the narrative that these men have created the cult for the purpose of exploiting impressionable women. The president reveals that the cult contains both living members and disembodied "spirit members." This detail sets an important precedent for the incorporeal vampire entities described by the Order of the Vampyre, the Temple of the Vampire, and Ordo Strigoi Vii.

The female cultists were given a list of people whom the president wanted "vamped"—that is, turned into vampires. The women set about this task by donning special red girdles. A cultist explained to O'Donnell that the girdles are made from "the bark of a stichimonious tree, growing in a notoriously vampirous district in Hungary, and were encased in goat skin, soaked in the blood of a Jew who had been murdered by Albanian brigands." O'Donnell adds, "She was quite serious when she told me all this, and I felt sure she believed it herself. And, perhaps, it was true."

The women were also given special flowers to eat. O'Donnell writes, "These flowers, she explained to me, came from the Balkans. There they were known among the natives there as vampire flowers, and if eaten shortly before midnight, to the accompaniment of certain incantations, they were deemed sufficient in themselves to develop vampire tendencies." Equipped with their special vampire girdles and having eaten their special vampire flowers, the women closed their eyes and entered a two hour trance. When they awakened, the women described having visited their assigned "targets" in their sleep and vampirizing them by gouging them with their nails and drinking their blood. (O'Donnell seems rather preoccupied with women's fingernails throughout the article.) Upon awakening, several cultists claimed they could taste the blood during this encounter. O'Donnell refers to this process as "projection." He is informed that these attacks will leave actual physical wounds on the target, but that these will be dismissed by the victims as insect bites or boils.

The story concludes with several humorous elements. One of the women was sent to vampirize a lawyer and objects that lawyers are already vampires to begin with. O'Donnell also adds, "One of the women, who was elderly . . . was very anxious to project herself into my room one night and make a vampire of me. Had she been pretty, I might, I confess, have given her the desired opportunity, but in the circumstances I preferred to put her on the wrong track; so I gave her the address of someone I disliked very much. Whether she succeeded in her designs or not with regard to him I do not know, but I hope she did."

Is there a kernel of truth to this story? If so, it represents a very early iteration of the vampire community. The story weaves together various elements that were already present in the vampire milieu by 1934. The method of vampirism by astral projection could easily have been adapted from Fortune's *Psychic Self-Defense,* published only four years prior. Girdles made from human skin appear in European folk tradition, although as a means to become a werewolf, not a vampire.[16] Finally, it should be noted that *Dracula* starring Bela Lugosi had been released in 1931.

Either O'Donnell invented the story, weaving together elements to make a plausible story or the story is true and a London occultist weaved together the same elements to lure impressionable vampire fans into a cult. Both possibilities seem equally likely. At any rate, O'Donnell's article suggests that it was certainly *possible* that some form of the vampire community existed in the early twentieth century. Curiously, Russo describes a group active in the United Kingdom known as The Ordo Anno Mundi (OAM). The OAM is a magical society that offers training in witchcraft as well as "werewolf and vampire transformation." The group was apparently founded in Staffordshire in 1985, but their mailing address has since moved to a box in Singapore.[17] If the OAM is not the descendent of the London vampire cult, it certainly appeals to the same audience as O'Donnell.

The 1970s

On Midsummer night 1970, Jim Morrison and Patricia Kennely were married in a Wiccan ceremony. Bride and groom cut themselves and mixed their blood in a cup of wine which they both shared. They also used blood to sign two versions of their wedding vows—one in English and one in witch runes. (Morrison fainted at the end of the ceremony—possibly due to nervousness about tying the knot, blood loss, or a combination of both.)[18] Elements of Paganism seem to have fed into the first vampire communities during the 1970s. A similar ritual of drinking blood mixed with wine is used today by the vampire group Ordo Sekhemu.[19] Although Morrison and his bride were not vampires, their wedding serves as a symbolic beginning to what has been dubbed "the vampire decade."

Although little is known about the vampire community in the 1970s, it does seem to have existed in a rather nebulous form. Damon, a British vampire interviewed by Rosemary Ellen Guiley, said that the vampires "came out" in 1971.[20] If this is true, then the vampire community predates the punk movement, the goth movement, and *Interview with the Vampire.* The form of vampirism espoused by Damon and his consort Damien was anti-Christian and Satanic. Peter Haining's *The Dracula Scrapbook* includes an article from the *The Daily Mirror* dated August 4, 1971, describing another similar Satanic model of vampirism in Wales:

> A magistrates court in Ruthin, Wales fined a local "vampire" and warned him not to drink anymore blood. Alan Dyche began telling friends he was a vampire and staged a number of "black magic ceremonies" in which he killed "six sheep, two lamps, four rabbits and a cat—and drank their blood." . . . The court was told that the ceremonies impressed witnesses who claimed that they twice heard thunder roll as Dyche lifted a cup of blood and declared, "Devil, this is your drink."[21]

It is possible that Damon simply read *The Dracula Scrapbook* and this article was the source of his date. But who was Alan Dyche and who were these "friends" attending his black magic ceremonies? As with O'Donnell's London vampire cult, it is difficult to draw any conclusions.

Meanwhile, in the United States there are rumors that "vampire biker gangs" existed in the 1970s. The closest I have come to substantiating these claims is Page's account of Misty and her Lost Shadows Gang. Misty claims that in the early 1970s she would discuss her vampiric habits with anyone who would listen via CB radio, eventually earning the nickname "Countess." She sent several pages to Page describing members of the Lost Shadows gang who had names like "Grim Reaper," enjoyed doing stunts on their motorcycles, and would allegedly pick up inebriated woman in bars to drain their blood while they were unconscious. It seems possible that truckers speaking to Misty about the Lost Shadows Gang could be the origin of the vampire biker gang rumor.[22]

There are two current vampire groups that claim to have been in existence for several decades. The Web site of House Dark Haven states that they were established in the mid-1980s, but that their lineage goes back to the 1970s. Lord Alistair, the group's leader, traces his tradition of vampirism to Canada and a "patriarch" named Sire Terrence Lightfoot. Lightfoot was apparently of Mohawk Indian descent and connected to some sort of countercultural group that involved punk rock, Pagan spirituality, and vampirism. Whatever he was doing was not well received in Canada and Lightfoot was briefly incarcerated. The mantle of leadership fell to one of Lightfoot's colleagues, Elder Julian DuBois (sometimes referred to as Father Julian). DuBois began instilling the group with the concept of maintaining both a positive dayside persona and a vampiric nightside persona.[23] The Web site of House Sahjaza in New York City explains that before becoming a vampire house, it began as a coven of "female Pagan vampyres," headed by a woman known as Goddess Rosemary.[24] My contacts within the vampire community tell me that House Sahjaza has a history going back several decades, but exactly how far back is unknown.

The 1980s

House Dark Haven's Web site argues that the cultural "vampire boom" of the 1980s and 1990s helped the vampire community to prosper.[25] In 1987, Inanna Arthen's article "The Story of Real Vampires" appeared in the Pagan journal *Fireheart.* The article described an awakened model of vampirism in which vampires are "incarnated" with "a certain way of dealing with the physical world." Although the article does not actually use the word "psychic vampires," it explains that vampires have energetic needs that can be satisfied by consuming either blood or energy.[26]

Certain documents describing "The Old Ways" of vampire society were accessed during research for this book and are attributed to the late 1980s and early 1990s. A contact explained that the two documents came from different sources who were not aware of each other. According to this contact, elements of the history were considered to be true if they were described in both documents. (This approach is not unlike New Testament experts comparing details in the gospels of Matthew, Mark, and Luke.) The documents show that certain vocabulary had already become widespread in the vampire community. The term "elders" appeared in both documents—a term that is also used in *Vampire: The Masquerade*. The term "mundanes" also appeared, used to refer to individuals who are not vampires and have no knowledge or expertise in the occult. One document stated that vampire houses have only a 15 percent survival rate and that when a house disintegrates it is often absorbed into a more prosperous house. Elders of the old house can petition the new house for a "rite of fire" to maintain their status. The rite of fire consists of testing the elder to measure their knowledge and, apparently, their martial prowess.

Vampires in Small Print

Sometime in the late 1980s, the vampire community began printing newsletters and zines.[27] (Zines are small, homemade print publications often making use of only a copy machine to reproduce a small number of issues for distribution.) One publication would typically have advertisements for another, forming a network. Jeff Guinn and Andy Grieser refer to this network as "the vampire underground" and report that every vampire they interviewed subscribed to several newsletters and publications.[28] (This is hardly surprising as ads were placed in *The Midnight Sun* on their behalf in order to solicit interviews.) Campbell, in his article on the cult milieu, argues that magazines are crucial to the growth and survival of the milieu.[29] Print publications allowed vampires on opposite sides of the continent to contact each other and caused the community to become more self-aware.

Underground vampire publications ranged from Gothic fiction and poetry to manifestos about vampirism. Belanger lists titles such as *Necropolis* by Chad Williams, *Onyx Magazine* by Chad Savage, and *Erebus Rising* published out of the United Kingdom.[30] Liriel McMahon of Seattle, Washington, published *VAMPS,* and Lady Dark Rose of Florida began her publication *The Dark Rose Journal.* Page lists *The Velvet Vampyre* and *Crimson.*[31] One of my contacts provided articles from another publication, the *Journal of the Dark.*

Belanger ran a group of journals under the banner of Shadowfox publications.[32] *Shadowdance* was a gothic literary publication that served as a "facade" to explore vampire beliefs. This led to the publication of a new journal *Midnight Sun* in 1995.[33] *Midnight Sun* was the official publication of the International Society of Vampires and was openly vampiric. New subscribers received a short paragraph in the publication where they answered questions such as, "Are you a vampire?" The pinnacle of the mailing networks may have been the *Vampire Theatre Videozine,* run by a group called Vampires of America. Vampire footage could be mailed to Vampires of America, who would select and edit the best footage and mail it to subscribers—essentially applying the zine concept to new media.[34]

Belanger describes many vampires becoming "awakened" during this era of the small print. A "quest for knowledge" fueled the zines and other publication as self-identified vampires tried to find others like them. According to Belanger, the Temple of the Vampire was one of the most organized vampire groups at the time and was successful at exploiting the new market for vampire lore[35] Many people who purchased the Temple's book, *The Vampire Bible,* had no intention of becoming active members of the organization, but they were willing to pay $25 for the opportunity to learn something about vampires. Guinn and Grieser describe an interview with "Gremlin" of Seattle, Washington. Gremlin's approach to the Temple of the Vampire appears to have been typical during this time:

> "I'll always continue to be a questioner," he added. "That's why I'm in touch with the Temple of the Vampire. They seem a little adamant in the way they run things. They sent me this brochure that said if I buy this book, buy this ring, and by this pendant, I'm an active member. In the book, they tell you certain things you have to do to get a higher rank. I haven't bought the book yet. I think it's twenty-five dollars, but I plan on it just to see what they're about. I'm a Khlysty. I'm a truth finder, and if they're not what I'm looking for, I'll know, and then I'm not going to deal with them."[36]

Once again, this attitude is not unique to vampires but applies to a broad spectrum of American spiritual seekers. Literary scholar Harold Bloom has recently argued that all American religion is inherently "Gnostic."[37] Bloom's thesis is that all Americans approach their religion as a form of radical self-discovery that can be both liberating and isolating.[38] The vampire community certainly seems to embody Bloom's Gnostic quest for self-knowledge.

Vampires on the Internet

Christopher Partridge has argued that the Internet draws those seeking "detraditionalized spiritualities."[39] Whether or not one considers vampirism to be a detraditionalized spirituality, it should come as no surprise that vampires have been active on the Internet for as long as it has existed. The Internet also became a place where the curious go to seek vampires out. Before the vampire community began to create its own resources, these seekers typically encountered pranksters, role-players, or worse.

An article entitled "Vampire? Fake! The Story of Vincent Tremaine," featured in the *Journal of the Dark* is the autobiographical story of a woman who was sexually exploited while searching for vampires online. The author met "Vincent Tremaine" using the Prodigy online service provider in 1990. She was only 15 at the time. Tremaine claimed to be an immortal vampire and strung out a long, detailed story about being born into vampire nobility in Eastern Europe. He promised to take the author away from her family as his immortal bride; however, he first required proof of her devotion. Tremaine asked the 15-year-old to mail him nude Polaroids of herself—a request to which she consented. After months of correspondence, Tremaine told the author that she had betrayed him and that he thought she was actually a vampire hunter. At the time the girl was crushed. It was not until years later that she realized she had been targeted by a sexual predator.[40] What is interesting about this case is how early it happened: Many people were not even aware the Internet existed in 1990. The vampire community is currently interested in creating resources for teens, in part to prevent this sort of incident from happening in the future.

In 1996, a chat room entitled "RealVampiresNoRP" appeared on America Online. (The suffix "NoRP" indicated that role-playing was not tolerated in the chat room.) Many real vampires including Belanger and Father Sebastiaan began finding others through this chat room.[41] In 1997 the Sanguinarius Internet Relay Chat (IRC) channel was launched. This was followed in 1998 by the creation of two large vampire e-lists run by Reverend Osirus in New York City and Daemonox in California.

Various support Web sites for vampires, featuring articles on how to feed, what it means to be a vampire, and other topics, also began to appear.[42] Arthen briefly created a series of "checklists" that readers could use to determine whether or not they were vampires. She later took the checklists down because she was being inundated with e-mails from possible vampires asking what their "scores" meant. The vampire community also complained about the checklists, claiming they were responsible for "a flood of newbies."[43]

While the vampire community existed before the Internet, the Internet has allowed it to flourish like never before. Even more so than the print publications, the Internet allowed independent and isolated vampires to join the vampire community. Vampires in rural areas could now instantly locate and speak to vampires on either coast. Vampire groups and houses were no longer limited by space. Many modern vampire groups have members across the country and indeed across the world. Partridge called the Temple of the Vampire "an Internet religion" because it appears to have no actual headquarters—only a network that has been facilitated first through print publications and then through the Internet.[44] However, such networks have become the rule, rather than the exception, for many vampire groups. This in turn, has made national gatherings all the more important for the vampire community because these gatherings provide an opportunity to meet face to face.

It is now so easy to find real vampires on the Internet that leaders of the community have become frustrated with neophyte vampires—typically teenagers—bombarding them with the same questions over and over. Transcripts of the 2008 "Voices of the Vampire Community" meetings describe frustration with young people who apparently refuse to read the numerous articles provided on the Internet. The latest innovation is a series of videos on YouTube. Questions about vampires can be e-mailed to a vampire known as Zilchy, who will record a video of himself answering the questions and post it online. It was hoped that a video format would be more palatable for the short attention spans of young vampires. So far, it remains to be seen if the videos are effective.[45]

The New York Vampire Scene

In the mid-1990s, a distinct vampire culture formed in New York City. Although vampire culture in other parts of the United States is quite different from that of New York, the New York vampire scene is a watershed in the history of the community. The *Vampire: The Masquerade* LARP served as a catalyst that led to a full-blown vampire life-style combining elements of gothic culture, Renaissance festival anachronism, fetish club culture, and esoteric movements.

Although only two vampires from the New York scene were willing to speak about their experiences, electronic correspondences between the vampire "courts" of New York were obtained. The signatures used in these documents speak volumes about their culture. The following signature is characteristic of the scene:

> Sir Shaolin MacPhee of House Sabretooth MacPhee
> Calmae to House Sabretooth MacPhee
> Proud and Loyal Son of Lord "O" MacPhee Orion, True Sheriff of Gotham
> GrandChilde of Father Vincent Orion, High Elder and KING OF KINGS of Gotham

There appears to be nothing analogous to this anywhere else in the vampire community. None of the vampires contacted for this book in the South or on the West Coast used titles more elaborate than "lord" or "lady." By contrast, New York vampires are divided into different clans, hold courts, and engage in political rivalries that can turn quite vicious. Initiation is more important in this culture, and New York vampires may refer to the vampire who initiated them as their "sire" or informally as their "father" or even "daddy."

Elements of the New York vampire culture have been exported throughout the world, but the same baroque aesthetic has never been fully replicated elsewhere. Many New York vampires describe vampirism as a life-style rather than an ontology, and the distinction between "lifestyle" and "real" vampires may have emerged as a reaction to the New York vampire culture. While being active in the New York vampire scene does not preclude being a "real vampire," some self-identified real vampires express suspicion toward their peers in New York.

More than any other individual, Father Sebastiaan was responsible for organizing and promoting the New York vampire scene. Sebastiaan, who currently resides in Paris, France, was described by many contacts as a bit of scoundrel. However, he is very charismatic and has a natural facility for networking and organizing people. Katherine Ramsland describes interviewing Sebastiaan for her book *Piercing the Darkness* only to end up agreeing to be an editor for one of his literary projects.[46] It is doubtful that the vampire community would exist in its current form without his efforts.

In a phone interview, Sebastiaan described himself as "a farm boy from Jersey." He attended a Quaker school in Pennsylvania where he met a Wiccan classmate. She first introduced him to the idea that there are Pagan covens that consume blood as part of their rituals. Sebastiaan became active in the first LARPs and moved to New York City where he worked to organize games. It was in New York that he began working as a promoter for the nightclub Limelight. He described having his first experience absorbing energy on New Year's Eve 1995, while sitting backstage during a concert by the band Hole. Sebastiaan said that he had been working all day and sat down in a state of complete exhaustion. From his position behind the stage, he was able to feel the energy that the audience was directing toward the band. Sebastiaan said that he had never tried heroin but that he imagined it felt much like that moment backstage.

Sebastiaan also worked at the Sterling Forest Renaissance Faire in Tuxedo, New York, where, in 1995, he founded Sabretooth Inc. The company created custom vampire fangs, contact lenses, and vampire-themed jewelry. Sebastiaan, a licensed dental technician, had received his first pair of fangs in 1992 from a company in Seattle called Strangeblades. When not at a Renaissance festival, Sebastiaan would run his fangsmithing business out of a body-piercing shop known as Andromeda. He took the title "Father" because he felt a close connection to his clients after creating custom fangs for them. "You feel like daddy," he said. In an interview with Ramsland he described his dream of developing, "a 'coven' in which the leaders of the various sections would be a network of fangmakers across the country." He added, "That's what I want to be remembered for, and I'll gain a sort of immortality from the vampire myth."[47] Sebastiaan eventually did succeed in his goal of creating a national network of vampires.

According to Sebastiaan, he was first introduced to vampire culture by a coworker at the Renaissance festival named Dmitri. In 1995 Dmitri took him to an underground vampire club located in a basement in East Village near Ave C. Sebastiaan writes of this experience:

> I remember a belly dancer in one corner with a slave in a straight jacket like a monkey on a leash, an altar with a pig skull on it and a pagan ritual taking place, people dressed in REAL victorian clothes not Hot Topic designs, a tarot card reader, a BDSM scene, and mixed tapes of really dark ethereal and eerie classical music. All in all there were about 20–30 people there at most and this vision has truly stuck in my mind from that point on. Any "donors," guests and slaves had to come on a leash.[48]

Sebastiaan's detractors believe that Dmitri never existed. But according to Sebastiaan he caught the tale end of a completely underground vampire community that is now extinct—in part due to gentrification and the "crackdowns" by mayor Rudolf Guiliani. He said that Dmitri and his coven, along with about 50 other people all vanished mysteriously in 1996. The story is corroborated somewhat by Vlad Marko and Sky Soro. Vlad and Sky are vampire performance artists who enjoy a sort of celebrity status within the New York vampire scene. Sebastiaan cited them as two survivors of this previous epoch. In an interview with *Bite Me* magazine they do make mention of underground vampire clubs in New York.[49]

Perhaps inspired by his experience with Dmitri, Sebastiaan began to modify LARPs, making them into more of a culture than a game. He told an amusing story about a LARP held in a nightclub in which an attractive girl played a go-go dancing vampire. She was enjoying herself wearing fangs and dancing in a cage when another player (Sebastiaan described him as a "fat, nerdy gamer") approached and announced he was using his domination power on her. The girl rolled her eyes and ignored him, breaking the rules of the game.

Sebastiaan wanted to preserve the sensual, aesthetic experience of the LARP without being burdened by rules or attracting "power gamers." So in 1995, he used his contacts as a club promoter to organize a series of "vampyre balls" at New York nightclubs. Favorite venues included The Bank (once an actual bank), The Cave, the Vault, and Limelight.[50] Sebastiaan said that in 1996, Limelight held a vampyre ball that was attended by 1,500 people. That year turned out to be an interesting year for Limelight. Now called Avalon, the club was originally an old Episcopal church on 6th street in Manhattan.[51] In 1996, another club promoter killed and dismembered Angel Melendez, a drug dealer who had been working in the club.[52] The Melendez murder created a scandal in the New York club scene and became the basis for the 2003 film *Party Monster* starring Macaulay Culkin.[53] Although most vampire groups condemn criminal activity and drug use, Sebastiaan seems to have been comfortable dealing with the seedier elements of New York City. He stated that he had known most of the drug dealers who frequented Limelight and described his relationship with them as "friendly but not friends."[54]

A gay club called Mother opened in 1996 and became an important club for the New York vampire scene. Sebastiaan worked with the club's owner to produce a weekly vampire night called The Long Black Veil. The Long Black Veil was successful and brought Sebastiaan widespread recognition. In 2000, Two *New York Times* reporters who attended the Long Black Veil quoted Sebastiaan, "We used to charge $20 to people who were out of dress if we deemed them worthy, but now we charge $50. . . . We don't want people just sitting and staring. We want members of our community to feel comfortable."[55] In 1998, Sebastiaan organized the first Endless Night festival held in New Orleans on the weekend of

Halloween. The Festival has now been running for over ten years and is one of Sebastiaan's greatest successes.

In 1996, Sebastiaan, along with another vampire, Father Vincent, formed Clan Sabretooth as a club for fangsmiths and their clientele.[56] By 1997, Sebastiaan was beginning to organize the different vampire groups. In March, the first Court of Gotham was held in New York. (Gotham is an old nickname for the city. It is believed to have been coined in 1807 by writer Washington Irving for the satirical magazine *Salmagundi*.)[57] A "court" in the vampire community refers to a social function attended by various vampire groups. The Court of Gotham met on a monthly basis, and those in attendance came to be known as SNOG, an acronym for Society Nocturnis of Gotham.[58] Courts gave expression to the themes of honor and chivalry that the vampire community had inherited from role-playing games and Renaissance festivals. At some courts, a herald would stand by the door, announcing each vampire by title as they arrived.

On the national level, Sebastiaan began a group known as The Sanguinarium as a sort of confederacy for different vampire groups. Known groups were offered membership as a "house" of The Sanguinarium. All that was required was that they create a special sigil (symbol) for their house.

The symbol for The Sanguinarium was a bladed ankh called the Legacy Ankh. The idea of a bladed ankh originates in the 1983 film *The Hunger*. Sebastiaan said he found an actual bladed ankh at a gothic jewelry store called Skincrawl. He commissioned his friend D'Drennan, a metal worker, to create a new one with a slightly different design. Legacy Ankh medallions were then bestowed on new members of The Sanguinarium.

The Sanguinarium created a common lexicon of vampire terms and a set of shared traditions. These elements became a sort of prototype that different vampire groups could tailor and gave the emerging community a sense of legitimacy and verisimilitude. Part of the original vision of The Sanguinarium was to create a "council of elders" to standardize a vampire terminology. Some have even said the group was charged with creating a vampire language. This entity became known as COVICA, an acronym for the Council of Vampyric International Community Affairs. Although vampires outside of New York were largely unconcerned with a self-appointed "council of elders," standardization occurred nevertheless.

Sebastiaan canonized the term "house" to describe a group of vampires rather than the word "clan" (used in *Vampire: The Masquerade*) or "coven," used by Anne Rice. Prior to Rice, the word coven was used only to refer to a group of witches. By avoiding this term, Sebastiaan also sought to distinguish the emerging vampire community from Pagan groups. The term "Elder"—also taken from the role-playing game—became more widespread and was expanded into a three-tier hierarchy. Those new to the life-style were dubbed "fledglings," and intermediates were "calmae." Sebastiaan envisioned a Sanguinarium court where

The Sigil of House Kheperu. (Courtesy of Michelle Belanger)

everyone would wear an ankh indicating their rank: Calmae would bear a red stone in their ankh, while elders would have a purple stone. Non-vampires associated with the community came to be called "swans." A "black swan" is a donor or another individual who is friendly toward vampires. A "white swan" is antagonistic toward vampires. (Thus a black swan may be invited to court, but a white swan may not.) Although not all vampire groups use these terms, the Sanguinarium lexicon became a sort of *lingua franca* that can now be found throughout the vampire community.

Sebastiaan also produced two documents for vampires: a Donor's Bill of Rights and set of ethical guidelines known as the Black Veil. The Black Veil bears strong traces of the womb communities that inspired it. It is widely thought to have been based on the rules vampires must follow in the game *Vampire: The Masquerade.*[59] In 2002, Belanger worked with Sebastiaan to create the Black Veil 2.0. Revisions were intended primarily to distance the document from the role-playing game. Sebastiaan, however, said that he adapted the Black Veil from the creed of The Eulenspiegel Society, a BDSM education and support society.[60]

In 2003, the SciFi Channel aired a reality show entitled *Mad, Mad House.* The show featured five "alts," each of which represented an alternative life-style.

Don Henrie gained minor celebrity status on the show representing the vampire life-style. On the show, Henrie often compared vampirism to a faith and at one point referred to the Black Veil as a "sacred document." This elicited a surprised response from Belanger who stated, "I wrote the Black Veil. I thought a document could only become sacred once its original author was long dead and had faded into anonymity."[61]

Sebastiaan has said of the Black Veil:

> We are seeing something incredibly special and unique in the world develop and The Black Veil has been the center of this entire concept, something that has really spoken to people in all of its variations and incarnations. All The Black Veil is just common sense organized into a presentable form and is truly the center of the entire vampyre movement.[62]

This quote points to the true function of the document. One contact told me that these documents were never created because there were widespread problems with vampires acting unethically or abusing donors. Rather, they were created to "make progress." I think that by "making progress" she meant creating a set of traditions rich enough to give vampire culture—and hence the vampire identity—a greater sense of reality. Vampires wanted The Sanguinarium to feel more meaningful than a social club or a role-playing game and documents like the Black Veil contributed to this feeling. Although numerous vampire groups and Web sites refer to the Black Veil, I have never heard of any jurisprudence regarding it. This suggests that the Black Veil serves the community more as a symbol than as an actively enforced system of rules.

Forensic biologist Mark Benecke went to New York to study the vampire subculture from 1997 to 2000. He concluded that the social bonds between vampires served as a kind of pseudo-family. In Atlanta, I interviewed Stephen O'Mallie, who had been active in the New York vampire scene in the mid-1990s. He also described the scene in its heyday as feeling like a family. Sadly, he felt that this unity had yielded to infighting and political struggles.

O'Mallie was the founder of a New York vampire group, Clan O'Mallie, and had once held the title of "Sheriff of Gotham." Each member of his clan had a background in martial arts, and together they were responsible for self-policing the community. O'Mallie described how a rival vampire group had been attacking members of the Court of Gotham and stealing their ankhs. It fell to Clan O'Mallie to discourage this behavior, through force if necessary. O'Mallie described himself as a lifestyle vampire and confirmed that New York vampire culture evolved from LARP games. The title "Sheriff" originates from *Vampire: The Masquerade*. In the game, vampire courts would select a powerful vampire to be in charge of policing rogue vampires—exactly as O'Mallie had done in New York.

O'Mallie indicated that the community had been damaged by its own success. As the courts grew, positions of leadership became more coveted. According to

O'Mallie, "people began to stab each other in the back." If he missed court, politically minded vampires would attempt to use it against him. He described how participation in the culture had originally been a form of release, but instead it had become a source of stress. Rival vampire clans became territorial and increasingly began to act like street gangs. O'Mallie described some groups in which initiates were required to have sex with the head of the group in order to become a member. The last straw for O'Mallie was when D'Drennan, a leader in the New York scene, committed suicide. O'Mallie has largely retired from the vampire scene and now resides in Georgia where he works as a detective. His opinion was that the vampire community needs to become more exclusive and to go back underground.

Sebastiaan now resides in Paris and devotes much of his time to his new project, the Ordo Strigoi Vii. The Court of Gotham has now split into two groups: SNOG and the Court of Lazarus are independent, but each group sends diplomats to the other.[63] Father Vincent has now taken a place of seniority in the New York scene. At the time of this writing, he is attempting a "census" of the New York vampires. Some believe this is an attempt to monitor volatile younger vampires (referred to as "baby bats" by older vampires[64]). O'Mallie referred to this new generation of New York vampires as "some straight up thugs." One group in particular, Clan Hidden Shadows, was portrayed as the *hoi polloi* of the vampire community. The appearance, body language, and diction of this group is certainly consistent with a street gang. An informal list of "reckless vampires" is maintained by the vampire community in order to police these individuals. Having taught teenage gang members for several years, I find it unsurprising that they would take an interest in New York vampire culture. Elements of chivalry, loyalty, and secrecy are predominant in the cultures of both groups.

What will Father Sebastiaan's legacy be? Will he achieve the immortality he wants as the founder of a vampire society? I see Sebastiaan's Sanguinarium as a sort of midwife to the vampire community, just as the short-lived Hermetic Order of the Golden Dawn served as a midwife to modern occult movements. The Sanguinarium created a model culture that different vampire groups can modify to their tastes. More formal vampire groups still use terms like calmae, elders, and swans, while others find these terms pretentious. However, some Sanguinarium traditions such as the Black Veil are used by almost every vampire group.

Vampire Values

Not surprisingly, loyalty and secrecy are important in the vampire community. Vampirism is difficult for outsiders to understand and being "outed" as a vampire can have disastrous consequences in some parts of the country. Because of their efforts to maintain secrecy, vampires sometimes describe themselves as "paranoid." The majority of vampires use "community names" to refer to themselves and one another. In fact, I know the actual name of only one of my contacts in Atlanta—and that is only a first name. Instead, my cell-phone contacts list is full of vampire pseudonyms such as Merticus and Eclecta. An emphasis on loyalty comes largely from the importance of secrecy. During my research, there were times when I felt a contact wanted to tell me some detail of vampire history or politics, but refrained out of loyalty to the community at large.

Associated with the idea of secrecy are the concepts of "dayside," "nightside," and "twilight." According to Belanger, these terms actually originated with the Temple of the Vampire. However, they have since been adopted by many individual vampires as well as groups like Ordo Sekhemu and Ordo Strigoi Vii. "Dayside" refers to the identity that one presents to the world. One's career, personal finances, church affiliation, and family are considered dayside pursuits. Nightside refers to the vampire's hidden identity. Feeding practices, occult traditions, and community names are all part of the vampire's nightside persona. Many vampire groups emphasize the importance of nurturing both the dayside and the nightside persona. In fact, there seems to be more than a little contempt for vampires who attend all of the parties and rituals but cannot hold down a job. The Ordo Strigoi Vii has both a dayside and a nightside recommended reading list. The nightside list, as might be imagined, contains various occult texts. The dayside list contains books on subjects such as finance and politics including Machiavelli's *The Prince* and *Rich Dad, Poor Dad* by Robert Kiyosaki. The goal for many vampire groups is to achieve a state of "twilight" in which both spheres are in a productive state of equilibrium. A banner on House Sahjaza's Web site states, "Balance, Unity, Twilight!"[65] Each vampire separates his or her dayside and nightside personas to a different degree. Some vampires do not even use a pseudonym. Others maintain two separate personas that are kept entirely discreet.

It may come as a surprise that some vampires are politically conservative, describing themselves as republican or conservative libertarian. (Neal Boortz is said to be popular with more politically active vampires.) Although anything resembling an alternative life-style is often associated with liberalism, the political views of vampires often reflect the community's value of radical individualism. It is possible that this conservative streak is especially pronounced in the South, where I was doing my research. However, there is also evidence of conservatism among vampire communities in New York City and elsewhere. Many vampires support second-amendment rights and believe in a culture of self-defense. I met several vampires who practice martial arts or carry weapons for protection. Vampires also describe efforts to police themselves, showing a desire for political autonomy. Several conservative theorists have had an influence on the vampire community. Ayn Rand appears on the dayside reading list of Ordo Strigoi Vii. LaVeyan Satanism—which is prominent in some vampire groups—also expresses a conservative ideology emphasizing personal responsibility and even Social Darwinism.

Related to the value of personal autonomy is a desire for the community to be self-policing. One contact showed me some documents from the early 1990s describing "The Old Ways." These documents described remedies for internecine conflicts within the vampire community. One stated, "wars between rival clans is inevitable." Both documents described resolving conflicts through dueling—either to submission, to first blood, or to the death. The ideas of honor, chivalry, and romance associated with dueling are widespread in the vampire community. However, this contact added that to his knowledge there had never been an actual duel fought in the history of the vampire community.

As the old guard of the vampire community has gotten older and had children, they have learned the value of gaining positions in legal firms, law enforcement, and even local churches. "The community has gotten smarter," as one vampire put it. Those who step out of line are now effectively shut out of the community—they are blacklisted from all of the clubs and gatherings frequented by vampires, and community members who are active in law enforcement may be notified of their status. My contact implied that those banished in this way usually may continue to be active in the community only if they move to another city. He added: "We give you a plane ticket and send you on your way." When I asked what sort of transgression merited this treatment, I was given a short list of examples: abusing a donor, abusing a spouse, criminal activity, drug abuse. Although this streak of classic liberalism in the vampire community was unexpected, it reconfirms the American character of the community. Just as their ideas about religion are influenced by American thinkers ranging from Thomas Jefferson to William James, their social values of self-determination, antiauthoritarianism, and personal responsibility are the legacy of John Locke and other Enlightenment philosophers.

Metaphysical Communities: Awakened versus Mundanes

For many vampires, metaphysics plays an important role in how they form relationships with each other and how they see their community. Because vampires need to feed, they are ultimately dependent on other people and require the support of a community. For sanguinarian vampires, sharing blood with a donor or "a feeding circle" naturally leads to a certain degree of trust and intimacy. Psychic vampires may also form close groups for purposes of exchanging energy. Belanger has commented that not everyone's energy is equally nourishing and that energy taken from "mundanes" is not very sustaining.[66] Thus, psychic vampires must seek nourishment through consensual relationships with special donors and other vampires. In effect, the way vampires understand their own nature fosters community by counteracting their social value of radical individualism.

Feeding is only one way in which vampire metaphysics functions to create communities. The "Beacon" is another concept that functions to bring vampires together. Many vampires feel they possess a sort of sixth sense that allows them to identify each other. The most common term for this idea is the Beacon as promoted by Belanger in *The Psychic Vampire Codex.* Some contacts referred to the phenomenon as "pinging," as in, "That girl pinged when she walked in the room."[67] Daemonox, a leader in the vampire community, was once told she had an "etheric whistle" because of her ability to draw people together.[68] This is another variation on the idea of the Beacon. Some vampires believe that the purpose of the Beacon is to guide potential vampires to others who can help their awakening.

The concept of the Beacon bears a vague resemblance to the 1986 film *Highlander,* in which immortals can sense one another's presence. Interestingly, interviews with sanguinarian vampires from the early 1990s, which predate terms like "Beacon" and "pinging," also describe intuitively recognizing other vampires. Page includes three examples: Jack describes meeting another boy in his high school locker room and states, "I met this person and when I first met him I knew." The boy did not object when Jack then proceeded to lick a scrape on the boy's knee.[69] Shannon, another vampire, also had this ability and described it as "an antenna."[70] Monique from Boston was approached by a strange man in Kenmore Square who asked to share blood with her. (Despite being a vampire she ignored him and left quickly.)[71]

Belanger has commented that vampires are "marked by a strong sense of elitism."[72] Because of the role of metaphysical ideas in bringing vampires together, their collective identity sometimes resembles a religious identity more than a secular group. The idea of a "chosen people," or a community of the elect, has been a powerful one throughout Western culture from the ancient Israelites, to the Gnostic elite, to John Winthrop's "City on a Hill" sermon, to the American civil religion embodied by the phrase "God bless America." This idea of a community of the elect manifests in vampire discourse through the terms "awakened" and "mundane."

Non-vampires are normally referred to as "mundanes." (However, with the success of the Harry Potter franchise, the term "muggle" has been gaining usage.) The term "mundane" seems to have become popular through the New York vampire scene. The *New York Times* article about the Long Black Veil describes "mundanes" having to pay exorbitant fees to attend Sebastiaan's vampire party.[73] When I asked Sebastiaan about the origin of the term he told me, "The term was used by the Rennies at the New York, Tuxedo Renaissance Faire to refer to the 'normal' people who attended the faire. I started using this term with my fang clients and at my gatherings to refer to non-vamps."[74]

Ramsland has excoriated the use of the word "mundanes" by vampires as a way of dehumanizing those outside the community. She writes, "Obviously the word *mundane* has negative connotations, so to use this term is to convey a sense that what is done to those people is of little consequence. It's about being smug and dehumanizing."[75] There is an important social dynamic surrounding the term "mundanes," but to call it "dehumanizing" is overstated. SphynxCat features an article on her Web site entitled "Why do you use the term mundanes?" The article explains why she advocated the word "mundane" over other terms that were in use such as "mortal," "human," "normal," and "nil." These terms implied that vampires were not mortal, human, or normal. She felt that "mundane" was actually the least elitist of these terms. SphynxCat also confirms with Sebastiaan that the word was adapted from the Society for Creative Anachronism (a group that is intimately tied to Renaissance festivals.)[76]

The opposite of "mundane" is not "vampire" but "awakened." This term refers not only to vampires but to other categories of people who either have special esoteric training or are ontologically different from other humans. Belanger writes in *The Psychic Vampire Codex:*

> We are not the only beings that undergo a process of Awakening and who may recollect lives. There are the spiritually cultivated, sages and mystics, who have devoted previous lives to gaining spiritual awareness. These may Awaken in this lifetime as well. There are the psychically gifted, whose latent talents of spirit and mind require that they accept a greater reality. As their abilities manifest, these also undergo an Awakening. Additionally, there are the Othersouled, those that have come to this place from another. As they realize what they are, these undergo an Awakening, remembering and harnessing their Other nature.[77]

Some explanation is needed to unpack this text. By "Othersouled," Belanger is referring to other identity groups who, like vampires, feel that they are essentially different from normal humans. Describing these groups could easily become a book unto itself. Just as modern vampires use the vampire milieu to put their experiences into context and to construct self-narratives, others have formed identities around werewolf lore, mythological stories of faeries and elves, and other sources. These groups have formed their own communities through processes parallel to that of the vampires.

"Therians" identify with a particular animal. Much in the way that modern vampires identity with the vampires of legend, the therian identity has been shaped by stories of werewolves as well as other cultural traditions of shape shifting. "Otherkin" may identify as faeries or elves or even as mythological creatures like dragons or unicorns. The word "otherkin" is also used as a broader term to describe anyone who considers herself to be other than or essentially different from humanity. This broader use of the term includes vampires, therians, otherkin, humans with alien DNA, humans possessed by extra-dimensional entities, and things far stranger. It should be noted that vampires are often critical of the claims of otherkin and vice versa. These groups do not simply accept each other's subjective identities, but rather negotiate them through a variety of criteria. Some otherkin—for instance those who claim they are the earthly incarnation of characters from cartoons or computer games—are widely viewed as delusional. Nevertheless, otherkin in general are usually considered awakened and some vampires say that the Beacon effect applies to such individuals.

Psychics, occultists, and religious virtuosos are also classified as awakened, despite the fact that these individuals do not claim to be other than human. Pagans, especially, frequently interact with the vampire community without being considered as mundanes. (During my time with the AVA, I was invited to a "vampires versus witches" softball game.) Paganism is normally thought of as a religion rather than an identity group. However, Oliver Krueger has noted that as a result of "self-initiation rituals" disseminated through the Internet, the majority of Pagans are now "solitary practitioners" who have no affiliation with a Pagan coven or group. Thus, being a Pagan has become primarily a source of identity, just as being a vampire is a source of identity.[78] Furthermore, it should not be forgotten that terms like "witch" and "pagan" were highly negative terms for much of Western history. Describing oneself as a "witch" entails a process of identifying with an occult threat, de-otherizing that threat, and making it a technology of the self. In this way, the Pagan community established a prototype for the vampire community.

The dichotomy between awakened and mundane forms the cosmology of these essentialist identity groups and shapes the way they see the world. Lupa, the author of *A Field Guide to Otherkin,* offers a quotation that demonstrates this effect starkly, "Being an Otherkin effects my life in a very tremendous way. It effects [*sic*] who I socialize with, now that I know I am not human, socializing with regular humans (mundanes) I find rather boring, and dealing with them too often or in too large of doses is frustrating to me because they're just so, ugh, dull."[79] This led Lupa to remind her readers:

> Speaking of humans, it can be deceptively easy to fall into the attitude of "Otherkin are better than humans because we're all nice/we're better to the environment/we don't start wars/insert excuse here." This can lead to quite a superiority complex, accompanied by a lot of blind spots. First off there are more than enough Otherkin who are lying, quarrelsome, and otherwise generally unpleasant assholes.[80]

What is ultimately at stake with the use of the terms "awakened" and "mundane" is the creation of new paradigm of discourse. Ron Eyerman and Andrew Jamison argue that creating an "oppositional other" is an important part of the mental space created by successful social movements.[81] Journalist Christine Wicker, after interviewing vampires, otherkin, and other "magical people," wrote, "The magical and the muggle are separated by a river, wide and deep."[82] This comment shows that those outside the movement have begun to enter this mental space. The purpose of labeling others as mundane is not so much to dehumanize or abuse them but to shift the discourse from one in which vampires, therians, and otherkin are delusional and abnormal to one where they are a distinct yet valid category of people. Indeed, all vampire discourse can be read in this way, from the Black Veil code to the VEWRS.

The Current Vampire Community: The Lay of the Land

The VEWRS received responses from all 50 states with the exception of Alaska and the Dakotas. The states with the highest number of respondents were California, Georgia, Texas, Ohio, New York, and Florida.[83] A common misunderstanding is that all vampire groups function like the New York scene with a strong emphasis on hierarchy, glamour, and style. In fact, vampire cultures vary greatly from group to group and from region to region.

In the South, Atlanta has become a popular city for vampires. There are also said to be sizable populations in Savannah, Georgia, and Tampa, Florida. New Orleans used to have a high population of vampires but since hurricane Katrina it has become more of a tourist destination than a place of residence. A rumor within the occult community holds that Katrina had altered the "ley lines"— invisible lines of mystic energy that cross the earth. The effect of this shift was that the occult energy of New Orleans has now been transferred to Atlanta.

Although my contacts have found Atlanta to be a hospitable city for vampires, the Bible Belt has had a chilling effect on Southern vampires. An extreme

(From left to right): Michelle Belanger, Mistress Sophia, and Don Henrie on set for the production of the music video "Shadow Dancer" by Belanger's band, URN. Belanger described the video as an "over-the-top parody of the Vampire genre." (Courtesy of Michelle Belanger)

example of this occurred when a vampire consented to an interview with a reporter from *The Savannah Morning News.* An article ran on August 30, 2005, with the headline, "Vampire's Night Out."[84] Two days later, an anonymous post appeared in the "vox populi" section of the paper stating, "To the group of vampires, witches and druids, you are practicing collective madness by creating delusions that don't exist in reality. Sounds like fun."[85] A more vitriolic response appeared on September 4 in the form of a letter to the editor entitled, "Nauseating vampire story had no place in newspaper." It read:

> Tolerance for others' beliefs is one thing, but why was the tell-all on vampires necessary ("Vampires' night out," article, Aug. 30)? What's next? An exposé on why we're supposed to feel sympathy for members of the North American Man/Boy Love Association? Maybe you'll fill us in on every little detail of their practices, too?
>
> Your article was nauseating and disgusting. What happened to majority rule? I find it hard to believe the majority of your readers felt there was a void in their lives that only this article could fill.
>
> The Morning News doesn't even consider the children who might see mommy or daddy reading the paper. While a 4-year-old can only be scared by the picture, an 8-year-old could read the headline. And I wouldn't even want a teenager to read the contents of the article.
>
> For you to use God's name in the article was offensive to me and a sacrilege. Furthermore, for you to say that "vampirism resembles a religion when you strip away its taboos (drinking blood, etc.)" is like saying that pedophilia is a wonderful kind of love if you strip away the fact that it abuses children.
>
> There was one statement in your article with which I could agree. The person being interviewed stated that "most vampires . . . believe in God." The Bible says in James 2:19, "...the demons also believe, and shudder." Shame on the Morning News for presenting such a nauseating article to its readers.[86]

Although the vampire was referred to only by his nightside pseudonym, there was enough information in the article for local readers to "out" the vampire. As a result of granting this interview, he was asked to leave his church and to withdraw his children from the Christian private school they attended. It is easy to imagine how even a single incident like this can affect vampire culture. Because of this social climate, vampires in the South are more paranoid then their New York cousins and less interested in high-profile social gatherings.

West-Coast vampire culture is generally characterized as the most "laid back." California is home to so many new religious movements and alternative lifestyle groups that vampires are often not even noteworthy. West-Coast vampires also tend to be even more suspicious of organization than other vampires, making their culture the opposite of the New York vampire courts. Daemonox, a California native, cited a strong sense of individualism and self-sufficiency as a deterrent to a hierarchical vampire culture.[87] There are virtually no active vampire groups on the West Coast. Instead, vampires tend to network through a variety of social events and goth clubs.

A club night known as The Fang Club was started in 1996 by promoter Jack Dean Strauss. Strauss and Sebastiaan were said to be in contact with one another and shared ideas. In 1998, Daemonox created an informal group with locals she met through the chat room RealVampiresNoRP. The group began meeting regularly on Tuesdays in the San Fernando Valley and came to be called Near Dark. In 2000, Daemonox started "Wretched," a electronic mailing list specifically for California vampires. Today the Web site http://www.LAdead.com/ continues to serve as a resource for vampire-friendly club events.

Partly because of language barriers, little is known about vampires outside the Anglophone world. The VEWRS received international responses from 26 countries. Of these, most were from Canada, the United Kingdom, and Australia. However, there were also responses from Jordan, Kuwait, Japan, Malaysia, Brazil, Mexico, and many countries in Eastern Europe.[88] In the United Kingdom, there is rumored to be a sizable population of vampires in England and in Northern Ireland. Russo characterizes vampires in the United Kingdom as shyer than their American brethren and less likely to meet in person.[89] British vampires are also said to import their fangs from the United States.[90] Aside from the Countess Elizabeth's Vampire Coven, there was one other group for real vampires in the United Kingdom, known as The Scarlet Moon Organization. The Scarlet Moon Organization was an online network for sanguinarian vampires who would occasionally meet in public. The long-term plan of the group was to buy cheap property at auction and rent it out only to members. The group existed from 1999 to 2002; however, Russo believes the remnants of the Scarlet Moon Organization are still in contact with one another.[91] The Ordo Strigoi Vii is said to be prospering in France and the Netherlands, and the Temple of the Vampire is rumored to have made inroads in Germany. Australia is also rumored to have a sizable number of vampires, but these are mostly independents who have not become organized into groups.

Vampire Gatherings

Because vampires are often separated by great distances, national gatherings have a greater meaning for the community. Belanger has studied anthropologist Victor Turner's work on ritual and describes conventions as "a liminal space." That is, conventions seem to participants to occur outside of normal time and space.[92] Belanger describes how two people can meet at a convention and not see each other again for five years. Yet, when they next see each other at another convention, it feels as if no time has passed. Most large vampire gatherings are primarily social events, as characterized by the Endless Night Festival in New Orleans. However, in the last few years a second type of gathering has emerged that resembles an academic conference more then a gothic festival. These "scholarly gatherings" generally feature lectures and seminars and tend to appeal more to the awakened model of vampirism. Vampires are also likely to congregate at conventions hosted by the various womb communities. For example, DragonCon in Atlanta drew a sizable number of vampires. Johnson's book describes meeting vampires at a "Leather Conference" held for the fetish community. Conferences on the occult, Paganism, or holistic health also tend to attract vampires.

In 2008, the 11th Endless Night Festival was held. This festival has been featured on HBO, MTV, and Oxygen TV and has set the tone for other vampire and gothic gatherings.[93] Originally the festival featured a four day LARP. It has since branched out into a number of other activities including a "vampyre ball" and a "dark bazaar." This year the festival was held in the New Orleans Scottish Rite Temple, and it is rumored that Sebastiaan has already arranged to rent this venue for years to come. Several vampires have attempted to play up the venue by implying a connection between vampires and Freemasonry. (It is rumored that a number of vampires also have membership in Freemason lodges.) The festival's Web site states, "Many make the pilgrimage each year and now that we have the most perfect venue for the weekend, the mysterious Temple of the Scottish Rite, we can make this the best Endless Night Festival yet!"[94]

As the festival grows larger, new traditions have emerged such as a "Lost Boys Beach Party." The festival has also begun cross promotion with the Anne Rice Vampire Lestat Fan Club, which also hosts a festival in New Orleans on the weekend of Halloween. In the past, more metaphysically minded vampire groups such as House Kheperu and House Sahjaza have hosted rituals during the festival, but Endless Night remains primarily a social function.

The success of Endless Night has inspired a series of events known as "noir havens." These are vampire social gatherings held throughout the United States and throughout the world. A dress code is typically enforced and attendees are advised to follow the latest iteration of the Black Veil. Current annual festivals include Black Oaks in Savannah, Black Sun in Los Angeles, and Black Trillium in Toronto, Canada. Other noir havens have included Black Atlantis in Atlanta, Black Avalon in England, and Black Xion in Holland. According to Sebastiaan's *Vampyre Almanac 2006,* most noir havens begin with the word "black" in reference to the Long Black Veil parties held at Mother in New York City.[95]

AVA members have become interested in establishing more scholarly vampire gatherings. The events where they showed preliminary results of the VEWRS data tended to have an older crowd in less provocative dress. In 2007, I went with them to an "open house" run by House Kheperu at a hotel in Medina, Ohio. Although a party was held during the event, the weekend focused primarily on energy workshops, lectures, and seminars. The AVA gave a PowerPoint presentation on their survey data, citing previous academic articles on the vampire community. There was a round of applause when they showed their results for question 137, indicating that the majority of vampires did not consider themselves to be "goth."

Shortly after the open house in Ohio, the AVA presented their research again at the first Twilight conference. Twilight was established as a semiannual gathering modeled after an academic conference. The conference typically hosts panels and seminars on a variety of topics including the current state of the community, legal considerations for vampires, scientific perspectives of energy work, and representations of vampires in popular culture.

The first Twilight gathering was held on October 30, 2007, in Los Angeles. Twilight II was held in Atlanta in March 2008 and was invitation only. A downtown hotel was used as the venue. O'Mallie agreed to come out of retirement in order to give a lecture on vampires and law enforcement. (That weekend Atlanta also hosted the Southeastern Committee for the Study of Religion [SECSOR] Conference. Although I gave a paper at SECSOR, the vampires had a better venue and a much more sophisticated looking brochure. I seem to have chosen the wrong conference.)

Twilight III was held September 26–28, 2008 in Seattle, Washington. Organizers extended invitations to the Temple of the Vampire as well as the Order of the Vampyre to give lectures explaining their perspective; however, they did not receive a response from these groups. Topics for group discussion included "Vampirism: Lifestyle, Spirituality, Culture, or Something Else?" and "Vampire vs. Vampyre: The Myth of Solidarity Beginning with Lexicon." New England is being considered as a location for Twilight IV while London, Paris, and Canada are all being considered for Twilight V and VI.

In addition to these gatherings, several other occult communities host events that are "vampire friendly." Shadowlore is an online community consisting of vampires, Pagans, and otherkin. In 2001, Shadowlore began having two annual gatherings so that their online community can meet face to face. The group rents out a large estate known as The Lodge in Eagle's Mere, Pennsylvania. KinVention North is an annual gathering in Ontario, Canada. It is primarily intended for otherkin, but Belanger and Sebastiaan have both been guest speakers in the past.

Major Vampire Groups and Houses

Various Web sites have attempted to create a directory of vampire groups. Vampire groups are assembled and disbanded so quickly that maintaining such a directory is much like Sisyphus perpetually rolling his stone. The groups described here are not intended as a comprehensive list but rather serve to demonstrate the variety of organizations that exist with the vampire community. The community is not monolithic, and vampire groups—usually called houses or orders—have different orientations and goals. Many vampire groups might be termed "social houses." These groups tend to have younger members and are primarily interested in hosting gothic-themed social events. Although they often consider themselves "real vampires," they are more active in the vampire life-style and may wear prosthetic fangs or contact lenses to social events. More metaphysically minded houses are sometimes referred to as "teaching houses" or "mentor houses." These groups are concerned with providing resources for young people who are "awakening" to their nature as vampires and with transmitting metaphysical knowledge about vampirism. Finally, groups like the AVA consider themselves to be "working houses." AVA members spend most of their time and energy diligently producing research and organizing conferences like Twilight. They almost seemed to pride themselves on their lack of interest in goth parties and other social events.

House Sahjaza is often said to be one of oldest vampire groups. It evolved from a coven of Pagans headed by Goddess Rosemary. Originally a female coven, House Sahjaza now has two separate houses: house Mithu for men and house Kalistree for women. I could not discern when the original coven started, although some say it goes as far back as the 1970s. At any rate, the name "Sahjaza" was bestowed on the group by Sebastiaan. He explained that he heard the term from a Pakistani man on a flight to Dubai in 1993. Sebastiaan apparently recalled him saying it meant "visionary tiger" but later learned that it meant "spontaneous."[96] (According to a colleague who studies South Asia, "sahjaza" is not a word in Urdu, the national language of Pakistan. However, it could be a corruption of a word from one of Pakistan's many regional languages such as Balochi, Pashto, Punjabi, Sindhi, or Siraiki.)

In 1996, Sebastiaan encountered a strange symbol spray-painted on the concrete in front of his apartment. Sebastiaan, who was experimenting with the drug ecstasy when he made this discovery, began sketching and modifying the symbol. When he showed his sketches to Goddess Rosemary, this led to a conversation that eventually gave birth to House Sahjaza.[97] Sebastiaan seems to have intended House Sahjaza as a more private and esoteric group to compliment the open and secular Clan Sabretooth. ("Sahjaza" and "sabretooth" refer to two types of tigers: one more spiritual and one more predatory.)

Also in New York are several groups that are descendants of Father Sebastiaans's Clan Sabretooth, including Clan Hidden Shadows and House Pantheon. Clan Hidden Shadows is particularly active, regularly hosting vampire-themed parties and events. They use the Sanguinarium hierarchy of fledglings, calmae, and elders. Members also wear large medallions with their own version of the Legacy Ankh. The upper part of the ankh is actually a demon sporting large bat wings. New York is also home to the Society Nocturnis of Gotham and the Court of Lazarus, both descendents of Sebastiaan's Court of Gotham. The Court of Lazarus describes itself as a "noir salon." Its Web site states that it is "part ritual gathering, part dark performance space and part gothic cocktail party."[98]

House Kheperu, based in Ohio, is in many ways the opposite of the stylish New York vampire culture. Belanger's group of vampires and metaphysicans did not have a name until they were invited by Sebastiaan to join

Michelle Belanger presides over a "handfasting ritual" at Kinvention North. Handfasting is a ritual of commitment or marriage used in modern Pagan traditions. Belanger is a licensed and registered minister in the state of Ohio and often called upon to perform handfastings as legal marriages for vampires and Pagans. (Courtesy of Michelle Belanger)

The Sanguinarium. Belanger named the group House Kheperu after consulting a book entitled *Egyptian Mysteries* by Lucie Lamy. According to Lamy, "kheperu" is an Egyptian word meaning "to change," "to transform," or "to come into being."[99] Even more so than other vampire groups, House Kheperu is interested in past lives. Members of the house, known as "Kheprians," feel they are part of a family that has been reincarnated since before the days of ancient Egypt.

An important and often misunderstood aspect of House Kheperu is their use of a "caste system." Assigning someone a "caste" would seem to be antithetical to the radical individualism of vampire culture. Most people associate the word caste with the Indo-Aryan system of social hierarchy practiced in India. However, in vampire society, one's caste usually describes how a vampire consumes energy and their role in ritual, rather than position in a hierarchy. It may be that the appeal of the caste system is much like that of discovering past lives or assigning significance to one's horoscope: It presents a way to further define one's sense of self through occult lore.

House Kheperu acknowledges three castes, each of which are associated with a particular somatotype. Members of the priest caste are often tall and androgynous and require the greatest amount of energy to sustain themselves. Warriors tend to be stockier and require the least amount of energy. Warriors are also the least sensitive to changes in energy and are naturally "shielded" against any sort of energetic attack. Counselors are the most sensitive and intuitive caste. According to the group's myth, the counselor's role was once served by temple concubines. Individuals are never assigned their caste, instead they usually know their caste intuitively or else are guided in discovering it.

Priests serve the central role in Kheprian ritual. Counselors are typically assigned the role of generating ritual energy through tasks like dancing or circumambulating the ritual space. Warriors assist by "grounding" excess or negative energy and by preventing undesired energy (or beings) from entering the ritual space. A verse from Belanger's *Vampire Ritual Book* describes the role of caste in ritual:

> We are the Priest Caste,
> Shapers of spirit and form.
> With the Warriors as our Foundation
> And the Counselors as our Mortar,
> We build this structure brick by brick
> Through our Immortal Will.[100]

I participated in a very simple ritual at the Kheperu Open House. Everyone attending the conference stood in a circle holding hands in order to "attune" the energy of everyone at the event. The ritual lasted less than a minute; however, I noticed that the counselors of House Kheperu scurried about to make sure that they were evenly distributed throughout the circle.

The caste system has been adopted by a number of other vampire groups that have a heavy emphasis on metaphysics and ritual. As The Sanguinarium attempted to produce a standardized vampire language, Belanger's basic concepts were assigned more exotic names. Warriors became "mradu" and priests became "ramkht." Counselors were assigned the label of "kitra," which had originally referred to a donor. These terms are still used by Ordo Strigoi Vii and other groups that were associated with The Sanguinarium.

In Ordo Strigoi Vii rituals, kitra sometimes undress and their bodies are used as altars. Sebastiaan said of this practice, "When they are on the altar they are empowered, their egos are charged and with discipline and proper training they can control this power and help raise immense amounts of energy to fuel the purpose of the ritual."[101] This tradition of "human altars" is taken from the Satanic rituals of Anton LaVey, which have had a stylistic influence on Ordo Strigoi Vii. Belanger has noted that this is a completely different ritual role than that of the counselor caste in House Kheperu.[102]

House Eclipse, based in Baltimore, modified the castes even further. They added a fourth, "wizardly" caste known as a "nomaj" or sangomancer. They also created four "roads" within each caste, allowing members to define themselves even further. For example, a warrior under this system could be on the path of the guardian, the avenger, the wolfwalker, or the deathspeaker. Finally, House Eclipse added new names for all of these terms using Enochian.[103] (Enochian is a language created by sixteenth-century occultists Dr. John Dee and Edward Kelly. It is said to be the language of the angels and is still used by modern occult movements.)

In House Eclipse's system, it is possible to see the influence of fantasy role-playing games on vampire traditions. The vocabulary that makes it possible to define one's nature as a "guardian" or a "sangomancer" calls to mind games like *Dungeons and Dragons* in which players create characters modeled after a particular "character class" such as a warrior, a wizard, a priest, or a thief. This is not to suggest that House Eclipse *is* a role-playing game or that its members are unable to discern role-playing games from reality. Rather, it appears that games like *Dungeons and Dragons* have provided a vocabulary that the vampire community has developed into new technologies of the self. In my interview with O'Mallie, he made a direct reference to *Dungeons and Dragons* in order to explain the function and nature of his group Clan O'Mallie, "We're all 'warrior class.' You know what I mean?"

Ordo Sekhemu, founded by Reverend Vicutus, describes itself as the "sister house" to House Kheperu. Like House Kheperu, it has a strong interest in metaphysics and occult knowledge. The group's name is derived from Sekhmet, an Egyptian warrior goddess with the head of a lion. Sekhmet was said to have a great bloodlust and is sometimes described as drinking blood. Most "Sekhrians" consume blood either as part of ritual or privately with a donor. Like various left-hand path groups, Ordo Sekhemu encourages the cultivation and transformation of the self.[104]

Anton LaVey, the founder of the Church of Satan, presides over a Satanic wedding. Note the use of two scantily clad women as an altar. (AP Photo)

Many houses do not have a geographic location, but function more like networks. The House of the Dreaming is run by a woman known as Madam X. Madam X became involved with the New York scene and the Court of Lazarus. Her original idea for the House of the Dreaming was to create a house of ronin (independents). The group employs both the Black Veil and their own code, the Veil of Waking Dream. House Dark Haven, headed by Lord Alistair in Savannah, has also become an international network. This group employs some of the terminology of The Sanguinarium and a variation of the caste system referred to as warrior, concubine, and oracle. The House emphasizes a strict separation between dayside and nightside activities. Nightside activities are always to be attended in full Victorian, gothic, or fetish attire. Their Web site states, "We maintain strict formality in appearance and etiquette. Modern society has lost the sense of reverence, wonder and anticipation that comes with established standard and rituals. The fanciest restaurants and major corporations allow jeans and T-shirts; churches eschew dress codes and promote "contemporary" services."[105] Respect for hierarchy is also part of the nightside world. The group's tenets state, "Democracy has no place in our night side world, this is not to say that democracy between families is not to be expected. The patriarch holds absolute control and wields it for the benefit and protection of his family."

House Quinotaur, based in Canada, describes itself as "an international house for real vampires." According to their Web site, House Quinotaur has members in 16 countries and on six continents. While many vampire groups refer to their group as "a family," House Quinotaur is unusual in that they believe vampires are literally a family descended from the Merovingian kings. The group is involved in conducting genealogies to find evidence for this theory. Specifically, they believe that in the fifth century the pregnant mother of the Frankish king Merovich was raped by (or at least copulated with) an aquatic creature known as "the Quinotaur." Merovich therefore had two fathers—one a human and one a sea-monster, and his descendants are thought to be vampires. Membership is open to anyone who is of age, requires intake of energy to maintain their health, agrees to the *possibility* of what is called the "Merovich theory of vampirism," and will consent to the rules of the Black Veil. Genealogy also plays a role in the group's hierarchy. All self-identified vampires, even if they are not members, are known as "9th cousins," while those who can trace their lineage directly to Merovich are known as "1st cousins."[106]

The Future of the Vampire Community

Although the vampire community is characterized by radical individualism, a center has begun to crystalize from the cacophony of different vampire voices, and more fantastic elements have been pushed to the periphery. The community seems to have matured. A survey conducted by the vampire research institute in the mid-1990s reported that 72 percent of respondents believed in a Lestat-type vampire.[107] Today, this number would probably be closer to zero. Many of the interviews that appear in Guiley, Page, Guinn and Grieser, and Ramsland describe sinister cults that practice human sacrifice, vampires who cannot cross running water, or immortals who have lived for hundreds of years. These fantastic elements were totally absent in my study. Furthermore, anyone who expressed these ideas would probably not be tolerated on vampire chat rooms and forums or welcome in a vampire group. The model of vampirism that is emerging is more cogent and more practical. The awakened model seems to be gaining ground over the initiatory model of vampirism. Vampires seem to be increasingly portrayed as a naturally occurring category of person rather than a demonic foil.

It has been repeatedly suggested that the community is dying out. In the mid-1990s, McMahon of the Vampire Research Institute stated, "I know this vampire craze is still going on, but I think it might climax this year or next year. After that, not so many people will want to be acting like vampires."[108] Obviously this prediction proved false. This interview was taken when the New York vampires scene was still in its infancy, before The Sanguinarium and the Endless Night Festival. It was also before numerous "vampire specials" appeared on the History Channel, A&E, and other cable channels.

However, the AVA has noticed that even in the midst of massive media attention, the community is eroding instead of growing. An AVA member showed me a chart on his laptop measuring the amount of online activity by the vampire community over the last few years. (As he showed this to me, he added, "I got bored one day.") The chart indicated that online activity had been steadily declining for several years. "The community is contracting," he said, "It's going offline and underground." My contact believed that as more television shows seek vampires to film and interview, the old guard has become jaded and withdrawn from the community.

Sebastiaan also seems to acknowledge this trend. He writes in *The Sanguinomicon,* "Recently the Family has gradually distanced itself from the current incarnation of the 'vamp scene,' and such isolation, although understandable, has resulted in dissociation from each other and a worrisome downtrend for the Family. The *Sanguinomicon* has been compiled in this form to re-ignite the Black Flame within Our Blood and revitalize the time of Glamour, passion, romance, mystery, and secrecy."[109]

It is possible that in several decades people will speak of "the vampire movement" rather than "the vampire community." Eyerman and Jamison argue that social movements create "a cognitive space" within social discourse. In this model, a successful social movement alters the way society thinks about a particular issue and then dies out. This may be what we are seeing in the vampire community. The various vampire groups have successfully established the vampire as a valid category of person. The future will contain vampires, but the glamour and energy of the New York vampire scene may never be seen again.

Vampires sometimes compare their community to the gay community, as an emerging identity that is not yet accepted by mainstream society. Belanger writes, "For me, this is all about basic human rights, and I often turn to the human rights movement when I need inspiration. Fifty years ago, it was a terrible thing to be gay."[110] I find it telling that the early gay community also manifested as a secretive and romantic community, not unlike the vampyre courts of New York. The Order of Chaerona was formed in London in the 1890s by George Ives and is considered to be the first gay rights group in Britain. The Order took its name from the Battle of Chaerona in 338 BC in which a military unit known as the "Sacred Band of Thebes," consisting of paired homosexual lovers, fought to the death against the forces of Philip II of Macedon. Notable members of The Order included Oscar Wilde as well as vampirologist Montague Summers. Much like The Sanguinarium, the Order created its own set of rituals and passwords. Ives referred to equal rights for homosexuals as "The Cause" and worked with both sexologists and legislators to improve the status of homosexuals.[111] In the twenty-first century, the gay community can promote itself openly and no longer needs a secret society. I predict a similar future for the vampire community.

CHAPTER **6**

Vampirism and Religion, a Dialogue

It is in our lives and not our words that our religion must be read.

—*Thomas Jefferson*

Because I approach vampires from the perspective of religious studies, it is often assumed that I consider vampirism to be a religion. Instead, I find myself in the strange position of giving papers about vampires at religion conferences, only to end up arguing why vampirism is *not* a religion. At one point this led a colleague to ask, respectfully, what I was doing at a panel on new religious movements. What exactly is the relationship between the phenomenon of self-identified vampires and religion? Of course there are "vampire religions," but these represent only a small percentage of the vampire community. Is the identity as a vampire in some sense a religious identity? And if so, how does this affect a theory of religion? Does "religion" still connote affiliation with a church or has it become completely individualized? Perhaps most importantly, should the rights of vampires in America receive religious protection under the first amendment?

This chapter covers several issues at the intersection of vampires and religion. Individuals within the vampire community as well as researchers have already characterized vampirism as a religion. (It is these claims, by the way, that justify my presence at religion conferences.) In addition to the term "religion," vampires sometimes discuss "their faith," while researchers often claim that vampirism is a "new religious movement." After considering these claims, putting them into context, and qualifying them, it should become apparent that while there are "vampire religions," vampirism *as a whole* is not a religion. This will lead to a broader question: whether vampirism is in some way a religious phenomenon.

The vampire community has no unified position on religion, but several vampires have made claims about the nature of religion that are fascinating. The chapter closes with a proposal that the modern understanding of religion has become individualized and subjective and that these changes are reflected in the modern cultural concept of the vampire.

NRMs and "Ad-Hoc Vampire Religionists"

Several researchers have characterized self-identified vampires as a new religious movement. Others have suggested that vampires fill a space of meaning normally occupied by religion. Sociologist and Roman Catholic priest Andrew Greeley has described the appeal of the vampire in popular culture as "the junk food of spirituality."[1] There are also conflicting responses within the vampire community to this question of whether or not vampirism is a religion. The Temple of the Vampire is a registered church, but most vampires are not interested in "organized religion." Others might describe their vampirism as "spiritual," while still others do not see it as religious in any way.

The term "new religious movement" (NRM) is used by scholars of religion to describe small religious groups that are outside the religious mainstream. In America, the mainstream has been defined by Protestantism but is now expanding to include other world religions. Sociologists once referred to groups outside this mainstream as "cults." The word cult comes from the Latin *cultus* meaning "care" or "adoration." *Cultus* is also the root of the English word "cultivate." Classical cults literally nurtured and cared for their gods. After 1965, many such groups began to appear in America and, as part of a backlash against these movements, the word "cult" acquired an extremely negative connotation.[2] Thus, scholars have settled on the phrase "new religious movements" as a more neutral term to describe these groups.

The vampire community is undoubtedly outside the mainstream. What is less certain is whether it is religious and whether it is a movement. There are several formal groups within the vampire community that have a primary interest in religion, metaphysics, or magic that would qualify them as NRMs. In addition to the Order of the Vampyre, the Temple of the Vampire, Ordo Strigoi Vii, and Aset-ka discussed in Chapter 4, we can add to this list Michelle Belanger's group House Kheperu and its sister organization, Ordo Sekhemu. However, it must be reiterated that these groups represent a tiny minority of the overall community. Many vampire groups are secular and the majority of vampires are not part of any group.

The vampire community as a whole is not an NRM. The primary evidence for this is that most vampires identify themselves as practicing a religion other than vampirism, and a significant portion identify as having *no religion*. Question 155 of the VEWRS presents a list of 51 religions as well as Pagan and esoteric traditions. It asks, "Which faith, discipline, paradigm (spiritual/fraternal), or religion do you identify with? (Check all that apply.)" The seven groups with the highest number of responses were (1) Magick, (2) Wicca, (3) Neo-Paganism, (4) Occultism, (5) Christianity, (6) Shamanism, (7) Agnostic/Atheist/Humanist/Irreligious.[3] According to this survey, more vampires identify as Christians than as atheists or agnostics. Although I have not had access to individual survey responses, the AVA reports that almost every respondent listed more than one tradition. This is partly because of the way the question was worded, but it also indicates a spiritual marketplace at work in the vampire community. Like many Americans, vampires often take a "consumer" approach to religion, searching numerous traditions for ideas they find appealing.

Another claim made by researchers is that the vampire as an icon carries a level of meaning in popular culture that borders on the religious. Christopher Partridge, in *The Re-Enchantment of the West,* argues that as secularization has enervated mainline religious denominations, elements of popular culture have become "sacralized" and infused with religious meaning. The sacralization theory implies that even without an organized movement, dogma, or other trappings of religion, there is still a religious dimension to popular fascination with vampires. This is a more nuanced and less value-laden theory of Greeley's characterization of the vampire cult as "spiritual junk food."

Partridge has further posited the existence of what he terms "ad-hoc vampire religionists," for whom vampirism has become a religion of one.[4] On question 155 of the VEWRS, over 90 vampires checked "Other" as one of the traditions they identify with. Of these, five wrote in "vampirism" and two wrote in "vampyrism."[5] These responses seem to confirm Partridge's theory. San Diego vampire Don Henrie appears to follow an ad-hoc vampire religion. Henrie became a minor celebrity in 2003 when he appeared on the Sci-Fi Channel's reality show, *Mad, Mad House.* On the show, he explained that he consumes blood in order to achieve a higher state of consciousness and commented that, "vampirism is another type of faith."[6]

Vampire Perspectives on Vampire Religion

Some vampires of the awakened model do not see vampirism as a religion at all. According to vampire Dragan Dracul, "Vampyrism is the way one is born and lives, not a religion. Vampyres are free to worship and believe in what they want. There are Christian vampyres, Pagan vampyres, Satanic vampyres, even Buddhist vampyres. So the idea that vampyrism is a religion is wrong."[7] Sphynx-Cat writes on her vampire support Web site, "Personally, I consider it no more 'religious' than other people would consider being gay, diabetic or cancerous to be 'religious.'"[8] The claims of the awakened model are at stake here: If vampirism is a religion, this would seem to undermine the claims that vampirism is an essentialist identity rather than a social phenomenon. On the other hand, relatively few vampires would deny that vampirism has a spiritual dimension.

I asked some AVA members what they thought about Partridge's claim. One responded that there are ad-hoc vampire religionists but suggested that researchers would likely reverse cause and effect: An outsider would assume that individuals first become vampire religionists and then convince themselves they possess a vampiric nature. In keeping with the awakened model of vampirism, she argued that vampirism is an inherent nature that precedes religion. Thus, she qualified ad-hoc vampire religion as "a spirituality that is independently developed to address one's nature."

Belanger promotes the awakened model but is also the founder of House Kheperu, a metaphysical group that is widely considered to be an NRM. (On the VEWRS question 155, 45 vampires identified "Kheprianism" as one of their spiritual traditions.) Belanger delineates the spiritual elements of vampirism from the vampire ontology of the awakened model. In *The Vampire Ritual Book,* she writes:

> Because I recognize that the vampire as an archetype has grown into a potent symbol in the mythic imagination, I can see how a number of people may be attracted to this figure as a means of expressing certain aspects of themselves and of their spirituality. These individuals may not necessarily be vampiric in the respect that they regularly require energy in order to maintain their physical, spiritual, and emotional well-being. However, this fact does not undermine the vampire's allure to them, and it would be small of us who are legitimately vampiric to attempt to monopolize the archetype.[9]

Belanger identifies a "vampire spirituality" that is distinct from the vampire ontology. Both groups may use *The Vampire Ritual Book* and it is implied that awakened vampires may *also* practice vampire spirituality. Sanguinarius, who runs a support Web site for real vampires, makes a similar distinction between vampire religion and vampire nature. She compares vampirism and vampire culture to Judaism, which is an ethnic group as well as a culture and religious tradition.[10]

There seem to be three main schools of thought: First, there are initiatory groups like the Temple of the Vampire for whom vampirism is purely a religion and not an ontology. However, as described in Chapter 4, this perspective is a minority within the vampire community. Second, individuals such as SphynxCat, Dragan Dracul, and some members of the AVA seem to view vampirism as an ontology and not a religion. Finally, there are perspectives like those of Belanger and Sanguinarius who acknowledge vampirism as both a spiritual path and an ontology, which may or may not coincide with each other.

The "Religious" Dimensions of Vampirism

What about vampires who are neither part of a NRM nor ad-hoc vampire religionists? Must the entire concept be picked through on a case-by-case basis or is there some overarching aspect of vampirism that is "religious"? This naturally depends on what criteria are used to define something as religious. In 1912 James H. Leuba published *A Psychological Study of Religion,* which contained over 50 definitions of religion. This has led some to conclude that the effort to define religion is a hopeless task.[11] Can one even begin to discuss religious dimensions of vampirism without any precise definition? Anthropologist Clifford Geertz (1926–2006), who once described the study of religion as suffering from "the pigeon-hole disease," argues that you can. According to Geertz, an anthropologist of religion can "begin in a fog and try to clear it." By this he means starting with phenomena that are widely thought of as religious and then narrowing down what about them seems religious.[12] It is in this spirit—emphasizing phenomena over definitions—that I hope to explore the relationship between vampirism and the religious. Although some vampires have identified themselves as atheists, I am starting from the assumption that there is a religious dimension to vampirism. (There are, after all, a number of religions that do not promote belief in a deity or the supernatural.) What follows is a review of several conceptions of religion to see if this religious dimension can be qualified. Essentially, different perspectives of religion will be "tried on" to see if there is a fit. Religion scholar Jonathon Z. Smith points out that "religion" is ultimately a second-order term that was created by scholars for their own purposes.[13] In line with this thinking, what is important is not whether vampirism is or is not religious. What matters is *in what way* vampirism is religious and what insights arise from such a discovery.

The Legal Definition

While American law has no concise definition of religion, it has produced more case law and legal commentary on the subject than any other nation. The Temple of the Vampire is a registered church, but generally vampirism is not a religion in any legal sense and is not likely to become so in the future. That having been said, there are several interesting court cases that have questioned whether vampirism is a religion.

Legal definitions of religion are often challenged by cases involving prisoners, who frequently have special needs relating to their faith. Muslim prisoners have dietary restrictions and request prayer rugs, Sikh prisoners refuse to cut their hair in accordance with prison policies, and so on. Robert Paul Rice is serving up to a 15-year sentence in Utah for multiple felonies. Rice describes himself as a "Druidic vampire" and, in accordance with his religious beliefs, requested access to blood as well as conjugal visits with "a vampiress." (Utah does not grant conjugal visits to prisoners.) In 2002, Rice sued the Utah Department of Corrections for violating his first amendment rights by denying his religiously based requests. The case was thrown out.

Rice's claim of being a "Druidic vampire" must be considered a form of ad-hoc vampire religion. I know of no group, vampire or otherwise, that religiously requires its members to consume blood or engage in sexual contact. Rice's case was further undermined by the fact that he registered as Catholic when he began his sentence in 2000.[14] The AVA had little sympathy for Rice. One contact described him as a sort of con artist who trivialized the claims of real vampires in an attempt to receive a conjugal visit. Still, Rice will probably not be the last American to claim that vampirism is a religion protected under the first amendment.

The British courts have also debated the religious implications of vampirism. In 2003, Ben Lewis, a 25-year-old self-identified "reincarnated vampire," was sentenced to a 12-month jail sentence for "religiously aggravated harassment." Lewis and two friends are accused of harassing the local vicar, 45-year-old Reverend Chris Rowberry, and his family. Specific incidents include "howling" outside the church, posting obscene material on the church notice board, nuisance phone calls late at night, and launching fireworks outside the vicar's home. In the United States, these offenses would not add up to a jail sentence. However, in 2001, Britain passed the "Anti-Terrorism, Crime and Security Act." The Act defines a variety of crimes as "religiously aggravated" if either:

(a) at the time of committing the offence, or immediately before or after doing so, the offender demonstrates towards the victim of the offence hostility based on the victim's membership (or presumed membership) of a racial or religious group; or
(b) the offence is motivated (wholly or partly) by hostility towards members of a racial or religious group based on their membership of that group.[15]

It is rare in Britain that an offense is classified as "religiously aggravated," but the prosecution argued that Lewis had engaged in these activities specifically because he hates Christians. His identity as a vampire was deemed relevant to proving this fact.

Lewis described consuming blood and also referred to himself as "a psychic vampire." At one point, he was asked if he rose from a grave at night, which inspired laughter from the court. Lewis's musical tastes were also deemed relevant and the judge wrote down that he listened to the bands "Slipknot" and "Cradle of Filth." Lewis apparently did use the word "faith" in reference to his identity as a vampire. He explained that he was not a Satanist and added that he "identified with the Lord Jesus Christ" because he too was an outcast. Admitted as evidence were a collection of diaries and papers, many dating back to when Lewis was a young boy. At one point he had written: "I answer to no mortal and I spit on Christian beliefs."[16] After a seven-day trial, Lewis and his friend Scott Bower were found guilty.[17]

The Lewis case demonstrates many assumptions that are still being debated by the vampire community. The court clearly grasped that Lewis's identity as a vampire was a source of meaning to him; however, they seemed to have no idea whether this constituted a cultural phenomenon, a religion, or simply an elaborate fantasy. There also seemed to be no theory of how his identity as a vampire related to the alleged charges. As a result, an incredibly broad category of information was deemed relevant in order prove whether or not Lewis "hated Christians." In his diaries, Lewis described himself as a freak and an outcast. If Lewis were harassed for being a vampire, it would almost certainly not be pursued as a "religiously aggravated" case.

The Substantive Definition

Legal definitions of religion have evolved from what religion scholar Yves Lambert has called a "substantive" definition of religion. A substantive definition defines religion by certain elements: religious practice, the supernatural, ritual, and so on. Anything that does not contain these elements is excluded from the definition.[18] When people speak of religion in a quotidian sense, they implicitly use a substantive definition: Religions are often imagined as having certain elements such as a church, a congregation, and a sacred text. Vampirism will probably never conform to this conventional idea of religion. Interestingly, the Temple of the Vampire, which has legal status as a religion, denies being a religion in the conventional sense. They write, "The Temple of the Vampire is registered as a church of the religion of Vampirism with the US federal government. However, we are not a religion in the usual sense of the word. We have no doctrines of faith and we never worship. We practice a discipline that gives us a proven degree of control over death, among other things."[19] (This raises the question of why the Temple wanted to frame themselves as a religion in the first place.)

It is, however, interesting that vampires have adopted certain substantive elements of religion and given them new meaning. Viola Johnson modifies Jewish scripture in creating an origin legend for her vampire group, The Clan of Lilith. Her book, *Dhampir: Child of the Blood,* presents a myth in which Lilith, the first wife of Adam, becomes a vampire after she has been replaced by Eve. Unlike Jewish legend that depicts Lilith as a demoness, this story places Lilith firmly in God's good graces. Adam could not coexist with Lilith because of her superior knowledge and intelligence. Therefore, Lilith is separated from Adam and charged with being a sort of immortal naturalist: "The one decreed, 'Lilith, the world shall be the vessel of learning from which you shall drink. All the creatures of this planet shall be your teachers.'"[20] In fact, Lilith chooses to feed on blood because consuming "pre-digested meals" gives her more time to study the natural world. From here, the story departs further and further from the original narrative, ending with Lilith's grandson becoming the first werewolf.

Belanger also makes references to religious texts, although more conservatively. In *The Psychic Vampire Codex,* Belanger comments on her own writing style, "The opening will read a little like scripture. That is because it is the equivalent of scripture for our House, but it is our scripture alone."[21] Belanger uploaded

The Vampire Ritual Book as well as *The Vampire Codex* (an earlier, Internet version of *The Psychic Vampire Codex*) onto the Web site http://sacred-texts. com/, where they can be accessed along with the Bible and the Koran.

In 2001, Damien Deville created a Web site known as the Vampire Church. Visitors to the site may be surprised to read that, "The Vampire Church is not a religious entity." Instead, the site was established as "a haven and resource for the vampire."[22] The term "priest" has also been adopted and redefined within the vampire community. House Kheperu recognizes that some members are of "the priest caste" and this idea was borrowed and adapted by other vampire groups such as House Eclipse and Ordo Sekhemu. In this tradition, being a "priest," like being a vampire, is inherent to one's nature. Priests are defined not by having been ordained in a tradition, but by the character of their subtle energy body. In House Kheperu, "priests" are considered to be vampires who require a great deal of subtle energy and who take the role of directing subtle energy during rituals.

Terms like priest, church, and scripture have been uprooted from their original context and incorporated into the bricolages that vampires create. The use of these terms points to a religious element in vampirism, but they have been redefined and rewritten to suit a culture of radical religious individualism. Thus, the sacredness of scripture can be localized to a small group: "It is our scripture alone." Similarly, a priest is not defined by a religious institution, but by their innermost nature. This adaptation of religious language to describe a world of personal meaning is directly descended from Thomas Jefferson's claim, "I am a sect myself."

Soteriology

Soteriology is the branch of theology dealing with questions of salvation. Most world religions have some form of soteriology. For example, Christian evangelical soteriology emphasizes a personal relationship with Jesus, while Buddhist soteriology concerns the attainment of nirvana. The idea of immortality as a vampire is fundamentally soteriological—we are all mortals and will all die, unless we are turned into vampires first. This vampire soteriology has been fundamental to the Temple of the Vampire, as only initiated vampires will survive the coming apocalypse. Of course, the overwhelming majority of the vampire community does not believe in a coming apocalypse and regards physical immortality as a fantasy. Vampires often complain about individuals who appear on the Internet claiming to be hundreds of years old. None of my contacts ever expressed ideas that could be considered soteriological. However, a number of references to salvation appear in interviews with vampires from the 1990s. This suggests that for some individuals, identifying as a vampire entailed soteriological meaning.

Rosemary Ellen Guiley describes an interview with two self-identified vampires in London named Damon and Damien Vanien. Damien describes vampirism as a "stepladder." The first step on this ladder is simply dressing as a vampire, while the final step is immortality as a sort of disembodied vampire spirit. Guiley writes:

> "If the object is to gain eternal life as a vampire, how do you accomplish that while you're living?" I asked.
>
> Damien shrugged. "One doesn't know and one never will. It's a hope, as in any religion. I don't want to go to heaven, so there's only one other place to go and that's hell. It's obviously the better of the two. I'm better off than most vampires. Mine's quite a strange story. You see, I am in contact with a real vampire, Valan. I actually see him. Valan came to me the day I had the accident when I was three and he's stayed with me ever since. When I was growing up, I was told he was an imaginary friend. He's still here. I'm aware of him almost all the time, but I can't *bring* him into a room. I find it's getting harder to actually see Valan as I'm getting older. A clairvoyant I know says Valan is on a different plane. We keep each other alive, more or less. The idea is for me to get Valan into a form down here on earth so that he can eventually get me to where he is, so I can be a real vampire. We're not actually going to trade places, it's hard to explain. The thing is, I may be very old by the time this happens. There's a chance I could die first, but there's more hope for me for eternal life than for some other vampires. Valan is doing this for me.[23]

It should be noted that this interview was published a year before Anne Rice's novel, *The Tale of the Body Thief,* which involves a vampire and a human switching bodies. Damien's desire to trade places with Valan is essentially a vampire soteriology. It is literally his alternative to hell and achieving this state seems to be the highest concern of his life. It is particularly telling when he comments on his desire for immortality, "It's a hope, as in any religion."

Jeff Guinn and Andy Grieser describe another interview with a self-described vampire who is preoccupied with salvation. Twenty-one-year-old Gremlin of Seattle, Washington, claimed to be part of an ancient vampire clan called "the Khlysty," He is quoted:

> It all goes back to the time near Genesis . . . The clan, which wandered around the Eastern Hemisphere, was known as the Khlysty. . . . The theory behind the clan is that to sin is to forgive, forgiveness is salvation, therefore salvation is the ultimate sin. It's kind of a complex thing there. Basically, the way we feel is that if you're going to sin, it will be for the sake of the sin or else to hurt people. And we don't believe sinning to hurt people is the best way to go about it. . . . They called us vampires because we came into towns dressed in dark cloaks. . . . Anyone who said he did not sin was lying. So they would torture these people to actually admit to their sins, and, once they did, the sins were forgiven. I hold no pity toward hardly anyone. I help people because in a direct, hard way, I teach them what they need to know.[24]

Gremlin was probably not part of any group or clan. The Khlysty are actually an ascetic sect that broke away from the Russian Orthodox Church.[25] How Gremlin came by this name is unclear. Guinn and Grieser dismiss Gremlin's talk of salvation as a "rant" and imply that Gremlin is somewhat disturbed. In the interview, Gremlin admits that he grew up without a father and that he is a high-school drop-out. But the idea that "salvation is the ultimate sin" represents a sort of inverted soteriology, similar to Damien's comment that we would prefer to go to hell instead of heaven.

In 1998, 17-year-old Roderick Ferrell murdered a couple in Florida. At his trial, he stated that he was Vesago, a 500-year-old vampire (See Chapter 7). Prior to this act, Ferrell also expressed a sort of inverted soteriology in which God is evil. Ferrell allegedly told the members of his vampire group that God is evil and that they were, "put on earth to fight the Godhead."[26] What can be made of these three accounts? First of all, it should be noted that none of these individuals would be well received by the vampire community at large. In the 1990s, when these interviews took place, the community was less self-aware. Solitary vampires like Gremlin interpreted their meaning-worlds in isolation rather than in dialogue with a community. Claims of being immortal, of being part of an ancient clan of vampires, or of divine revelation have become far more rare in the vampire community of the twenty-first century.

Each of these individuals seems to have felt like a social pariah and to perceive the Christian tradition as fundamentally antagonistic and hypocritical. The inverted theological and soteriological models they created, in which hell is better than heaven, allegedly righteous people must be tortured, and God is evil, are undoubtedly religious. What is not clear is what relation these models have to their identity as vampires. Only for Damien is there a direct link between vampires and soteriology. Roxana Stuart has commented that Anne Rice succeeded in turning vampires from a symbol of terror to a symbol of the outcast.[27] Those who create these inverted soteriologies may be attracted to the figure of the vampire because it expresses their own feelings of persecution. (Recall Lewis's comment that he identifies with Jesus as a fellow outcast.) While this is certainly a religious dimension of the vampire identity, it does not appear to be a very common one. None of the vampires I met described these sorts of dark cosmologies, and a significant number of vampires identified with the Christian tradition.

Psychological Definitions

Henrie described vampirism as a faith and claimed that drinking blood leads to altered states of consciousness. Many vampires describe the act of feeding in spiritual terms. The clearest connection between vampirism and the religious may be the transcendent quality of these experiences. Ramsland has noted transcendent elements within vampirism, which she characterizes as "limit experiences" in the tradition of French theorists Michel Foucault and Georges Bataille.[28] Liriel McMahon, relating her own period experimenting with auto-vampirism, described consuming her own blood as a type of "communion."[29] Carol Page interviewed a vampire who said of consuming blood, "It's happiness . . . It's like making love. It's like the orgasm. It is the most inwardly erotic, sensual, warm, spiritual, uplifting thing that I do in my life. It gives me goose bumps to really express it."[30] Martin V. Riccardo received one letter that described the feeling after feeding as "blood peace." Another described this state as "like the universal 'ohm' resides in my head, vibrating through every atom I possess."[31] Riccardo expressed his theory that these sensations are psychosomatic. He then added, "I think this is comparable to the feelings some Christians might get from receiving Holy Eucharist."[32] Is it possible that religious experience and vampiric experience are two expressions of the same psychological phenomenon?

Transpersonal psychology is a controversial field that studies transcendent or spiritual aspects of human experience, especially mystical experiences and altered states of consciousness. The *Journal of Transpersonal Psychology* was started in 1969 by Abraham Maslow, Stanislav Grof, and Antony Sutich; however, a number of psychologists wrote on religious experiences prior to this date and are considered to have set the stage for transpersonal psychology. These include William James, Sigmund Freud, Otto Rank, and Carl Gustav Jung. These thinkers have promoted theories of religion that are the most widely applicable to the experience of vampires, particularly James, Jung, and Maslow.

William James (1842–1910) was a professor of physiology, anatomy, psychology, and philosophy at Harvard University. He also had an interest in alternative medicine and spiritualism, and from 1894 to 1895 he was the president of the Society for Psychical Research. From 1901 to 1902, he gave a series of lectures on "Natural Theology" at the University of Edinburgh, which were edited and published as a book, *The Varieties of Religious Experience*. Although this book has become a classic for the modern study of religion, when it was written it had a popular appeal in occult circles. *Modern Vampirism: Its Dangers And How to Avoid Them,* written by Albert Osman Eaves in 1904, begins by encouraging readers who "require proof of his ideas" to first read *The Varieties of Religious Experience*.[33] James's perspective on religion yields several points that are relevant to vampirism.

James states that his lectures are concerned only with what he calls "personal religion," and makes a clear distinction between personal and institutional religion.[34] For the purposes of his work, he defines religion as "the feelings, acts, and experiences of individual men in their solitude, so far as they apprehend themselves to stand in relations to whatever they may consider divine."[35] This definition is a good fit for the religious dimension of vampirism, which is so focused on subjective experience. James was also an early advocate of religious pluralism. He believed that different people were suited for different religions due to their constitution, worldview, and other factors.[36] This reflects the attitude toward religion and metaphysics expressed by Belanger and other vampires who emphasize self-discovery. The motto of House Kheperu is to "seek your own truth"—a sentiment that James would likely have agreed with.[37]

As a psychologist, James described personal religion in terms of different states of consciousness. In this way, his work set the foundation for transpersonal psychology. James is considered one of the first psychologists to write extensively on the "subliminal" or subconscious region of the mind, which he saw as intimately connected to religious experience. In the final lecture, he offers a theory that the subconscious acts as a sort of bridge that connects humanity to the divine.[38]

Carl Gustav Jung (1875–1961) was originally a student of Freud. However, his ideas about religion have more in common with James than his mentor. Jung believed in a collective unconscious to which everyone has access. The theory of a collective unconscious was used to explain similar images, stories, and ideas that appear across different cultures. Jung furthered James's ideas about the unconscious and its relationship to the divine, to claim that the unconscious effectively *is* the divine. Jung believed that the unconscious exists outside the ego and that when the two realms meet it produces a sense of fear and wonder that is the source of religious experience. Ancient people interpreted these encounters with the subconscious as the presence of the gods, and in this sense the subconscious and the divine are synonymous.[39] James had described mystical and religious experiences as "invasions" from the subconscious.[40] Jung named these god-like forces of the subconscious "archetypes."

Although Jungian archetypes sometimes function like autonomous entities, he compared them to different "organs" within the collective unconscious. Jung believed that prophets received revelations from the subconscious through the archetypes. While this contact can be a source of great meaning, he also cautioned that archetypes could potentially be dangerous and lead to psychosis.[41] Jung and his theory of archetypes are extremely popular with vampires. In fact, Jung interpreted vampire legends as being part of a larger archetype he called "the shadow."[42] Belanger describes the vampire as depicted in popular culture as an archetype and dedicates an entire chapter of *The Vampire Ritual Book* to rituals working with this archetype.[43] Jung's work also appears in the bibliography of *The Psychic Vampire Codex*. The Order of the Vampyre attributes their order's secrets to divine revelations given to them by vampire archetypes.[44]

Finally, Jung saw the function of religion as integrating the conscious with the unconscious in order to produce a healthy and unified entity—"a self." He termed this process "individuation" or "becoming what you were meant to be."[45] From this perspective, the awakened model of vampirism—in which vampires discover essential aspects of themselves that were previously unknown to them—could be interpreted as a religious function.

Abraham Maslow (1908–1970), considered one of the fathers of transpersonal psychology, further modified Jung's notion of "individuation." Maslow is most famous for his theory that humans experience a "hierarchy of need." The most basic needs are physiological (air, food, water, for example) while the highest and least often fulfilled need he calls "self-actualization." Self-actualization is equated with the striving for health, the search for identity and autonomy, and the yearning for excellence. People come closer to self-actualization through heightened states of consciousness that Maslow calls "peak experiences" that allow the individual to be more free and more autonomous. Peak experiences include profound experiences of "ecstasy, rapture, bliss, greatest joy, awe, mystery, complete perfection, humility, surrender, and worship."[46] Borrowing James's distinction between institutional and personal religion, Maslow argues that institutional religion does not lead to peak experiences, but that personal religion does.

Like Jung's notion of individuation, Maslow's ideas of self-actualization run parallel to many ideas of vampirism. The left-hand path traditions and their concepts of apotheosis seem indebted to Maslow. Consider the following statement from the Temple of Set:

> Glorification of the ego is not enough; it is the complete *psyche*—the entire self or soul—which must be recognized, appreciated, and actualized. The process by which this exaltation of the *psyche* is sought is called by the name *Xeper* [pronounced "kheffer"; it is the Egyptian hieroglyphic term for "to become" or "to come into being"].
> The means by which Setians seek to *Xeper* are many.[47]

The idea of integrating the "complete psyche" comes from Jung, while the term "actualization" stems from Maslow. The fact that there is no prescribed means of pursuing *xeper* also calls to mind Maslow's notion of peak experiences. The Temple of Set's notion of *xeper* or "becoming" has been adopted by several religious vampire groups. House Kheperu admittedly derives its name from the same Egyptian word that the Temple of Set renders as *xeper*.[48] As with the Temple of Set, this term relates House Kheperu's goal of personal transformation. Ordo Strigoi Vii has modified this term yet again, presenting it as "*Zhep'r*," which they define as "the evolution from a mortal's perspective to that of the Immortal."[49]

While vampirism as a whole is not a religion, there are aspects of vampirism that may reasonably be called "religious." The most widely applicable criteria of religion appears to be the emphasis on self-discovery and self-transformation that preoccupies so many vampires. This does not mean that all vampires regard vampirism as supernatural or with the same gravity that we associate with religious convictions. But the religious elements are strong enough and widely expressed enough that vampirism can be safely classified as a religious phenomenon.

Is Religion a Form of Vampirism?

How do vampires see religion? Jung and Maslow interpreted religion as fulfilling important psychological processes. Other theorists have attributed hidden functions to religion. Karl Marx saw religion essentially as a ploy used by the elite to maintain control over the working class. Voltaire actually equated the vampire with the clergy "bleeding people dry."[50] In the same way, many vampires have reinterpreted religious traditions in light of their own psychological and social theories.

The Temple of the Vampire shares Marx's suspicion of religion, but as an order of elite predators, they have naturally cast themselves as the manipulators rather than the manipulated. A four-page information sheet from the Temple stated that ancient vampires, "created Christianity, Buddhism, Hinduism, Islam, and all other major world religions to produce docility and compliance with the Rule of the Masters."[51] Thus, the world's religions are actually only methods of control created to serve vampires—an idea that Marx would likely agree with. Ordo Strigoi Vii shares this skepticism of religion, although they do not claim to be openly manipulating it. Father Sebastiaan Tod van Houten writes, "The Awakened Strigoi Vii have come to the mutual agreement that religion is a system of arbitrary belief used by humans to excuse their behavior and create a false sense of security."[52]

Belanger, a psychic vampire, sees both vampirism and religion in terms of energy. She writes:

> When groups of people gather to worship, they generate a significant amount of energy and this energy is charged with the emotions experienced by everyone in the group. The fundamental purpose of ritual is to encourage the generation of this energy and ultimately give it a direction. Many of the world's organized religions have lost touch with their knowledge of energy, however.[53]

She adds that Pentecostal services produce a particularly large amount of energy as does the old Catholic High Mass. Like Maslow, Belanger implies here that religion has a common purpose, which institutional religion has forgotten. The idea that energy is put forth in religious ritual is not new. Sociologist Emile Durkheim (1858–1917) described Aboriginal totemism as "the religion of a kind of anonymous and impersonal force," and argued that all forms of religious expression have evolved from rituals similar to those of Australian Aborigines. He adds:

> When I speak of these principals as forces, I do not use the word in a metaphorical sense; they behave like real forces. In a sense, they are even physical forces that bring about physical effects mechanically. Does an individual come into contact with them without having taken proper precautions? He receives a shock that has been compared with the effect of an electrical charge.[54]

Unlike Belanger, Durkheim did not literally believe in a metaphysical or subtle energy. Rather, he made the point that the social weight of religious ritual has effects that are *indistinguishable* from physical forces. Despite this distinction, the connection is worth making. One contact in the AVA had read Durkheim and mentioned that she liked his analysis of religious ritual. Durkheim may inadvertently be responsible for some of the concepts of energy that permeate the discourse of new and alternative religions.

How do vampires, the energy-workers *par excellence,* play into this energy-based interpretation of religion? Belanger states that it is unethical for vampires to attend church services simply to feed on religious energy. However, she proposes that vampires can essentially, "pay their dues" by using their abilities to manipulate and enhance the energy of the service as they feed.[55] This would seem to make vampires almost like a sort of religious faerie godmother, anonymously raising congregations into higher states of religious experience.

In fact, Belanger took on this very role in the church where she was brought up. She was raised in a Catholic environment and very active in her church, where she founded a youth choir and assisted in teaching Sunday school. At age seven, she expressed her desire to be a priest, only to be told that women cannot join the priesthood. (Belanger states that her habit of wearing black is tied to this early desire for the cloth.) Her enthusiasm waned as she began to notice gossip and pettiness among churchgoers. She has stated, "The stink of hypocrisy drove me from my church."[56]

Before leaving the church, Belanger's desire to replace the petty impiety of her congregation with religious meaning led her to conduct a strange experiment: Sitting in the choir loft between songs, Belanger would concentrate intensely on the large crucifix that dominated the church. She stated, "I wanted to make it so that it would move, look like it was breathing, or look like it was bleeding so that there was something miraculous for the people to see." The experiment continued for weeks until one day Belanger found that the cross had been removed from the church. She later found it, sneaking into the church garage, where it had been dismantled and left in a corner. There were eventually unconfirmed rumors that "someone had been called in to run an exorcism on the cross."[57]

Belanger's second experiment was an attempt to create an apparition of the Virgin Mary. What she described as "A Marian cult" had already begun to form at her church, and she attempted to create a miraculous experience through energy work. Belanger also reasoned that a disembodied apparition could not be removed from the church, as had the cross. Church members did indeed begin to have visions of the Virgin Mary, and the church has since constructed a $35,000 shrine. Although Belanger does not accept sole responsibility for the visions, some people did associate their experience of Mary with Belanger's singing. When Belanger left the choir, she was reportedly "stalked" by members of the Marian cult, asking her to return.[58] While not all of Belanger's story can be proven, Our Lady of Grace Church in Hinckley, Ohio, does indeed have a shrine. According to the church's Web site, The Marian Society had the idea to build a shrine in the early 1990s, which fits with Belanger's chronology.[59]

Vampires, Religion, and Modernity

It is interesting that the definitions of religion that apply best to vampirism are associated with transpersonal psychology, while vampire ideas about religion seem indebted to thinkers like James and Jung. Did James's study of personal religion really open up new areas for analysis? Or is it that he *redefined* religion as a personal matter, fueling an American tradition of radical religious individualism that vampires now exemplify? In other words: Did James anticipate the religiosity of vampires or did he help to create it?

The idea that religion, and indeed all aspects of life, have become subjective and private is usually considered a consequence of modernity. Modernity has also been associated with the rise of secularism, a rejection of religious authority and hierarchy, and the "disenchantment" of the world.[60] What I find interesting is that our cultural concept of the vampire has undergone changes that parallel the effects of modernity on religion. Vampires were once part of a cosmology divided between supernatural forces of good and evil. However, movies and literature have begun to secularize the vampire. In contemporary vampire fiction, the vampire has become a complex character, and the old dualistic cosmology has dissolved into a world of moral ambiguity. A consequence of modernity appears to be that our ideas about vampires and our ideas about religion have begun to converge. Thus the vampire—whether it is regarded as an archetypal ideal or an ontological identity—appears as an increasingly religious concept.

The decline of the supernatural is reflected in modern vampire narratives. This trend seems to have begun in 1954 when Richard Matheson wrote a vampire story entitled *I Am Legend*. Matheson's vampires are not supernatural creatures at all: They are simply humans that have been genetically altered by a virus. Genetic and viral vampires have increasingly replaced the old model of supernatural vampires as seen in films like *Blade, Underworld,* and *Ultraviolet.* In our modern, disenchanted world, the virally explained vampire seems more compelling, and it is easier for the audience to suspend disbelief. Meanwhile, the old trope of vampires being repelled by the authority of crucifixes and religious objects has become increasingly rare. J. Gordon Melton states of the impotency of crucifixes in contemporary vampire fiction, "It includes a protest against the authority of any particular religion and its claims of truth in a religiously pluralistic world."[61] Thus cross-resistant vampires indicate not only secularization, but also pluralism, and the radical doubt associated with modernity.

Vampire fiction has become preoccupied with a quest for evidence that reflects modernity's skepticism of religious claims. Reluctance to believe in the supernatural is one of the themes of Bram Stoker's *Dracula*. This search for evidence becomes overtly theological in the writings of Anne Rice. Rice breaks with tradition as her characters cast a reflection when they look into a mirror. Rice interpreted this piece of vampire lore as indicating that vampires are damned: The reflection is an image of the soul and the vampire casts no reflection because its soul is in hell.[62] Rice gave her vampires a reflection because she wanted to emphasize that even vampires are plagued by theological doubt. Katherine Ramsland quotes Rice, "If Louis failed to see himself in a mirror, he would know that some force was at work."[63]

Rice is also credited with shifting the vampire from a figure of consummate evil to a morally ambiguous character. Dark Rose, a vampire from Florida, commented on Rice, "The lifestyle of the vampire is not presented as a facet of evil, but rather as an inevitable quirk of nature."[64] Moral ambiguity is also considered a consequence of modernity as religious traditions are seen as having less authority to dictate good from evil. Mary L. Carter also notes that the modern vampire is to be judged by an ecological rather than a cosmological standard. She asks, "Is a vampire any more guilty than a man-eating tiger?"[65] (The idea of a "food chain" is referenced frequently both in vampire literature and by real vampire groups.) These appeals to a natural order also reference modernity. As early as the Enlightenment, nature was seen as an alternative source of authority to the dictates of the monarchy and the church.[66]

The Vampire Lestat closes with a scene in which the vampire, posing as a human rock star, gives a concert. The lyrics of Lestat's song "Age of Innocence" reflect the demise of supernatural evil and a dualistic cosmology in the disenchanted modern age:

> This is the Age of Innocence
> True Innocence
> All your Demons are visible
> All your Demons are material
> Call them Pain
> Call them Hunger
> Call them War
> Mythic evil you don't need anymore.
> Drive out the vampires and the devils
> With the gods you no longer adore.

Finally, where the vampire of folklore was simply a monster, modern vampire literature focuses on individual vampires. Lestat is a metaphor for the modern cult of the self. Rice made Lestat a rock star because rock stars are expected to be "completely wild, completely unpredictable, and completely themselves, and they are rewarded for that."[67] As a rebel vampire, Lestat has no moral authority to guide his existence as a vampire. Throughout The Vampire Chronicles, he continually attempts to create a moral code on his own terms. Lestat's attempt to create "a moral code of one" is a stark example of the radical religious individualism that self-identified vampires participate in.

Religion scholar Wade Clark Roof discusses the phenomenon of "religious privatism" in which meaning-worlds have become exclusively personal and subjective.[68] Roof sees this especially in his study of the baby-boomer generation. He comments that baby-boomers' modern conception of the self has led to their being characterized as narcissistic and self-absorbed. I find it telling that these same characterizations have been applied to vampires. (Amusingly, Guinn and Grieser complain that whenever they interviewed vampires in their homes, the vampires would help themselves to snacks or coffee without offering any to their guests.[69]) The subjective meaning-worlds of vampires and their groups are not so different from the privatized religious worlds described by Roof. If the phenomenon of self-identified vampires strikes us as religious, it may be because the modern image of the radically autonomous, morally ambiguous vampire has become the perfect symbol of the private meaning-worlds that have come to occupy the religious landscape of the contemporary Western world.

CHAPTER 7

Out of the Shadows

It's funny how people will bash vampires until you step up and say that you are one. Their tune changes quite remarkably.
—Mora Zoranokov, quoted in A Field Guide to Otherkin

The AVA and other vampires have worked to establish the vampire as a valid category of identity and to disseminate resources for recently awakened vampires. However, some in the community object to this exposure and wish to remain "in the shadows." The AVA's survey was initially regarded with suspicion. A rumor briefly circulated on the Internet that the AVA was actually a government agency trying to collect data on vampires for nefarious purposes. This rumor came to be called "the X-Men Scenario" in which the government would monitor all vampires and attempt to control them for their powers. One AVA member commented on the likelihood of this scenario, "Our powers really aren't all that impressive." A more cogent fear was that exposure would bring unwanted attention from the religious right. Religion scholar David Keysworth does describe the existence of a Christian vampire slayer movement that is opposed to the vampire community.[1] While I never heard of vampire being identified and murdered by a slayer, vampires have received threats of physical violence. According to one contact, "There have been people that will try to jump you in the Denny's parking lot."

Regardless of this debate, the vampire community's exposure to mainstream society seems inevitable. It should be remembered that people were hunting the undead long before there were self-identified vampires. A cultural preoccupation with vampires provides plenty of incentive to either seek out modern vampires or else create them where they do not exist. The vampire hunters of the twentieth century include self-styled occultists, some evangelical Christians, and occult-crime experts. These individuals have re-enchanted the modern world by populating it with Satanists, blood cults, and vampires. They tend to publicize the existence of the vampire community to further their goals, using it as a demonic foil to their own heroic self-narrative.

The media is another factor that brings unwanted attention to the vampire community. Vampire headlines sell, and the media is quick to label anything as vampiric—especially murder cases. Disturbed individuals who do not identify as vampires are often labeled as such if they committed a crime that involved drinking blood. Meanwhile, criminals who do call themselves vampires are rendered larger than life: Their actions can be presented as typical examples of gothic or vampire subcultures and in some cases they are interpreted as agents of wide-reaching vampire cults.

Finally, real vampires who are not criminals also attract media attention. In the 1990s several real vampires as well as numerous posers appeared on daytime talk shows. Many vampires complain that these television appearances attract only "prima donna" vampires in search of celebrity status. Another complaint is that when respected members of the community appear in documentaries, the interview is inevitably accompanied by ominous music and stock footage of Hollywood vampires.

In the last year, there has been a resurgence of vampires in popular culture exemplified by the *Twilight* series of romance/horror novels by Stephanie Meyer and the HBO series *True Blood*. In the wake of these pop culture vampires, there is increasing pressure on real vampires to appear in documentaries and on reality television. At the time of this writing, the AVA has received no less than 14 e-mails within the previous 15 months from researchers and production assistants trying to solicit vampires for documentaries and talks shows. The vampire community is highly ambivalent about this newfound attention. Some feel that a greater media presence will attract support for more serious scientific and medical research. Others feel that this attention threatens the community's culture as well as the families and careers of vampires and is generally unbecoming of vampirism. However, if real vampires will not appear for interviews, attention seekers and vampire hunters will. It seems that one way or another, the community must find a way to exist above ground.

The Vampire Hunter Fantasy

Before anyone ever identified as a vampire, people identified as vampire hunters. In some parts of Eastern Europe, vampire hunting could even become a livelihood. Hunters would travel from village to village charging a fee to exhume and dismember corpses. Often the hunter's son would inherit his father's vampire detection abilities and continue the family business.[2] In our modern society, the motivation for vampire hunting is rarely money but instead the desire to live in a re-enchanted world.

Even those who do not believe in the paranormal use the vampire community to re-enchant their worlds by imagining it as exotic and potentially dangerous. Many otherwise rational people seem to think field research with vampires is a Romantic quest for forbidden knowledge and totally different from field work with other groups. Shortly after I made contact with the AVA, a graduate student asked if she could accompany me on an observation. "I should come with you," she said, "I'm pale." Her research interests were unrelated to vampires, and this strange request seemed to be rooted in a fantasy of infiltrating an AVA meeting "disguised" as a vampire.

In addition to teaching high school and moonlighting as a religion scholar, I also study martial arts. When one of my instructors found out I was writing this book, he (only half-jokingly) offered to give me extra training to get ready for my research. Specifically, he recommended I work on my fighting skills using a type of hooked knife from Indonesia called a karambit. Not even Indiana Jones— arguably the worst anthropologist ever imagined—packs a knife. (By the time you are engaged in a knife fight with your research subjects, the validity of your data has been seriously compromised.) I still ponder the folly of showing up at an AVA meeting in faux-gothic attire with my karambit concealed in my black trenchcoat, only to find an innocuous group of computer-savvy people arguing about the banalities of research methodology.

Incidentally, the only sincerely dangerous situation reported by a vampirologist comes from Stephen Kaplan. In his book *Vampires Are,* he describes how his collie Nova died after eating cookies found in Kaplan's backyard. The cookies were laced with strychnine and had been meant for Kaplan's children. Following the death of his dog, Kaplan received a threatening phone call by someone claiming to be a Satanist.[3] If this story is true, it is not because Kaplan's research brought him close to exposing a group of Satanists. Rather, it is because he allowed his Vampire Research Center to become a media spectacle without taking precautions to protect his private life.

Susan Walsh

The crescendo of the vampire hunter fantasy occurred in July 1996 when Susan Walsh disappeared while researching the New York vampire scene for *The Village Voice.* Tony Thorne says of the Walsh disappearance, "The notion of enchanted underworlds existing somewhere beneath the streets of the metropolis had become a potent pop-cultural myth."[4] Despite the numerous factors in her disappearance, no one seemed able to look past the vampires. Even media sources who ought to have known better suggested the tantalizing possibility that Walsh had learned too much about vampires—and had been silenced.

What really befell Walsh is almost certainly less glamorous. An aspiring journalist, Walsh hated her current full-time job as a stripper. She already had a history of alcoholism and, according to her family, had begun drinking again as well as abusing the prescription drug *Xanax* prior to her disappearance. She was also described by her friends as manic-depressive, and it was rumored that she had recently made a suicide attempt. More importantly, Walsh had recently produced a story on figures in the Russian mafia who were forcing Russian girls to dance and prostitute themselves at New York strip clubs. Walsh even told friends that she feared she was being stalked by the Russian mob.[5]

The New York vampire community was briefly investigated and exonerated. This was likely only a formality as the Russian mafia obviously had both the motive and the means to cause Walsh's disappearance. I spoke with Stephen O'Mallie, who was active in the investigation of the New York vampire scene following Walsh's disappearance. Being from a cop family, he described how he had easily noticed an undercover police officer in the vampire club. As the Sheriff of Gotham, he felt obliged to approach the officer and ask what he was doing. The officer explained that he was from an occult-crime investigation unit within the NYPD. For the next month, O'Mallie became a consultant on the case.

O'Mallie, who is now a detective himself, called the investigation "a half-hearted effort." He added, "no one evaporates without a trace" and suggested that only organized crime had the resources to cause so complete a disappearance. Despite the evidence, the Walsh case remains a high-water mark in the history of the vampire community, and some vampires have capitalized on the story's mystique. AVA members have described frustration at vampires who appeared in filmed interviews and were asked, "What happened to Susan Walsh?" only to answer, "I can't say." These coy responses deliberately play on the vampire hunter fantasy. Father Sebastiaan Tod van Houten, who seemed to believe Walsh was still alive, felt that only New Yorkers were qualified to comment on the disappearance. Incidentally, Sebastiaan said that Dmitri along with about 50 other vampires disappeared at the same time as Susan Walsh.

The Highgate Vampire

When combined with a belief in the supernatural, the vampire hunter fantasy can result in full-blown hysteria. Such was the case in London's Highgate Cemetery in 1970. Founded in 1829, many famous and historical figures are interred at Highgate including Karl Marx and British novelist Douglas Adams. Rosemary Ellen Guiley believes that Highgate appears in Stoker's *Dracula* as "the cemetery near Hempstead Heath" where Lucy Westenra is entombed.[6] Today, the cemetery is most famous for the Highgate vampire case. The Highgate vampire has become the stuff of legend, spawning several books and at least one academic article. It has also become a source of embarrassment and great inconvenience to the cemetery's caretakers.

By the late 1960s much of the cemetery had become dilapidated and overgrown. This attracted the attention of vandals as well as a variety of occultists. David Farrant allegedly spent the night in the cemetery where he glimpsed an apparition of "a gray figure." This sparked numerous other stories of apparitions at Highgate, none of which had any features in common. In addition to gliding white ghosts and disembodied voices, witnesses also described seeing a tall man in a hat, a ghost riding a bicycle, a woman in white, a face glaring through the bars of a gate, and a figure wading into a pond.[7]

The stories attracted the attention of Sean Manchester, who claimed to know the source of the trouble at Highgate: a "king vampire" from Wallachia that had been brought to England in a coffin by his supporters at the start of the eighteenth century.[8] Manchester succeeded in acquiring a great deal of media attention with this claim, and Farrant was not eager to give up his spotlight. The two began spreading competing theories of what exactly was happening at Highgate. Both men claimed that a supernatural evil dwelled in Highgate and that they were qualified to destroy it. This climaxed in March 1970 when a mob of self-appointed vampire hunters swarmed the cemetery, defiling graves and corpses and inflicting immense property damage.

Manchester has since published several books describing his exploits in defeating the vampire. In 1985 he published *The Highgate Vampire,* which describes how he and his companions chased the vampire from grave to grave using garlic, communion wafers, and other traditional techniques, before finally tracking it back to an abandoned house and killing it with a wooden stake. (Upon death, the vampire's body disintegrated.) Manchester also founded the International Society for the Advancement of Irreproducible Vampire and Lycanthropy Research (ISAIVLR), which published a newsletter, *The Cross and the Stake.* For good measure, he also started his own religious order, The Church of the Holy Grail.[9] Not to be outdone, Farrant wrote his own book, *Beyond the Highgate Vampire,* and formed a rival society, the Highgate Vampire Society with its newsletter *Suspended in Dusk.*[10]

Manchester and Farrant continued to antagonize each other and ultimately declared that they would fight "a magician's duel" in 1973. (Neither combatant made an appearance.) Meanwhile, vandalism continued at the cemetery, and in 1974 Farrant was arrested for damaging memorials and desecrating corpses. Farrant and an associate allegedly sent dolls stuck with pins to detectives who intended to testify at the trial. He conducted his own defense and blamed damage to the cemetery on Satanists. Farrant did admit to conducting a ritual that involved a nude woman dancing inside one of the vaults, but said that this had been an exorcism. He was sentenced to four years and eight months in prison. The feud between Manchester and Farrant continues to this day. A contact from the AVA suggested that anyone making posts critical of Farrant on an Internet forum is probably Manchester and vice versa. As for the cemetery itself, the hysteria inflicted massive property damage. The cost to repair damaged tombs far outweighed the Highgate's funds, and in 1981 the famous cemetery was sold for only 50 pounds.[11]

Bill Ellis, a professor of English and American Studies, points out that England has a history of similar episodes of mass hysteria. On September 23, 1954, a cemetery in a Glasgow suburb was swarming with children armed with sticks and stones. They were hunting "a vampire with iron teeth" and nearly succeeded in dragging an adult into their hunt. In the nineteenth century, panics were inspired by "Spring-heeled Jack" and other legends.[12] These hunts for the supernatural can also be read as a form of re-enchantment. Imagining a cosmological evil works against the banality of the modern world and allows men like Farrant and Manchester to create heroic, even epic, narratives for themselves. However, it is not necessary to believe in the supernatural to construct such a narrative: Cultists and Satanists create an equally suitable demonic foil.

Cult Cops

The term "cult cops" refers to a movement within law enforcement to train police to combat occult crime. What exactly makes a crime occult? The category does not appear in FBI's uniform crime reporting system alongside rape, homicide, and arson.[13] A contact in Atlanta stated flatly, "I don't think there is such a thing as occult crime." In theory, officers trained to fight occult crime would be knowledgable of dangerous occult groups and be able to identify occult symbols that might appear at crime scenes. But do occult symbols appear at crime scenes often enough to justify such training? Even if they did, these symbols are not emblematic of large occult organizations with a common set of symbols. More often, they are chosen by the criminally insane working alone for reasons known only to the individual perpetrators. In this critique, there are crimes and crime scenes with occult symbols, but "occult crime" is a false category.

Whether or not occult crime exists, training seminars are held every year, funded by tax dollars that have been designated for law enforcement. The 1980s were an especially prosperous decade for occult-crime training. Robert D. Hicks shows that 50 training seminars were held in 1984–1990. In addition to police officers, occult-crime training was made available to educators, social workers, mental health personnel, victim advocates, probation officers, corrections officials, and clergy. These training sessions would often use props including altars, candles, and human skulls. While these effects were supposed to give police an idea of what to look for, Hicks argues that their actual purpose was to "dissuade critical, analytical thinking." In addition to Satanic groups, Afro-Atlantic religions such as Santeria were also popular targets of the seminars.[14] Advice given to law enforcement on these groups had grim implications for a democratic society. It was argued that although groups like the Church of Satan condemn criminal behavior, they espouse philosophies that may naturally attract criminals, and, therefore, these groups warrant increased police surveillance. Occult-crime training would often elide into a battle against supernatural evil, not unlike Sean Manchester's alleged struggle against the Highgate vampire. Hicks quotes a 1987 newsletter created by the Cult Crime Impact Network with the help of a Boise police officer. It informs police officers, "you may be battling with forces which are impervious to your wrist-twists, your batons, or your service firearms—and they may destroy you."[15]

Hicks describes police administrators who simply wanted to make training available for as many types of crime as possible. The existence of these seminars shows the power of a category: A crime does not have to be a serious problem to receive funding, it only needs to have been designated as its own "type" of crime. There are several other dubious categories in which the vampire comunity has been implicated. Kaplan describes the category "blood cults," which may include modern vampires as well as Afro-Atlantic religions. Another is "hemocide," invented by John L. Vellutini in the *Journal of Vampirology*. He defines "hemocide" as "murder committed in order to assuage a craving for blood."[16] Simply coining a term like "hemocide" implies that the world is inhabited by "hemocidal maniacs" who commit several hemocides every year. Someone with the right connections might even find funding to lecture on hemocide prevention. But none of this means even one actual case of hemocide ever took place. Before the category of occult crime was created, calls to police involving cults or the supernatural were often dismissed as "nut calls." In the 1950s, Anton Szandor LaVey, founder of the Church of Satan, worked as a psychic investigator and had police contacts direct such nuisance callers to him. When callers were not happy with the rational explanations provided by LaVey's investigation, he would invent supernatural ones.[17] So, in a great irony, the first cult cop was the founder of the Church of Satan.

The cult-cop phenomenon began to change in the mid-1990s. Whereas Satanists were the most popular target in the 1980s, the gothic and vampire communities by the mid-1990s offered a more immediate and tangible source of menace. Academics had been typically dismissed by cult cops; their insights were considered irrelevant to "real police work."[18] However, this changed in the late 1990s when some academics became more conducive to the cult-cop agenda. Dawn Perlmutter is the director of the Institute for the Research of Organized and Ritual Violence and gives seminars on "violent religious groups." She has also appeared on *The O'Reilly Factor* and other news programs and has even been consulted by prosecutors in murder cases. In addition to the usual suspects of Pagan, Satanic, and Afro-Atlantic religious groups, Perlmutter has also targeted fetish culture and the vampire community. She has written a number of articles portraying the vampire community as a hierarchical religious group that is responsible for "numerous crimes ranging from vandalism to murder."[19] She has also written the entry on "Vampire Culture" for the book *Religion and American Cultures: An Encyclopedia of Traditions, Diversity, and Popular Expressions.* Needless to say, the AVA are upset by these characterizations and frequently cite Perlmutter's work as part of their motivation for the VEWRS project.

An article about Perlmutter in *The Baptist Standard* indicates that she may have actually been recruited by cult cops. Originally a professor of art and philosophy, Perlmutter was first contacted by a New Jersey police officer for help with a murder case. Perlmutter suggested that local gangs were behind the murder and, not surprisingly, this proved correct. According to the article, Perlmutter was then asked to speak to an unspecified, "law-enforcement related agency."[20] This was probably a cult-cop organization similar to the Cult Crime Impact Network. This led to more consultations and more speaking engagements. Thus began the career of an occult-crime expert.

Detective O'Mallie had a different perspective on law enforcement and the occult. O'Mallie is a Pagan and lifestyle vampire and has tried to quietly help the community through his work as a detective. He told me a story about entering the home of a suspect who happened to be Pagan. Another officer spotted a ritual dagger known as an athame and moved to confiscate it. O'Mallie stopped him and explained that the dagger was part of the suspect's religious beliefs and not evidence of criminal activity. When asked if he had an interest in giving seminars to police on Paganism and vampirism, O'Mallie said he would love to if only there were a way to do so without harming his career. O'Mallie did attend the Twilight Conference in Atlanta where he helped with security and spoke to the vampire community about law enforcement. Before the conference, he told his police partner of many years about his life-style as a vampire. His partner was surprised but accepting.

Slayings

Just as self-identified vampires form their identities in reference to the vampire milieu, self-proclaimed vampire hunters and cult cops are influenced by a slayer milieu. Breaking into graveyards to hunt vampires or showing police an altar adorned with stage blood makes one larger than life. A slayer is no longer part of our disenchanted world but has become a mythic figure armed with occult knowledge much like the fictional Dr. Van Helsing or Buffy's mentor, Rupert Giles. Unfortunately, this form of re-enchantment requires the slayer to impose a fantastic identity onto others, assigning them to be their vampiric foil. When combined with mental illness, the slayer fantasy has been a factor in several homicides.

In 2001, 28-year-old Kirk Palmer of Colorado killed Antonio Vierira with a shotgun because he believed that Vierira had turned his girlfriend into a vampire. He told a psychologist that four days before the shooting in July 2001 he had removed a splinter from his girlfriend's thumb and saw Vierira come out of her body to tell him that she had been bitten and was now a member of his vampire gang. On March 10, 2004, he was found not guilty by reason of insanity and committed to a mental hospital.[21]

On March 12, 2004, Timothy White of Jacksonville, Florida, shot a coworker twice at a Domino's pizza delivery store. White had no criminal record and was described as a born-again Christian who was obsessed with vampires. He believed that he was a slayer and that his victim and longtime friend, David Harrison, was a vampire. Prior to the shooting, a witness had spotted him lingering outside the store. Asked why he was there, he replied that he was "vampire hunting." When taken into custody, he was armed with a knife, a sawed-off shotgun, and three handguns. There have been other cases of modern slayings, but these two examples are sufficient to demonstrate the pattern. Fortunately for the vampire community, these disturbed individuals usually turn on those closest to them rather than seeking actual vampires. However, these stories do justify much of the "paranoid behavior" demonstrated by the community.

Vampires in the Headlines

When the vampire community appears in the newspaper, it is usually for one of two reasons: Either a new vampire movie has just come out and a human interest story about the vampire community appears in the movies section, or there has been a violent crime. Vampires sell papers, and, therefore, it is good capitalism to include the word "vampire" in as many headlines as possible. Unfortunately, this practice causes the community to be associated with and implicated in many gruesome crimes. It also fuels the theories of cult cops and vampire hunters who see these headlines as evidence of some dark organization rather than as isolated acts committed by the criminally insane.

The vampire community—defined as the networks and institutions used by self-identified vampires—can be almost completely exonerated from the various murders and assaults that have been labeled as vampiric. Most stories of "vampire criminals" fall into one of two categories. In the first case, a criminal does not identify as a vampire at all and has not been influenced by either the vampire milieu or the vampire community. This sort of criminal is labeled a vampire after the fact because his crimes were excessively bloody and heinous. In the second case, the criminal does claim to be a vampire or else desires to become one. These individuals are influenced by the vampire milieu: Their delusion may have originated from abuse, a chemical imbalance, or other causes, but it has been shaped by Anne Rice, White Wolf games, or some other cultural representation of vampires. However, these criminals typically act alone and rarely have contact with other self-identified vampires. Therefore, they are not part of the vampire community. Only a handful of cases remain in which a violent crime had connections to both the vampire milieu and the vampire community.

The case of Fritz Haarmann (1879–1925), the so-called Hanover vampire, demonstrates the first category of "vampire criminal." Haarmann was a child molester and a serial killer and is believed to have killed more than 50 people. He also practiced cannibalism and in at least one case bit one of his victims and consumed their blood. For this reason, Haarmann has been described by the media as suffering from "clinical vampirism."[22] However, for all of Haarmann's problems, he never actually *claimed* to be a vampire. Melton points out that Haarmann's story is more relevant to the annals of serial killers than vampirism.[23] Similarly, Vlad Tepes, Elizabeth Bathory, and variety of modern serial killers did not see themselves as vampires. Whatever motivated their actions, it was independent of vampire lore.

Joshua Rudiger is a prime example of the second category of "vampire killer." In 1998, 22-year-old Rudiger began using a knife to attack homeless people in San Francisco. He injured three men and killed a woman who had been sleeping in a doorway. At his trial he declared that he was a 2000-year-old vampire and that he needed to drink human blood. He added that his existence as a vampire was punishment for a crime he had committed in a previous lifetime. In addition to being a vampire, Rudiger also claimed to be a ninja warrior.[24]

Rudiger's trial revealed a failure by the state to help someone suffering from an obviously dangerous mental illness. A forensic psychiatrist stated that Rudiger had been diagnosed as psychotic at the age of four. He had grown up in various foster homes and psychiatric hospitals where he had been caught licking the chests of other patients. At one point he informed a therapist of his intentions to drink the blood of those around him. Despite these obvious warning signs, he was released at age 18, after which he immediately began attacking people. In 1997 he shot a man with a bow and arrow before the 1998 murder of a homeless woman.[25] Unlike Haarmann, Rudiger was influenced by the vampire milieu and did claim to be a vampire. However, Rudiger had no contact with the vampire community or anyone else identifying as a vampire. Like Haarmann, he was mentally ill and motivated by reasons known only to him.

A similar high-profile case occurred in 2003, when 17-year-old Matthew Hardman stabbed an elderly woman to death in North Wales. Hardman arranged two fire pokers in a cross formation at the victim's feet before removing the heart and placing it in a saucepan wrapped in paper. He also drained blood from her leg into a saucepan. Investigators found a tide mark on the pan, suggesting that Hardman had drunk from it. Like Rudiger, Hardman was mentally ill and obsessed with vampires. He hoped that this ritual would allow him to become immortal.[26] Hardman appears to have devised this murderous ritual on his own. While cult cops no doubt had a field day interpreting the symbolism of this ritualistic murder, it is highly unlikely that it had any meaning to anyone other than Hardman.

There remain only two murder cases in which the murderer both identified as a vampire and worked with others: Manuela and Daniel Ruda of Germany and

Roderick Ferrell and his "vampire clan" of Murray, Kentucky. The Ferrell case in particular has brought more negative attention to the vampire community than any other event. There were numerous factors in both cases, but the connection to the vampire community cannot be easily dismissed.

The Rudas met after Daniel placed an ad in a music magazine that read, "Pitch black vampire seeks princess of darkness who hates everything and everyone." In 2002, 23-year-old Manuela and her 26-year-old husband Daniel stabbed

Manuela Ruda showing off for the courtroom at her murder trial in Bochum, Germany. (AP Photo/Michael Sohn)

Frank Haagen 66 times.[27] The Rudas proceeded to carve a pentagram in the victim's chest, drank his blood from a bowl, and then had sex in a coffin where Manuela usually slept.[28]

Manuela claimed that she had learned about Satanism in the United Kingdom. In 1995, at only 16, Manuela ran away from her family in Germany to Scotland. Apparently in search of unusual subcultures, she visited Tom Leppard, an enigmatic figure better known as "The Leopard Man." Until 2008, Leppard lived as a hermit on a remote part of the island of Skye. He is tattooed from head to foot with a leopard pattern design and wears a set of custom-made fangs. However, it was in Islington, north London, where she claims she met vampires and Satanists, attending secret meetings in cemeteries and drinking blood from donors. She also claims that she was once buried alive in order to "see what it feels like." The Rudas explained that their souls belonged to Satan, and that they had been commanded to make a "sacrifice."

Although the Rudas were deemed to be criminally insane, they did seem to have some involvement with Satanic elements of the vampire subculture. The extent of this involvement is purely speculative; however, Ramsland points out in her analysis of this crime that the Rudas' behavior was neither characteristic of nor

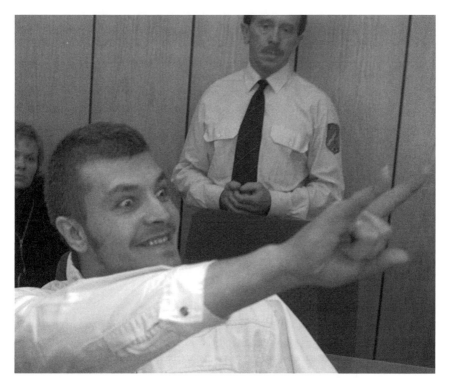

Daniel Ruda gives "the sign of the horns" in the courtroom. (AP Photo/Frank Augstein)

condoned by the vampire community.[29] *The Islington Gazette* ran an article describing a "secret colony of vampires" based on the Rudas' testimony, but there does not appear to have been a formal investigation in the United Kingdom.[30] While it seems plausible that a coven of Satanic vampires existed in Islington, there is no evidence for this claim other than the testimony of the criminally insane.

Ferrell, a 16-year-old self-described vampire, murdered a couple in Eustice, Florida, in 1996. This event, which occurred in the same year as Susan Walsh's disappearance and the murder of Angel Melendez in New York, brought unprecedented media attention to the vampire community, all of it negative. The Ferrell case served as fuel for vampire slayers and cult cops, "proving" to them the existence of dangerous vampire cults. By contrast, the vampire community has stated that Ferrell was simply a delusional teenager and not a vampire. The Wendorf murders are a complex case: Ferrell was undoubtedly delusional, but he was also in contact with other self-identified teenage vampires. His actions cannot be generalized to large social trends as has been done by the media, but his association with the vampire community cannot be easily dismissed as with most other vampire murder cases.

The events leading up to the murders began when Ferrell met Heather Wendorf at Eustice High School in Eustice, Florida. Both teens had few friends and shared a gothic aesthetic and an interest in the occult and vampires. The two were separated when Ferrell and his mother, Sondra Gibson, moved to Murray, Kentucky. It was in Kentucky that Ferrell began forming a coterie of friends interested in vampires. Although Ferrell was a misfit and expelled from the local high school, he had charisma that allowed him to influence other teens. He claimed to be a vampire and at various times the antichrist. He also had a gift for storytelling and was able to invent realistic details about previous incarnations in France and elsewhere. He gave diatribes to other teens on occult philosophy, impressing them with snippets of Shakespeare or Plato. Teenagers who had low self-esteem and an interest in the occult saw him as a leader. Several teenage girls found Ferrell charming and slept with him. Ferrell and his friends would also regularly drink one another's blood. The group had no structured belief system about drinking blood but seemed to engage in this practice for social and emotional reasons. Ferrell liked to cut himself in public as an attention getting device while some of the female members of his circle practiced self-injury as a way of coping with stress. Because they never claimed to *need* blood for their health, Ferrell's group would not be considered to be sanguinarian vampires by the real vampire community.

Somewhat surprisingly, Murray, Kentucky, was already home to another teenage vampire. Steven Murphy went by the vampiric name "Jaden" and had already formed his own coven of vampires before Ferrell arrived. Both Ferrell and Jaden seemed to have narcissistic tendencies but managed to build off on each other's fantastic claims. In fact, their relationship is reminiscent of the rivalry between

Farrant and Manchester in the Highgate vampire case. The two briefly participated in a *Vampire: The Masquerade* LARP held at Murray State University but
lost interest in it. Like Farrant and Manchester, they had a falling out and formed
two rival vampire groups or covens. At one point, Ferrell had a restraining order
placed on Jaden following an altercation.

While it may seem unusual for a rural town to possess rival covens of teenage
vampires, this behavior was probably far more common than one might imagine.
In the 1990s, teenagers all over America were forming identities around alternative
spiritualities and the occult. Many vampires, therians, and otherkin "awakened" as
teenagers. Leaders in this community describe how they had been far less critical
of each other's subjective claims as teenagers. In many cases, groups of teenagers
who adopted these identities would find themselves in a state of paranoia bordering
on hysteria. Lupa, a leader in the therian community, describes a similar situation:

> At the tender young age of seventeen, struck in a small town with hardly any resources
> beyond Montague Summers' *The Werewolf*, I was fully convinced that I was a Child of
> Gaia Philodox straight out of White Wolf's *Werewolf: The Apocalypse*. I counted as
> friends another were, a vampire, and a faerie-blooded vampire hunter (who somehow
> never attacked our vampire friend). And, of course, we were at war with a rival group
> of local vampires and werewolves who never seemed to manifest physically, though we
> seemed to experience an awful lot of psychic attacks, complete with Salem-witch-trial-
> style convulsions and panic attacks. Thankfully, I grew out of it pretty quickly.[31]

Tragically, were it not for Ferrell's actions, the teenagers of his vampire clan
would likely have grown out of this paranoid phase, as did Lupa, and today be
productive members of society.

While in Murray, Ferrell still remained in phone contact with Wendorf and
her friend Jeanine in Florida. The two girls came from affluent families and
dressed in gothic attire as a form of rebellion. They talked to Ferrell for hours
over the phone. Wendorf often complained that her parents were too controlling.
Allegedly, their conversations also included running away and even killing her
parents. For the two girls, this was probably just a dark fantasy, but for Ferrell
it was not. Ferrell blended obvious falsehoods with actual beliefs so frequently
that it was difficult for his friends to tell when they were playing an imaginary
game with him and when they were feeding a genuine delusion.

In November 1996, Ferrell drove to Eustice, Florida, to get Wendorf. He was
accompanied by the members of his coven: Dana Cooper, Charity Lynn Keesee,
and Howard Scott Anderson. Ferrell had managed to form a very tight group and
had assigned nicknames to each member of his coven. He was "Vesago," Anderson
was "Nosferatu," Heather would be "Zoey," and so on. The teens had brought a
great deal of luggage (Cooper had apparently brought over five bags of clothing
and personal effects). Innocuous items found in the teens' vehicle included teddy
bears, Disney tapes, baby pictures, and even a resume.[32] They apparently saw the
expedition to Florida as an opportunity to run away and start a new life.

It is unclear when Ferrell made the decision to murder the Wendorfs. After picking up Heather Wendorf, Ferrell and Anderson entered the Wendorf home through the garage. Upon entering the garage, the two boys found a variety of potential murder weapons including a machete, a chainsaw, and an axe. However, Ferrell eventually settled on a crowbar.[33] Once inside Ferrell beat both Wendorfs to death using the crowbar. Seemingly as an afterthought, Ferrell burned a "V" into Richard Wendorf's body. It was never determined whether the "V" stood for Vesago, for vampire, or had no meaning at all. Anderson reportedly froze and did not participate in the murders. It is possible that he never thought Ferrell was sincere about his plan to murder the Wendorfs. Neither teen consumed any of the victims' blood, as was later alleged.

After the murders, the teens transferred their belongings into the Wendorfs' Explorer and began driving toward New Orleans. Ferrell told Wendorf that he had murdered her parents, but she assumed this was simply another one of his outrageous claims. They were eventually arrested in New Orleans and sent to Florida to stand trial for murder. Ferrell, Anderson, Cooper, and Keesee all pled guilty. Only Heather was acquitted. Ferrell was given a death sentence and is currently on death row. Anderson was given life in prison without parole. The two girls were only found guilty of third degree murder and were given lighter sentences. Cooper received 17 years, Keesee 10. Keesee was allegedly seen exchanging blood with another inmate after her sentencing.[34]

From the moment Ferrell and his coven were arrested, a media circus ensued. Everyone involved with the case was pursued by reporters from as far away as Japan and Australia. *Jenny Jones* hosted an appearance by Jaden to talk about vampirism. *Maury* did a show entitled "I'm Scared My Teen is Evil," in which he interviewed Ferrell and his mother. *Hard Copy* sent reporters to Eustice High

Four of the five teens arrested following the murder of Richard and Naoma Ruth Wendorf. (AP Photo/WPSD-TV [Ferrell's name was misspelled as "Farrell" by WPSD-TV])

During Rod Ferrell's sentencing, a crime analyst displays the shirt worn by Richard Wendorf when he was murdered. (AP Photo)

in search of vampires.[35] Anne Rice stated that she wanted nothing to do with the story and that it was unfortunate that some of her books were found in the stolen Explorer.[36] Numerous groups and subcultures were blamed. Not only vampires, but LARPs, Paganism, and gothic culture in general were all cited as corrupting and dangerous influences.

In reality, it is much more likely that numerous mundane factors set Ferrell on the road to murder. He was being raised by his mother, a former prostitute and stripper who had never held down a steady job in her life. An expert witness during the trial testified that Gibson had the emotional maturity of a 12-year-old. Gibson dressed in gothic fashion like her son and told several people involved with the investigation that she wanted to be initiated into Ferrell's coven. Gibson had also sent sexually explicit messages to Jaden's younger brother, Jamie, and allegedly had built a shrine to him in her room. The boy's parents eventually found these messages, and Gibson was charged with soliciting rape and soliciting sodomy. These charges occurred only a few days before Ferrell left for Florida.[37] It is baffling how often this detail has been overlooked in accounts of the murders. It is possible that Ferrell took his coven to Florida simply because he was emotionally unable to deal with the situation created by his mother.

Ferrell also testified that he was the victim of sexual abuse. He stated that at age six, his grandfather presented him to a "Black Mass Cult" where he was sodomized by several men.[38] Expert witnesses stated that some of Ferrell's behavior was consistent with a survivor of sexual abuse. Finally, Ferrell abused a variety of drugs including LSD. Members of his coven described episodes where Ferrell feared that his couch was going to eat him.[39] Ferrell testified that he was under the influence of LSD, marijuana, and various prescription drugs throughout his road trip from Kentucky to Florida; however, no one from his coven seemed to notice him in the act of taking drugs.[40] With a dysfunctional mother, drug abuse, and possible sexual abuse, it was unlikely that Ferrell would come to a good end whether or not he developed an interest in vampirism.

Ferrell seems to have constructed a vast fantasy world for himself of which vampirism was only one part. This was almost certainly an escape mechanism that allowed him to cope with a toxic environment. Ferrell frequently described a coming apocalypse that combined elements of the Book of Revelation, Nostradamus, fears of environmental devastation, and nuclear war. He colored this prophetic vision with vague references to current events and leaders such as Saddam Hussein. Paperback books on the occult were also significant in the world Ferrell was constructing. *The Necronomicon* and *The Witches' Bible* were both found in the stolen Explorer following the murder. Finally, Ferrell and his coterie borrowed extensively from movies and television. The phrase "brought over"—which Ferrell and his friends used to describe initiation as a vampire originates from the television series *Forever Knight* about a vampire cop.[41] Ferrell's persona "Vesago" is the name of a Satan-worshipping villain in the film *Hideaway*.[42] At the trial, Gibson referred to herself as "Star."[43] This is the name of a sympathetic female vampire in the film *Lost Boys*. Even Jaden admitted that his nickname was borrowed from an episode of *Star Trek*.[44]

The narrative of a "teenage vampire clan" appears to have been created *post factum*. The media was quick to sensationalize the story, claiming that Ferrell drank the blood of his victims or that the murders were part of a Satanic belief system. Law enforcement officials may have also contributed to this narrative when they interrogated impressionable teenagers. In her book on the Ferrell case, Aphrodite Jones presents the following description based on taped conversations between Heather Wendorf and Detective Gussler:

> "What rank in the organization does Rod hold?"
> "Organization?"
> "Or group?"
> "Group of what?" Heather wondered. "All of us or just Rod?"

"I guess, I mean, how many of them is there? Other than the five of you?"

"Oh, you mean all over."

"Oh, they're *all over* huh?"

"Yeah."

"Vampires."

"Vampires"—the detective winced—" 'cause you like blood?"

"Yeah."

"Any blood?"

"Yeah."

"You like to see blood?"

Heather had no response for that.

"I mean it's okay," Gussler told her, scratching his head, "we're just trying to understand. This is new to us."[45]

Wendorf may have thought of her interactions with Ferrell as an elaborate game. However, in this conversation, the detective seems already to assume that Wendorf is part of large vampire "organization." He may have made this assumption based on seminars hosted by cult cops. Wendorf is badly frightened and clearly an impressionable 15-year-old girl. By trying to cooperate with law enforcement, she may have given answers that confirmed these assumptions.

The cult narrative was also strengthened when a girl named Amber Blood contacted the Crime Stoppers Hot Line with information about the case. Blood had gone to Eustice High and claimed that she had been friends with Ferrell and Wendorf. She stated that the two of them were in a vampire cult. Blood eventually failed a polygraph and repudiated her story. But by this time, the vampire cult story was already at full strength.[46]

Ferrell and his friends had formed some connections to the larger vampire community, which were incorporated into their fantasy world. Although most of Ferrell's associates no longer claim to be vampires, Ferrell still does. This presents a problem for the vampire community: How can a community with no clear definition of vampirism place themselves in a separate category from a disturbed killer like Ferrell? When Belanger was asked this question in a phone interview, she described her desire to say that Ferrell is not a vampire and that his actions were completely unrelated to the community but conceded that she could not do so.

There is evidence that Ferrell and Jaden had access to the print media used by vampire networks in the mid 1990s. Belanger mentioned that Lady Dark Rose claimed she had received a letter from Ferrell, suggesting that Ferrell read *The Dark Rose Journal*. Jaden had purchased a copy of *The Vampire Bible* from the Temple of the Vampire. Jones describes him as offering his life force to the undead gods at the local Hardees[47] (probably not the Temple's prescribed locale for vampire initiation).

Belanger also suggested that there may have been some legitimate form of vampire spirituality through Ferrell's use of *The Necronomicon. The*

Necronomicon was conceived by horror writer H. P. Lovecraft. It was an evil spell book capable of summoning "elder gods" that appeared in several of his short stories. Despite Lovecraft's repeated claims that the book was the product of his imagination, occultists were always fascinated by the idea that he had based his story on a real book.

In fact, modern occultists (known as "chaos magicians") believe that the entities of Lovecraft's horror stories can be magically summoned even though they are a work of fiction. According to chaos magicians, Lovecraft's entities now exist as thought-forms, and therefore spells to summon them will have tangible effects— at least psychologically.

In 1977, obsession with Lovecraft led an enterprising writer under the pseudonym Simon to write an "authentic" copy of *The Necronomicon*. This book may have originally been marketed as a joke or a novelty, but it became wildly popular. Teenagers from all over the country could now purchase a forbidden spell book in the metaphysical section of almost any bookstore. Following the murders, Ferrell and his friends performed a summoning ritual using *The Necronomicon* in a New Orleans cemetery.[48] (Bear in mind that casting spells in cemeteries was a regular activity for Ferrell and that this ritual may have had no direct relationship to the murder.)

Belanger indicated that in 2008 she was contacted by Heather Wendorf who had begun listening to her podcast, *Shadowdance*. Belanger was initially skeptical that this was "the real Heather" and mentioned that she did some research to confirm her identity. After this contact, Belanger feels she had a better understanding of Ferrell's interest in the paperback *Necronomicon*. The book contains of short glossary of Sumerian words, one of which, *akhkharu*, Simon translates as "vampire."[49] Belanger explained her theory that Ferrell was attempting to summon the *akhkharu* so that they would bestow their vampiric condition onto him and his friends. Interestingly, there is precedent for using *The Necronomicon* to become a vampire in this fashion. The vampiric publication *The Midnight Sun* contains an article in which the author pleads for help for her friend who summoned *akhkharu* and is now showing symptoms of psychic vampirism.[50] This article appeared in May 1996—only six months before Ferrell made his fateful drive to Florida. Even though Ferrell was living in an escapist fantasy, woven together from all manner of fantastic sources, Belanger conceded that his use of *The Necronomicon* could be considered an initiatory model of vampirism. To categorically deny that Ferrell is part of the vampire community would potentially exclude a number of other self-identified vampires who see vampirism as an occult initiation.

Logically a single tragic event does not indicate a link between the vampire community and murder. In fact, there is still no motive for the murder of the Wendorfs. It was not, as has been claimed, based on an occult belief. An early report on the murders cites a police statement that, "There were no ritualistic signs connected with the deaths."[51] Ferrell is quoted as saying, "I really don't understand it myself. There's really no reason. There never was."[52] Jaden testified that Ferrell had broken "vampire codes" by committing murder.[53] What codes he was referring to are unclear, but this does suggest that there was a vampire subculture that had been forming in Murray and that it did not condone murder. Belanger's theory is that Ferrell saw himself as protecting Heather Wendorf from overly controlling parents. She added that if there was anything at all about the murders related to the vampire community, it was the sense of family common to vampire groups. For Ferrell, this value became twisted and violent.

The Ferrell case presents a problem to the vampire community that is shared by many religious groups. While the overwhelming majority of Muslims are not terrorists, some are. While the overwhelming majority of Christians would never bomb an abortion clinic, some have. No group should be judged by its violent periphery; however, there is a problem in categorically excluding people like Ferrell from the group with which he identifies. Religion scholar Robert Orsi has written on how scholars were asked to delineate "good" and "bad" Muslims after September 11, 2001. He writes, "There was tremendous pressure to define a normative 'Islam' in contradistinction from whatever it was that motivated the men who flew their planes into the World Trade Center, who we were told (by the president of the United States among others) did not represent 'real' Islam."[54] Orsi points out that while this distinction is well intentioned, it is arrogant for American scholars to proclaim to the world what "real" Islam is. By the same token, a serious approach to the vampire community can neither generalize Ferrell's crimes to the entire community, nor dismiss Ferrell from the community *ipso facto* because he is a murderer.

Vampires on TV

In 2004, the SciFi channel's reality show *Mad, Mad House* introduced the world to Don Henrie. That same year, *CSI* did an episode called "Suckers" in which a murder leads crime scene investigators into the vampire subculture. Belanger believes that most of the research for this episode was done by looking at the Web site for The Sanguinarium. The Black Veil as well as other Sanguinarium terminology are cited throughout the episode. James Haven played a vampire in this episode and wore a vial of his lover's blood around his neck. This idea first appears in one of Anne Rice's books where a mortal wears a necklace containing his vampire patron's blood. The necklace serves as a signal to other vampires that he is protected and not to be eaten. (Not surprisingly, vials filled with FX blood are now a popular accessory among goths in the United Kingdom.)[55]

Interestingly, Haven's sister is actress Angelina Jolie, who has also expressed a fascination with vampires. She is rumored to have married her first husband, Jonny Lee Miller, while wearing a shirt with his name written on it in her own blood. She and her second husband, Billy Bob Thornton, were also rumored to have worn vials of each other's blood around their necks. These details seem to have at least some connection to an interest in vampires. Jolie was quoted in *The Daily Telegraph:*

> When I was 14, I collected knives. My first boyfriend and I ended up getting into some fighting in bed and being silly. People think that happens every time I go to bed. . . . It was actually something he never wanted to do again. It was a mistake and we really hurt ourselves. It was just being young, you know, when you're curious about vampires and that kind of thing. Just experimenting. It was an accident and I ended up in hospital.[56]

Jolie has since clarified that she did not wear a vial of blood but a bloody fingerprint more like "a flowerpress."[57]

If Jolie ever comes out as a vampire, it will be the media event of the year. In the meantime, producers are aggressively seeking less famous vampires to appear in numerous documentaries, talk shows, and reality television shows. Said one of my contacts:

> You have no idea how many inquiries members of the real vampire community actually receive in their mailboxes on a yearly basis—especially this last year alone. The media has gotten much better at actually locating the members in the community worthwhile to speak with, however, when it comes to an agreement to be signed to go in front of a camera—95% of us respond with the answer "No way."

At the time of this writing, HBO is vigorously promoting its new series *True Blood,* based on *The Southern Vampire Mysteries* by Charlaine Harris. Part of the campaign has involved "viral marketing" in which the lines between fiction and the real vampire community are deliberately blurred. *True Blood* briefly created a Web site claiming to have obtained via a hacker secret communications between vampires. Visitors to the site could watch clips of vampires from around the world talking to each other about the prospects of synthetic blood. There were also several clips in which vampires threatened the humans who had stumbled across their secret society. The Website did not say that it was promoting a television show on HBO but instead presented itself as an actual underground community of vampires. The strategy was that vampire fans would be intrigued and forward the Web site to their friends. Even as they sowed confusion, HBO media relations was fully aware of the real vampire community and sent a press release to Suscitatio Enterprises promoting the show. HBO's viral marketing is only the latest way in which the media has attempted to package the vampire community for a vampire-hungry public.

The Tyra Banks Show, Sean Hannity's America, and even *Good Morning America* have recently sought guests for vampire episodes. The reality show *Trading Spouses* attempted to find a vampire family, but was universally turned down by the community. Documentaries receive more consideration from vampires but are still regarded with suspicion. I was forwarded numerous e-mails from television producers in search of vampires. The requests ran the gamut from polite and informed to foolish and insensitive. Some even contained spelling errors. The majority of the projects were not actually about vampires, but rather wanted a vampire to appear alongside other "unusual characters."

A television station in the United Kingdom sought a vampire for a show about "incredible people from around the world." The History Channel wanted a vampire for a documentary on "Blood Rituals." The Women's Entertainment Channel found a female vampire to appear with a Wiccan and a Satanist for a show on women and the occult. The National Geographic channel offers a show called *Taboo* that explores exotic cultural practices. An episode on relationships had been planned to feature an African tribe in which men dance to attract wives and a man who had scarred the outline of his wife's hand into his chest. To complete the episode, they wanted a vampire couple to discuss blood drinking in their relationship. Finally, a vampire was sought for a Canadian show entitled, *TV Made Me Do It.* This may have been the most galling of the requests because it made no attempt to hide its assumption that vampirism is simply an imitation of television. An agent for the show stated, "My ideal character is a regular joe-shmoe type (ie. full-time student, housewife, stockbroker) who has a tightly knit vampire social network by night."

It is easy to see how frustrating these requests must be for vampires. The format of these programs offered no chance for vampires to explain themselves on their own terms: They could only present themselves within whatever category the show's producers had already cast them. I thought of my own identity as an Irish-American Catholic and how I would feel if producers wanted to contact my family members for documentaries such as "Incredible But True: People Who Pray to Saints" or "Immigrants Who Drink!" Not surprisingly, few vampires respond to these requests. However, a few vampires still hope that they can further their movement through an appearance on the right documentary.

Vampire Celebrities

While the majority of vampires are wary of the media, a few actively seek media attention. Misty was one of the earliest of these "vampire celebrities." She was approached by both Norine Dresser and Carol Page in their early works on the vampire community and apparently succeeded in annoying both writers severely. Misty claimed that she was dedicated to the cause of "vampire rights," however, Page portrays her as a somewhat disturbed woman who is profoundly starved for attention.[58]

Vlad, of Chicago, was another vampire celebrity who achieved widespread recognition in the 1990s. In addition to being the front man for the rock band Theatre of Darkness, Vlad would speak openly about drinking blood and achieving "serial immortality" through reincarnation. A self-described "media whore," he has appeared on numerous talk shows including *Sally Jessy Raphael, Joan*

Rivers, and *Montel Williams.* However, Martin V. Riccardo indicates that Vlad has since dropped out of the vampire scene.

Perhaps the most entertaining vampire celebrity is self-proclaimed "Satanic vampire" Jonathon "The Impaler" Sharkey. Sharkey filed with the Federal Election Commission as an independent candidate for president in 2004 and 2008. He has also run for congress in various states and under various conservative parties and ran for governor of Minnesota in 2006. In 2007, an independent filmmaker in Australia released a documentary about Sharkey entitled *Impaler.* In 2008, Sharkey ran for president as an independent, representing "The Vampyres, Witches, and Pagans Party," which he founded in 2005. The two pillars of Sharkey's campaign appear to be tolerance for alternative life-styles and the public execution by impalement of child molesters, rapists, drug dealers, terrorists, and George W. Bush. (Sharkey claims he was visited by the Secret Service in 2006.)

Sharkey is quoted in an interview with Citypages.com, "I *want* criminals to fear me. I want bin Laden and all his al Qaeda buddies to think back to when their ancestors, the Turks, were trying to invade Romania, and Vlad Tepes, Dracula, impaled them for it. I want them to think they're dealing with another Vlad Tepes. I want them to think of me as the impaling governor-slash-president." He is also quoted describing how he hates child molesters and has killed one using black magic, "And believe it or not, Satanists are against child molesters. I've had people from the Church of Satan contact me to deal with a pagan high priest who was molesting teenage girls. I'm into witchcraft and the black arts, so I cast a spell on this S.O.B. and he suffered a massive heart attack. He's not molesting children anymore."[59] It is sadly ironic that Sharkey sees himself as an advocate for minority religious and lifestyle groups yet simultaneously seeks political power by appealing to a xenophobic hatred of Muslims and Arabs.

Sharkey is not very active in the vampire community, although several of my contacts in Atlanta said that they had been contacted by him. The AVA regards Sharkey as a source of embarrassment and advised their members not to dignify his e-mails with a response. Vampire celebrities like Misty, Vlad, and Sharkey complicate the community's relationship with the media. They serve as a reminder that if vampires turn their back on the media, producers will always find *someone* who wants to be on television.

Out of the Shadows

Because most vampires value secrecy, the general public knows of the community only through questionable journalism and extremely peripheral figures such as Sharkey, or worse, Ferrell. Slowly the vampire community has begun to realize this and adopted strategies toward a more positive (but also more public) image. In 1999, Darkness Against Child Abuse (DACA) and Darkness Against Domestic Violence (DADV) were founded.[60] These groups are networks formed by the "dark community" defined as Pagans, Satanists, vampires, and others with "dark life-styles," for the purpose of improving society. DACA and DADV sponsor Web sites with resources on a variety of topics including child abuse and drug addiction. DACA's Web site features an Amber Alert ticker and photos of missing children. The site is currently maintained by Shadow Villanueva, who claims to be a licensed counselor.[61]

The AVA's survey is another method of countering negative characterizations of the vampire community by the media and academics. They have stated that by presenting statistical data on vampires they hope to raise the standard of evidence required to make statements about the community. They currently plan to release several books of qualitative and quantitative analysis from their survey. While these efforts may make life easier for vampires, it will also mean sacrificing some of the secrecy and mystique that many vampires still value. The shadows can no longer hold the vampire community: The only question now is how they choose to emerge from them.

CHAPTER 8

Vampires and the Modern

Americans may have no identity, but they do have wonderful teeth.

—*Jean Baudrillard*

One theory making its way through the vampire community is that vampires represent a new phase of human evolution. The VEWRS as well as other projects continue to search for evidence of a medical or scientific basis for modern vampires. Whether or not such evidence is ever found, the reality of vampires as an identity and as a community is a product of the modern world. We now live in an era of communication technology in which mainstream media can be circumvented and ignored, ideas can be disseminated with incredible speed, and global networks can be formed overnight. Modernity has heralded a new, more fluid notion of the self in which one's identity and life-style must be achieved in order to be meaningful. Vampires have emerged from these conditions and are uniquely adapted to them. The essentialist claims of real vampires represent a radically new form of self-narrative and a new type of community. They are a sign of the times and, for this reason, we ignore them at our peril.

Anthony Giddens and other social theorists have described how social identity has become disconnected from the contexts, communities, and expectations that once defined the individual's relationship to society. As an example of this, he describes his own modern identity crisis, "Here I am a name on a page; there I am a web-site address; elsewhere I am a national insurance number in a government computer."[1] Notice that Giddens's insight into the fragmented character of modern cultural identity is remarkably similar to the vampire philosophy of dayside and nightside personas. When our institutions no longer have the authority to tell us who we are, more and more aspects of identity are seen as achieved rather than ascribed. Vampires, along with therians and otherkin, represent the next phase of this process in which not only social identity but ontological and metaphysical identity have become subjective.

Furthermore, I predict that our society will not be able to ignore these identity claims. Sociologist Peter Berger argued that every society contains "a repertoire of identities."[2] As the community continues to evolve and crystalize, there will be an increasing awareness of vampires as a category of person. This will not only affect the vampires: All of our identities will be modified to accommodate this new category, causing us to think about ourselves in new ways. I was not born thinking of myself as a white, heterosexual, Irish-Catholic male. To achieve this identity, I had to form a concept of other races, sexual orientations, ethnic groups, religions, and genders. Because I am aware of the vampire community, I add "non-vampire" to my list of social markers. This is not merely political correctness. Discourse about vampires causes us to make these reactionary shifts in identity without realizing it. The self-appointed vampire slayers who have posted onto vampire forums and sent menacing e-mails to vampires are defining themselves in contradistinction to the vampire identity. Christine Wicker felt it necessary to state in her book *Not in Kansas Anymore: A Curious Tale of How Magic is Transforming America,* "I am *not* a vampire, a witch, a fairy, a wizard, an elf, a werewolf, an angel, or a devil."[3] These are only the first non-vampires whose identities will be changed as the vampires and other communities continue to affect discourse.

The community that has formed around the vampire identity is equally unprecedented and has no direct analogue. Vampirism is not a religion and the community does not resemble formal identity groups such as churches, clubs, or advocacy groups. Nor will the community as a whole ever have such a structure as long as vampires see their identity as essential rather than participatory. Because the community is united by a shared identity, it resembles an ascriptive identity group such as a race, gender, or sexual orientation. However, unlike a race or a gender, being a vampire is an identity that is not yet fully recognized by mainstream culture. In this way, the vampire community resembles the transgendered community: Mainstream culture has been critical of the claims of both identity groups, and both vampires and transgendered people have been characterized as mentally ill.

On the other hand, the claims of transgendered identity are relatively circumscribed. Outsiders can understand these claims, even if they do not accept them. By contrast, what it means to be a vampire is in a state of flux. There is no authority to assert a definition of vampirism, so the community defines itself through a continuous reflexive process. This is why the VEWRS is so significant: The data generated by this survey will ultimately serve to define the category.

Because of this reflexive quality, the closest analogue to the vampire community may actually be the autistic community. Like vampirism, the definition of the autism spectrum is in a state of flux. Survey data have had a vital role in how those who have autism as well as parents of autistic children define the condition. Several Web sites such as http://www.autismdata.org have been created by and for the autistic community to collect survey data. Indeed, this is the only other community that seems to be as preoccupied with introspective surveys as the vampire community.

Because autism is a condition endorsed by the medical establishment, it may seem to be "real" in a way that vampirism is not. Identity as a vampire is assumed to be subjective and contingent on cultural representations of vampires, and by contrast autism is thought to be an objective condition with a neurological basis that exists independently of culture. However, the experts who create the categories and ascribe people to them do not exist independently of culture. Autistic writer Rich Schull in *Autism: Pre Rain Man,* describes his suspicion of autistics who were diagnosed following Dustin Hoffman's portrayal of an autistic man in the 1988 film *Rain Man.* Schull argues that were it not for the effect of this film on our culture, many people would never have been diagnosed with autism and would have lived much happier lives. In a chapter entitled "Rain Man's Curse," he writes, "Just look at the Autistics in a group home after Rain Man and just find one pre-Rain Man?"[4] This *Rain Man* effect indicates that culturally based and scientifically based categories of people are not distinct, but run together.

Like vampires, advocates for the autistic community are in a process of redefining the definition of their shared social marker. Both vampirism and autism were originally conceived as highly negative conditions. The effort by some vampires to reframe themselves as "energy manipulators" rather than parasites is mirrored in the autistic community by the "neurodiversity movement." This movement, spearheaded by Web sites such as http://neurodiversity.com and http://autistics.org, argues that autism is not a disease but an alternative way of seeing the world with its own strengths and weaknesses. As with vampires, the Internet has been vital in bringing autistics together and allowing such advocacy efforts to form.[5] It may come as no surprise that Lupa's survey of otherkin found several respondents who identified as being on the autistic spectrum as well as several transgendered people.[6]

As a new and poorly understood identity group, the vampire community presents a challenge that a democratic society must ultimately address. How will mainstream culture adapt to a world inhabited by vampires, therians, and otherkin? The first court cases involving vampire identity have already taken place and at least one piece of anti-vampire legislation has been proposed. In 1990, Wisconsin senator James Baumgart proposed a bill that would have made it illegal to drink the blood of minors.[7] The proposed "vampire law" was a response to Philip K. Buck, also known as the "Sheboygen County Vampire." Buck had allegedly lured teenage girls into his home and convinced them to cut their wrists.[8] Because the girls had come of their own accord and Buck had not actually touched them, he could only be charged with fourth degree sexual assault, to which he pled no contest. Baumgart was quoted,

"If adults want to drink each other's blood, that's one thing, but kids have to be protected."

As the general public becomes aware of vampires, more legal questions will be raised. A high-profile discrimination case seems inevitable if someone is fired for being a vampire. When this case does happen, it will set an important legal precedent as to whether vampirism a religion, a life-style, a medical condition, or something else. Family law will also become significant as more vampires are having children. Pagans have long complained that their religious beliefs are used against them in custody battles. One can only imagine what visitation rights a divorced vampire might expect. Some vampires see their condition as genetic, which will in turn raise legal issues about raising children to be vampiric. Lady CG, a Canadian, described how all four of her children are vampires and that one of her grandchildren has already begun to show signs of being a vampire. In America, vampire families will play into a larger debate that has troubled this country: At what point does a parent's right to raise a child in their own culture infringe on the child's autonomy?

In April 2008, the Texas Department of Family and Child Protective Services removed 462 children from the Yearning for Zion Ranch, a community affiliated with the Fundamentalist Church of Jesus Christ of Latter-day Saints, on the grounds that they were potential victims of child abuse. The American public is far more familiar with fundamentalist Mormons then with vampires. If Child Protective Services is not reformed, it seems likely that vampire families will also be required to prove that they do not abuse their children.

Lady CG was understandably reluctant to speak to me at length about her family. However, she seemed considerate of her children's autonomy. She stated that she did not mention vampirism to them until they "showed signs of awakening and craving blood."[9] In an online article for other vampire parents entitled, "Raising a Crop 'O Vampires (Or HELP! My Teenager Wants to Eat the Dog!)," she states that no one under the age of 18 should be drinking human blood and that young sanguinarian vampires should sustain themselves on bloody steaks.[10] The tone in the final pages of Lady CG's book is optimistic: She closes by describing her vampire son playing with a non-vampire in the back-yard as a vision for a harmonious future.

With so many challenges ahead, it is easy to understand the sentiment of vampires like Stephen O'Mallie who feel the community should go back under-ground. But the community has received too much exposure to return to the shadows. Although the vampire community is a small minority, the questions such a group poses to a democratic society must inevitably be answered. Further-more, if the vampire community were to dissolve, the conditions that allowed it to thrive would still exist. The clock cannot be turned back: We now live in a world where ontological identity is subjective and achieved. The Ordo Strigoi Vii claims that we are seeing the dawn of the "Fifth Aeon of Humanity," in which mankind will become free of the bonds of religion and tradition. The idea of a Fifth Aeon does make a rather poetic illustration of the forces of modernity and the subjective notion of the self: It is possible that vampires come as the heralds of a brave new world of "ontological diversity." This will not mean the end of humanity, but it may mean that one's status as a member of the human species can no longer be taken for granted.

Notes

Preface

1. Bob Curan, *Encyclopedia of The Undead: A Field Guide to Creatures that Cannot Rest in Peace* (Franklin Lakes: Career Press, 2006), 36.

2. Sharon Schlegel, "Spiritual Sleuth Studies Violent Religions to Fight Crime," *Baptist Standard* 7 (November 2003).

3. Nancy Ammerman, "Religious Identities and Religious Institutions," in *Handbook of the Sociology of Religion,* ed. Michelle Dillon (Cambridge: Cambridge University Press, 2003), 215.

4. Katherine Ramsland, *Piercing the Darkness: Undercover with Vampires in America Today* (New York: HarperPrism, 1998), x.

5. Anthony Giddens, *Modernity and Self-Identity: Self and Society in the Late Modern Age* (Stanford: Stanford University Press, 1991), 2.

6. Ibid., 80–85.

7. Ibid., 5.

8. In analyzing the vampire identity, I am not taking a position on the reality of the vampire phenomenon. Many real vampires believe that they have an undiagnosed condition that may one day be discovered through empirical testing. However, if such a condition does exist, those who have it have not referred to themselves as vampires until the late twentieth century. Thus the vampire identity has a specific historical context that is distinct from the idea of a vampire phenomenon.

Chapter 1

1. Jan L. Perkowski, *The Darkling: A Treatise on Slavic Vampirism* (Columbus: Slavica Publishers Inc., 1989), 18.

2. "Archaeologists Find Grave of Suspected Vampire," *Prague Daily Monitor,* July 18, 2008, http://www.praguemonitor.com/en/377/czech_national_news/25427/ (accessed August 4, 2008).

3. Eric Nuzum, *The Dead Travel Fast: Stalking Vampires from Nosferatu to Count Chocula* (New York: Macmillan, 2007), 39.

4. Ibid.

5. Martha Rose Crow, "Are Vampire Capitalists About to Descend on Crisis Wrought Myanmar?," *Atlantic Free Press,* May 9, 2008.

6. Jeff Guinn and Andy Grieser, *Something in the Blood: The Underground World of Today's Vampires* (Arlington: The Summit Publishing Group, 1996), 19.

7. Norine Dresser, *American Vampires: Fans, Victims, Practitioners* (New York: Vintage Books, 1989), 30.

8. Maureen Dowd, "Desperately Seeking Street Cred," *New York Times,* April 27, 2008, Opinion section.

9. Rosemary Ellen Guiley, *The Complete Vampire Companion* (New York: Macmillan, 1994), 98.

10. Rosemary Ellen Guiley, *Vampires Among Us* (New York: Pocket Books, 1991), 85.

11. Ramsland, *Piercing the Darkness,* 53.

12. Katherine Ramsland, *The Science of Vampires* (New York: Berkeley Boulevard Books, 2002), 176.

13. Giddens, *Modernity and Self-Identity,* 80.

14. Margaret Mittelbach and Michael Crewdson, "To Die For: Painting the Town Red and the Capes and Nails Black," *New York Times,* November 24, 2000, Movies section.

15. Guinn and Grieser, *Something in the Blood,* 128–29.

16. Ramsland, *Science of Vampires,* 185.

17. Father Sebastiaan, personal communication with the author, July 20, 2008.

18. Suscitatio Enterprises, LLC, "Vampirism and Energy Research Study," http://www.suscitatio.com (accessed June 1, 2008).

19. Ibid. The Vampire and Energy Work Research Study surveyed 650 self-identified real vampires and energy workers between 2006 and 2007. Gaining any sort of quantitative data from real vampires is extremely difficult, and the results of the survey may not meet some scholarly standards for quantitative research. However, the preliminary results of the survey do contain some useful information that are almost certainly representative of larger trends within the vampire community.

20. Ibid.

21. Guinn and Grieser, *Something in the Blood,* 100.

22. Lady CG, *Practical Vampyrism for Modern Vampyres* (LuLu, 2005), 20–21.

23. Norma Myer, "First Rule of 'Bite' Club: Vampires Are People Too," *Copley News Service,* October 19, 2007, http://www.signonsandiego.com/news/features/20071019-9999-lz1c19vampire.html (accessed June 1, 2008).

24. Michelle Belanger, ed., *Vampires in Their Own Words: An Anthology of Vampire Voices* (Woodbury: Llewellyn, 2007), 100.

25. Guinn and Grieser, *Something in the Blood,* 83.

26. Sarah Dorrance, "Vampyres: Blood Safety and Feeding," Sanguinarius.org. For Real Vampires, http://www.sanguinarius.org/articles/feedprop.shtml (accessed June 1, 2008).

27. Lady CG, *Practical Vampyrism,* 72.

28. Suscitatio Enterprises, LLC, "Vampirism and Energy Research Study," http://www.suscitatio.com (accessed June 1, 2008).

29. Arlene Russo, *Vampire Nation* [uncorrected proof edition] (Woodbury: Llewellyn, 2008), 51.

30. Guiley, *Vampires Among Us,* 89.

31. Michelle Belanger and Chris Miller, "Vampires and Otherkin and Therians, Oh My!," *Shadowdance Podcast,* October 23, 2006.

32. Suscitatio Enterprises, LLC, "Vampirism and Energy Research Study," http://www.suscitatio.com (accessed June 1, 2008).

33. Guiley, *Vampires Among Us,* 19.

34. Lady CG, *Practical Vampyrism,* 77.

35. Father Sebastiaan, personal communication with the author, July 20, 2008.

36. Guinn and Grieser, *Something in the Blood,* 69.

37. Dresser, *American Vampires,* 23.

38. Guinn and Grieser, *Something in the Blood,* 84.

39. Lady CG, *Practical Vampyrism,* 52.

40. Roxana Stuart, *Stage Blood: Vampires of the 19th Century Stage* (Bowling Green: Bowling Green State University Popular Press, 1994), 19–20.

41. Guinn and Grieser, *Something in the Blood,* 156.

42. Kamara, "Inside the Life of a Real Vampire," *Journal of the Dark* no. 7 (1996): 44.

43. Ibid., 85.

44. Ramsland, *Science of Vampires ,* 244.

45. Martin V. Riccardo, *Liquid Dreams of Vampires* (St. Paul: Llewellyn, 1996), 201.

46. Brian J. Frost, *The Monster with a Thousand Faces: Guises of the Vampire in Myth and Literature* (Bowling Green: Bowling Green State University Popular Press, 1989), 89.

47. Guiley, *Vampires Among Us,* 76–77.

48. Ibid., 77–81.

49. Dresser, *American Vampires,* 29.

50. Russo, *Vampire Nation,* 125.

51. Guinn and Grieser, *Something in the Blood,* 68.

52. Ramsland, *Piercing the Darkness,* 191.

53. Terrence Hines, *Pseudoscience and the Paranormal* (Amherst: Prometheus Books, 2003), 113.

54. Michelle Belanger, research interview with the author, July 15, 2008.

55. Riccardo, *Liquid Dreams of Vampires,* 201.

56. Belanger and Miller, "Vampires and Otherkin and Therians."

57. Belanger, *Vampires in Their Own Words,* 33.

58. Konstantinos, *Vampires: The Occult Truth* (St. Paul: Llewellyn, 1998), 148.

59. Ramsland, *Piercing the Darkness,* 203–4.

60. Belanger, *Vampires in Their Own Words,* 32.

61. Michelle Belanger, *The Psychic Vampire Codex* (Boston: Weiser Books, 2004), 96.

62. Ibid., 100.

63. Ibid., 101.

64. Ibid., 104.

65. Ibid., 105.

66. Belanger, *Vampires in Their Own Words,* 22.

67. Ibid., 80.

68. Michelle Belanger, *Sacred Hunger* (Fort Wayne: Dark Moon Press, 2005), 22.

69. Paul Barber, *Vampires, Burial, and Death* (New Haven: Yale University Press, 1988), 30–31.

70. Dawn Perlmutter, "Vampire Culture," in *Religion and American Cultures: An Encyclopedia of Traditions, Diversity, and Popular Expressions,* ed. Gary Laderman (Santa Barbara: ABC-CLIO, 2003), 279–83.

71. Chris Barker and Paul Willis, *Cultural Studies: Theory and Practice* (Los Angeles: Sage Publications, 2003), 221.

72. BDSM is a complex acronym derived from the terms "bondage and discipline," "domination and submission," and "sadism and masochism." The community that engages in these activities generally prefers this acronym to the term sado-masochism.

73. Suscitatio Enterprises, LLC, "Vampirism and Energy Research Study," http://www.suscitatio.com (accessed June 1, 2008).

74. Mircea Eliade, *Shamanism: Archaic Techniques of Ecstasy* (Princeton: Princeton University Press, 1964), 18.

75. Belanger, *Psychic Vampire Codex,* 14.

76. Amy Gutman, *Identity in Democracy* (Princeton: Princeton University Press, 2003), 9.

77. Corvis Nocturnum, *Embracing the Darkness: Understanding Dark Subcultures* (Fort Wayne: Dark Moon Press, 2005), 107.

78. Montague Summers, *The Vampire* (New York: Dorset Press, 1991), 78.

79. Bram Stoker, *Dracula* (New York: Scholastic Inc., 1999), 398.

80. Emily de Laszowska Gerard, "Transylvanian Superstitions," in *The Nineteenth Century: A Monthly Review,* vol. 18, ed. James Knowles (London: Kegan Paul, Trench & Co., 1885), 136.

81. Eric Nuzum, "How to Become a Vampire in Six Easy Lessons," Eric Nuzum dot com, http://ericnuzum.typepad.com/eric_nuzum_dot_com/2006/03/how_to_become_a.html (accessed June 1, 2008).

82. Ramsland, *Science of Vampires,* 91.

83. Guiley, *Vampires Among Us,* 11–13.

Chapter 2

1. Dresser, *American Vampires,* 10.

2. Ibid., 174–81.

3. Tony Thorne, *Children of the Night: Of Vampires and Vampirism* (London: Indigo, 1999), 134.

4. Philip D. Jaffé and Drank DiCataldo, "Clinical Vampirism: Blending Myth and Reality," in *The Vampire: A Casebook,* ed. Alan Dundes (Madison: The University of Wisconsin Press, 1998), 144.

5. Ibid., 148.

6. Ibid., 143.

7. The American Psychiatric Association, *The Diagnostic and Statistical Manual of Mental Disorders: DSM-IV-TR* (Arlington: American Psychiatric Association, 2000).

8. Guiley, *Complete Vampire Companion,* 179.

9. Guiley, *Vampires Among Us,* 75.

10. Ramsland, *Science of Vampires,* 191–92.

11. Suscitatio Enterprises, LLC, "Vampirism and Energy Research Study," http://www
.suscitatio.com (accessed June 1, 2008).

12. Lady CG, personal communication with the author, July 26, 2008.

13. Inanna Arthen, "'Real Vampires' Revisited: In which I Clarify, Correct, and
Recant Some Things," http://bylightunseen.net/revisit.htm (accessed August 21, 2008.).
Inanna Arthen, also known by her community name "Vyrdolak," holds Master of Divin-
ity from Harvard and is an intellectual leader in the vampire community.

14. J. Gordon Melton, *The Vampire Book: The Encyclopedia of the Undead* (Detroit:
Visible Ink Press, 1999), 551.

15. Ibid., 552.

16. Ibid., 553.

17. Ramsland, *Science of Vampires,* 185.

18. Dresser, *American Vampires,* 38.

19. Transcript from Voices of the Vampire Community, Public Meeting, April 27,
2008.

20. Arthen, "'Real Vampires' Revisited."

21. Ian Hacking, "Making up People" in *Reconstructing Individuality: Autonomy, Individuality, and the Self in Western Thought,* eds. Thomas C. Heller, Morton Sosna, and
Daved E. Wellbey (Stanford, CA: Stanford University Press, 1986).

22. Montague Summers, *Werewolf* (Whitefish: Kessinger Publishing, 2003), 230–34.

23. Belanger, *Psychic Vampire Codex,* 65.

24. Belanger and Miller, "Vampires and Otherkin and Therians."

25. Guiley, *Vampires Among Us,* 12.

26. Claire Fanger, "Mirror, Mask and Anti-Self: Forces of Literary Creation in Dion
Fortune and W. B. Yeats," in *Esotericism, Art, and Imagination,* ed. Arthur Versluis et al.
(East Lansing: Michigan State University Press, 2008), 174.

27. Michel Foucault, "Technologies of the Self," in *Technologies of the Self: A Seminar
with Michel Foucault,* ed. Luther H. Martin, Huck Gutman, and Patrick H. Hutton
(Boston: University of Massachusetts Press, 1988), 18.

28. David A. Palmer, *Qigong Fever* (New York: Columbia University Press, 2007), 8.

29. By describing vampirism as a technology of the self, I do not mean to imply that
the subjective experiences reported by vampires are psychosomatic or have no basis in
reality. Like other researchers, I have no way to evaluate these experiences, and it is not
my place to do so. Rather, I suggest that vampire discourse has provided a context by
which these experiences can be described and incorporated into a meaningful identity.
By arriving at this identity and attending to the needs that this identity entails, vampires
are able to "attain a certain state of happiness, purity, wisdom, perfection, or immortality." (Michel Foucault et al., *Technologies of the Self: A Seminar with Michel Foucault*
[Amherst, University of Massachusetts Press, 1988], 18).

30. Voice of the Vampire Community.

31. Christopher Lasch, "From the Culture of Narcissism," in *The Eighties: A Reader,*
ed. Gilbert T. Sewall (New York: Perseus Books, 1998), 4.

32. Ibid.

33. Stacey Abbot, *Celluloid Vampires: Life after Death in the Modern World* (Austin: University of Texas Press, 2007), 206.

34. Anne Rice, "Essay on Earlier Works," AnneRice.com, http://www.annerice.com/Bookshelf-EarlierWorks.html (accessed June 25, 2008).

35. Michelle Belanger and Chris Miller, "Drama, Roleplay, and Ritual," *Shadowdance Podcast,* June 25, 2007.

36. Guinn and Grieser, *Something in the Blood,* 172.

37. Tony Walter and Helen Waterhouse, "A Very Private Belief: Reincarnation in Contemporary England," *Sociology of Religion* 60, no. 2 (1999): 195.

38. Paul Heelas and Linda Woodhead, *The Spiritual Revolution: Why Religion Is Giving Way to Spirituality* (Malden: Blackwell Publishing, 2005), 2.

39. Christopher Partridge, *The Re-Enchantment of the West,* 2 vols. (London: T&T Clark International, 2004–2005).

40. Max Weber, "Science as a Vocation," in *From Max Weber, Essays in Sociology,* ed. Hans H. Gerth and C. Wright Mills (New York: Oxford University Press, 1958), 139.

41. Ibid., 7.

42. Daniel Martin and Gary Alan Fine, "Satanic Cults, Satanic Play: Is 'Dungeons and Dragons' a Breeding Ground for the Devil?" in *The Satanism Scare,* ed. James T. Richardson, Joel Best, and David G. Bromley (New York: Aldine de Groyer, 1991), 121.

Chapter 3

1. Colin Campbell, "The Cult, the Cultic Milieu, and Secularization," in *The Cultic Milieu: Oppositional Subcultures in an Age of Globalization,* ed. Jeffrey Kaplan and Helene Loow (Oxford: AltaMira Press, 2002), 12–15.

2. Massimo Introvigne, "The Gothic Milieu," in *The Cultic Milieu: Oppositional Subcultures in an Age of Globalization,* ed. Jeffrey Kaplan and Helene Loow (Oxford: AltaMira Press, 2002), 138–51.

3. Ramsland, *Piercing the Darkness,* 109.

4. Barber, *Vampires, Burial, and Death,* 46.

5. Ibid., 25.

6. Johnson, V. M., *Dhampir: Child of the Blood* (Fairfield: Mystic Rose Books, 1996), 23.

7. Suscitatio Enterprises, LLC, "Vampirism and Energy Research Study," http://www.suscitatio.com (accessed June 1, 2008).

8. Ramsland, *Piercing the Darkness,* 66.

9. Ann Swidler, "Culture in Action: Symbols and Strategies," *American Sociological Review* 51 (1986): 273–86.

10. Dresser describes the constant stream of vampire puns that her colleagues subjected her to while doing her research. I had the same experience during my own research. Typically these puns reference teeth, blood, biting, and sucking. None of these vampire puns are actually funny, and Dresser suggests that their function is actually to deal with the anxiety that vampires create as powerful symbols of sex and death. (Dresser, *American Vampires,* 166).

11. Dressser, *American Vampires,* 82.

12. Clay Thompson, "Slaying Vampire Energy Is Easy—Just Unplug Idle Appliances" in *The Arizona Republic,* June 29, 2008.

13. Stuart, *Stage Blood,* 131.

14. Belanger, *Psychic Vampire Codex,* 37.

15. Stuart, *Stage Blood,* 27–28.

16. Ann Radcliffe, *The Italian* (Oxford: Oxford University Press, 1981), 34–35.

17. Guinn and Grieser, *Something in the Blood,* 20–24.

18. Ibid.

19. Fear of immigrants continues to play a heavy role in French politics as in America. See Gerald M. DiGusto and Seth K. Jolly, "French Xenophobia and the Radical Right: Public Attitudes Toward Immigration," (Paper presented at The Workshop on the Politics of Change at the Felix Meritis Centre for Arts, Culture, and Science in Amersterdam, 13–14 June, 2008.) http://www.unc.edu/depts/europe/conferences/poc2008/papers/Jolly_FrenchXenophobia.pdf (accessed October 5, 2008).

20. Stuart, *Stage Blood,* 58.

21. Guiley, *Complete Vampire Companion,* 55.

22. Peter Haining, *The Dracula Scrapbook* (London: Chancellor Press, 1992), 13.

23. John L. Flynn, *Cinematic Vampires: The Living Dead of Film and Television* (Jefferson: McFarland and Company, Inc., 1992), 11.

24. Beth E. McDonald, *The Vampire as a Numinous Experience: Spiritual Journeys with the Undead in British and American Literature* (Jefferson: McFarland and Company, 2004), 87.

25. Ibid.

26. Nuzum, *The Dead Travel Fast,* 58–59.

27. Curan, *Encyclopedia of The Undead,* 64–65.

28. William Patrick Day, *Vampire Legends in Contemporary American Culture* (Lexington: The University Press of Kentucky, 2002), 35.

29. Deborah Wilson Overstreet, *Not Your Mother's Vampire: Vampires in Young Adult Fiction* (Lanham: The Scarecrow Press, Inc., 2006), 109.

30. Day, *Vampire Legends,* 35.

31. Abbot, *Celluloid Vampires,* 81.

32. Belanger, *Psychic Vampire Codex,* 260.

33. Ramsland, *Piercing the Darkness,* 71.

34. Ramsland, *Science of Vampires,* 48.

35. Dresser, *American Vampires,* 126.

36. Day, *Vampire Legends,* 41–42.

37. Melton, *Vampire Book,* 50.

38. John Clute and John Grant, *The Encyclopedia of Fantasy* (London: St. Martin's Griffin, 1999), 314–15.

39. McDonald, *Vampire as a Numinous Experience,* 129.

40. Abbot, *Celluloid Vampires,* 80–81.

41. Anne Rice, "Essay on Earlier Works," August 15, 2007, http://www.annerice.com/Bookshelf-EarlierWorks.html (accessed June 25, 2008).

42. Stuart, *Stage Blood,* 183.

43. Anne Rice, *Interview with the Vampire* (New York: Ballantine Books, 1976), 284.

44. Riccardo, *Liquid Dreams of Vampires,* 227.

45. Ramsland, *Science of Vampires,* 207.

46. Belanger, *Vampires in Their Own Words,* 35.

47. Ramsland, *Science of Vampires,* 223.

48. Bruce A. McClelland, *Slayers and Their Vampires* (Ann Arbor: University of Michigan Press, 2006), 178.

49. Mark Allen Peterson, "Consuming Youth: Vampires, Cyborgs, and the Culture of Consumption (review)," *Journal of American Folklore* 117, no. 464 (2004): 215.

50. Lynn Schofield Clark, *From Angels to Aliens: Teenagers, the Media, and the Supernatural* (Oxford: Oxford University Press, 2003), 4.

51. "500,000 Women Abandoning Church Every Year as Buffy the Vampire Slayer Turns Them on to Witchcraft," ThisIsLondon.co.uk, http://www.thisislondon.co.uk/news/article-23543421-details/50,000+women+abandoning+church+every+year+as+Buffy+the+Vampire+Slayer+turns+them+on+to+witchcraft/article.do (accessed August 26, 2008).

52. James Ellis, "Don Henrie," *The Metro* (September 15, 2004), http://www.metro.co.uk/fame/interviews/article.html?in_article_id=80&in_page_id=11 (accessed August 26, 2008).

53. Anonymous, "From Dusk 'Til Dawn—Don't Give up the Day Job," *Midnight Sun* 1, no. 5 (1996): 7.

54. Rhonda V. Wilcox and David Lavery, eds., *Fighting the Forces: What's at Stake in Buffy the Vampire Slayer* (New York: Rowman and Littlefield Publishers, 2002), xix.

55. Mary Alice Money, "The Undemonization of Supporting Characters in *Buffy,*" in *Fighting the Forces: What's at Stake in Buffy the Vampire Slayer,* ed. Rhonda V. Wilcox and David Lavery (New York: Rowman and Littlefield Publishers, 2002), 101.

56. Thorne, *Children of the Night,* 199.

57. Carol A. Senf, "Daughters of Lilith: Women Vampires in Popular Literature," in *The Blood is the Life: Vampires in Literature,* ed. Leonard G. Hildreth and Mary Pharr (Bowling Green: Bowling Green State University Popular Press, 1999), 211.

58. Paul Barber, "Forensic Pathology and the European Vampire," in *The Vampire: A Casebook,* ed. Alan Dundes (Madison: The University of Wisconsin Press, 1998), 109.

59. Dom Augustine Calmet, *The Phantom World; or, The Philosophy of Spirits, Apparitions,* trans. Henry Christmas (London: Richard Bentley, 1850), 324.

60. Ibid., 283.

61. Gary Laderman, *The Sacred Remains: American Attitudes Toward Death* (New Haven: Yale University Press, 1996), 170.

62. Hines, *Pseudoscience and the Paranormal,* 50.

63. Frost, *Monster with a Thousand Faces,* 15.

64. Eliphaz Levi, *Dogma et Ritual de la Haute Magie,* trans. A. E. Waite (London: Rider and Company, 1896), 68.

65. Ibid.

66. Melton, *Vampire Book,* 522.

67. Z. J. Piérart, *Review Spiritualiste* (Paris: Bureaux, 1861), 106.

68. Calmet, *Phantom World,* 327.

69. Helena Petrovna Blavatsky, *Isis Unveiled* (Point Loma: Aryan Theosophical Press, 1919), 453.

70. Charles W. Leadbeater, *The Astral Plane: Its Scenery, Habits, and Phenomena* (New York: Cosimo, Inc., 1995), 42–43.

71. Henry Steel Olcott, "The Vampire," in *The Theosophist: October 1890–April 1891,* ed. Henry Steel Olcott (Whitefish: Kessinger Publishing, 2004), 385–93.

72. Melton, *Vampire Book,* 330–31.

73. Helena Petrovna Blavatsky, *Studies in Occultism,* vol. 2 (Boston: New England Theosophical Corporation, 1895), 56.

74. Summers, *Vampire,* 123.

75. Ramsland, *Piercing the Darkness,* 41.

76. Reverend Vicutus, "Recommended Reading," http://www.ordo-sekhemu.org/, (accessed June 30 2008).

77. Alex Owen, *The Place of Enchantment: British Occultism and the Culture of the Modern* (Chicago: University of Chicago Press, 2004), 72.

78. V. H. Frater Resurgam, "Thoughts on the Imagination" in *Flying Roll No. V,* http://www.osogd.org/library/rolls/roll05.html (accessed April 8, 2008).

79. Belanger, *Psychic Vampire Codex,* 259.

80. William James, *The Principles of Psychology* (New York: Dover Publications, 1950), 162–76.

81. Frater Sup Spe, "An Exorcism" in *Flying Roll No. XXXIV,* http://www.golden-dawn.org/gd_fr34.htm (accessed April 8, 2008).

82. Laurence Oliphant, *Scientific Religion or Higher Possibilities of Life and Practice through the Operation of Natural Forces* (London: William Blackwood and Sons, 1888), 171.

83. Ibid.

84. Albert Osborne Eaves, *Modern Vampirism: Its Dangers and How to Avoid Them* (Harrogate: Talisman Publishing, 1904), 19.

85. Summers, *Vampire,* 176.

86. Mary K. Greer, *Women of the Golden Dawn: Rebels and Priestesses* (Rochester: Park Street Press, 1995), 452.

87. Dion Fortune, *Psychic Self-Defense* (York Beach: Samuel Weiser, Inc., 1997), 48.

88. In 2001, Red Wheel publishers produced their sixth printing of this book.

89. Belanger, *Sacred Hunger,* 32.

90. Ibid., 34.

91. Eugene Robinson, "Interview with Anton LaVey" in *Birth of Tragedy,* no. 4 (November 1986), http://www.churchofsatan.com/Pages/BOT.html (accessed July 21, 2008).

92. Anton Szandor LaVey, *The Satanic Bible* (New York: Avon Books, 1977), 25.

93. Stephen Kaplan and Carol Kane, *Vampires Are* (Palm Springs: ETC Publications, 1984), 154.

94. Ramsland, *Piercing the Darkness,* 191.

95. Judith Orloff, "Energy Vampires," http://www.oprah.com/health/omag/health_omag_200204_energy.jhtml (accessed April 11, 2008.)

96. Catherine L. Albanese, *A Republic of Mind and Spirit: A Cultural History of American Metaphysical Religion* (New Haven: Yale University Press, 2007), 6–7.

97. Barber, *Vampires, Burial, and Death,* 178–79.

98. Summers, *Vampire,* 122.

99. Sanford E. Marovitz, "Poe's Reception of C. W. Webber's Gothic Western, 'Jack Long; or, The Shot in the Eye'," *Poe Studies* 4, no. 1 (1971): 11.

100. Jean L. Silver-Isenstadt, *Shameless: The Visionary Life of Mary Grove Nichols* (Baltimore: The Johns Hopkins University Press, 2002), 86.

101. Ibid.

102. Stoehr, Taylor. *Hawthorne's Mad Scientists: Pseudoscience and Social Science in Nineteenth Century Life and Letters* (Hamden: Archon Books, 1978), 202.

103. I. Bernard Cohen, *Science and the Founding Fathers* (New York: W.W. Norton and Company, 1995), 185.

104. Albanese, *Republic of Mind and Spirit,* 226.

105. Charles W. Webber, *Yieger's Cabinet: Spiritual Vampirism: The History of Etherial Softdown and her New Friends of the "Inner Light"* (Philadelphia: Lippincott, Grambo, and Co., 1853), 15.

106. Albanese, *Republic of Mind and Spirit,* 402.

107. Guiley, *Vampires Among Us,* 203–4.

108. Glenn T. Morris, *Path Notes of an American Ninja Master* (Berkeley: North Atlantic Books, 1993), 144.

109. Inanna Arthen, personal communication with the author, July 22, 2008.

110. Belanger, *Sacred Hunger,* 32–33.

111. Ramsland, *Science of Vampires,* 78.

112. Shannon Appelcline, "A Brief History of Game #11" February 1, 2007, http://www.rpg.net/columns/briefhistory/briefhistory11.phtml (accessed August 26, 2008).

113. Ibid.

114. Frater Shinobi, "Vampire/Lycanthrope: As Above, So Below," *Midnight Sun* 1, no. 1 (1995): 6.

115. Frater Shinobi, "Of the Undead/Vampyre Order," *Midnight Sun* 1, no. 5 (1996): 4.

116. Thorne, *Children of the Night,* 193.

117. Sebastian Cade Blackstock, "Suspension of Disbelief," *Journal of the Dark* no. 2 (Spring 1995): 26.

118. Ramsland, *Piercing the Darkness,* 105.

119. Johnson, *Dhampir: Child of the Blood,* 101.

120. Ramsland, *Piercing the Darkness,* 213.

121. Belanger, *Psychic Vampire Codex,* 19–25.

122. Johnson, *Dhampir: Child of the Blood,* 135–38.

123. Ibid., 50. I should mention here that Johnson's book is peripheral to the vampire community. I showed a copy of it to one AVA member who had never heard of it.

124. Belanger, *Psychic Vampire Codex,* 21.

125. Sam Chupp, personal communication with the author, August 12, 2008.

126. Aphrodite Jones, *The Embrace* (New York: Pocket Books, 1999), 308.

127. Ibid., 26.

128. Melton, *Vampire Book,* 802.

129. Guiley, *Vampires Among Us,* 73.

130. Ibid., 91.

131. Kaplan and Kane, *Vampires Are,* 66.

132. Guiley, *Vampires Among Us,* 84–86.

133. Frost, *Monster with a Thousand Faces,* 20.

134. Ibid.

135. The Vampire Empire, "The Vampire Bookshop," http://wiki.benecke.com/index.php?title=2007-07-23_The_Vampire_Empire (accessed June 30, 2008).

136. Guinn and Grieser, *Something in the Blood,* 14.

137. Suscitatio Enterprises has continued to receive questionnaires since the survey was officially closed. As of February 2009, 908 people have completed the basic survey.

138. A selected bibliography from Suscitatio Enterprises included John W. Creswell, *Qualitative Inquiry and Research Design: Choosing among Five Traditions* (Thousand Oaks, CA: Sage Publications, 1998.); John W. Creswell, *Research Design: Qualitative, Quantitative, and Mixed Methods Approaches* (Thousand Oaks, CA: Sage Publications, 2003); Floyd J. Fowler, *Improving Survey Questions : Design and Evaluation* (Thousand Oaks, CA: Sage Publications, 1995); Etzel Cardena, Steven Jay Lynn, and Stanley C. Krippner, *Varieties of Anomalous Experience: Examining the Scientific Evidence* (Washington, DC: American Psychological Association, 2000).

139. Suscitatio Enterprises, *Definitions and Precedent* (2008), http://www.suscitatio.com/research/definitions.html (accessed January 8, 2008).

140. Guiley, *Complete Vampire Companion,* 179.

141. Hacking, *Reconstructing Individuality,* 226.

142. Ron Eyerman and Andrew Jamison, *Social Movements: A Cognitive Approach* (University Park: Pennsylvania State University Press, 1991), 20.

Chapter 4

1. Graham Harvey, *Contemporary Paganism: Listening People, Speaking Earth* (New York: New York University Press, 1997), 97.

2. Douglas Renfrew Brooks, *The Secret of the Three Cities: An Introduction to Hindu Shakta Tantrism* (Chicago, University of Chicago Press, 1990), 28.

3. Georg Feuerstein, *Tantra: The Path of Ecstasy* (Boston: Shambala, 1998), 101.

4. Ibid., 8.

5. Ibid., 81.

6. Westerners probably interpreted *dakshinachara* and *vamachara* in reference to Matthew 25:31–46. In this passage, Jesus gives a parable about a shepherd sorting his flock, assigning sheep to his right hand and goats to his left. The sheep represent the righteous who shall receive eternal life. The goats, however, are bound for eternal punishment in "the eternal fire prepared for the devil and his angels." (Matt 25:41 [New Revised Standard Edition]). This passage may have led Blavatsky and others to equate vamachara with the demonic.

7. Richard Sutcliffe, "Left-Hand Path Ritual Magick: An Historical and Philosophical Overview," in *Paganism Today,* ed. Charlotte Hardman and Graham Harvey (San Francisco: Thorsons, 1996), 131.

8. Partridge, *Re-Enchantment of the West,* vol. 2, 223.

9. Dresser, *American Vampires,* 33.

10. Joe Abrams, "The Temple of Set," December 8, 2000, http://web.archive.org/web/20060828130023/religiousmovements.lib.virginia.edu/nrms/satanism/tempset.html, (accessed August 26, 2008).

11. Dresser, *American Vampires,* 34.

12. Abrams, *The Temple of Set.*

13. Lilith Aquino et al., "The Order of the Vampyre" http://www.xeper.org/ovampyre/ (accessed August 26, 2008).

14. Ibid., 34.

15. Dresser, *American Vampires,* 35.

16. Aquino et al., "The Order of the Vampyre."

17. Ibid.

18. Partridge, *Re-Enchantment of the West,* vol. 2, 226.

19. Christopher Partridge, "The Temple of the Vampire," in *New Religions: A Guide,* ed. Christopher Partridge (New York: Oxford University Press, 2004), 353.

20. Nocturnum, *Embracing the Darkness,* 124.

21. Partridge, *New Religions,* 353–54.

22. Russo, *Vampire Nation,* 164.

23. Ibid., 55.

24. Belanger, *Psychic Vampire Codex,* 27.

25. Belanger, personal communication with the author, July 15, 2008.

26. *The Vampire Bible,* August 12, 1996, http://www.arcane-archive.org/religion/ satanism/the-vampire-bible-part-one-1.php (accessed June 6, 2008).

27. Temple of the Vampire, http://www.vampiretemple.com (accessed June 1, 2008).

28. Ibid.

29. Guinn and Grieser, *Something in the Blood,* 52.

30. Ibid., 51.

31. Nicholas, personal communication with the author, August 9, 2008.

32. Introvigne, *Cultic Milieu,* 148.

33. Ibid., 126.

34. From my observation, I did not see any evidence that vampires were preoccupied with eschatology. The Temple of the Vampire was the only group to promote eschatological themes and they have since ceased to discuss this belief publicly.

35. Temple of the Vampire, http://www.vampiretemple.com (accessed June 1, 2008).

36. Radu Florescu and Raymond T. McNally, *Dracula: A Biography of Vlad the Impaler, 1431–1476* (New York: Hawthorn Books, 1973), 167.

37. Theresa Bane, *Actual Factual: Dracula, a Compendium of Vampires* (Randleman: Ne Deo Press, 1997), 272.

38. Michelle Belanger, "Living Vampires in Romania," in *Midnight Sun,* vol. 1, no. 2 (1995): 5.

39. Belanger, *Psychic Vampire Codex,* 31.

40. Sebastiaan van Houten, http://fathersebastian.livejournal.com/ (accessed August 8, 2008).

41. Michelle Belanger, http://michellebelanger.com/v-web/bulletin/bb/viewtopic.php ?t=1260 (accessed June 6, 2008).

42. Father Sebastiaan, *The Sanguinomicon: Book III, Liber Calmae, Limited 666 edition* (New York: Rakasha Books, 2004), 89. Romanian uses a variation of the Latin alphabet. While most writers transliterate this term as "strigoi mort," the Ordo Strigoi Vii consistently uses the spelling "strigoi morte" to describe this type of vampiric entity.

43. The Sanguinarium, *The Scroll of Elorath* (Lulu, 2007), 16.

44. Father Sebastiaan, *Saguninomicon-V Edition* (Netherlands: The Sanguinarium, 2007), 13.

45. Ibid., 16.

46. "Kemetic Order of Aset-Ka," http://www.asetka.org/asetians.html (accessed August 8, 2008).

47. Russo, *Vampire Nation,* 177–84.

48. Ibid.

49. Suscitatio Enterprises, *Definitions and Precedent* (2008), http://www .suscitatio.com/research/definitions.html (accessed January 8, 2008).

50. Robert Bellah et al. *Habits of the Heart* (Berkeley: University of California Press, 1985), 233.

51. Ibid.

Chapter 5

1. Guinn and Grieser, *Something in the Blood,* 95.

2. Belanger, *Psychic Vampire Codex,* 17.

3. Belanger, *Sacred Hunger,* 40.

4. Father Sebastiaan, personal communication with the author, 2008.

5. Carol Page, *Bloodlust: Conversations with Real Vampires* (New York: Dell, 1991), 96.

6. Riccardo, *Liquid Dreams of Vampires,* 215.

7. Guinn and Grieser, *Something in the Blood,* 27.

8. Neil Steinberg, "Out of Time, Nearly: Feast of Fools," in *Chicago Sun-Times,* August 15, 2007.

9. Belanger, *Psychic Vampire Codex,* 20.

10. Dawn Perlmutter, "The Sacrificial Aesthetic: Blood Rituals from Art to Murder," *Anthropoetics,* 5, no. 2 (2000), http://www.anthropoetics.ucla.edu/ap0902/sacrifice.htm (accessed June 1, 2008).

11. Sylvere Lotringer, *Overexposed: Treating Sexual Perversion in America* (New York: Pantheon, 1988), 22.

12. Sebastiaan van Houten, *Vampyre Alamanac 2006* (New York: Rakasha Books, 2005), 78.

13. Haining, *Dracula Scrapbook,* 135–39.

14. Frost, *Monster with a Thousand Faces,* 14.

15. Haining, *Dracula Scrapbook,* 135–39.

16. Noll, *Bizarre Diseases of the Mind,* 91.

17. Russo, *Vampire Nation,* 171.

18. Jerry Hopkins and Danny Sugerman, *No One Here Gets Out Alive* (New York: Grand Central Publishing, 1995), 295–96.

19. Ordo Sekhemu, http://www.ordo-sekhemu.org/blackFAQ.shtml (accessed June 25, 2008).

20. Guiley, *Vampires Among Us,* 33.

21. Haining, *Dracula Scrapbook,* 174.

22. Page, *Bloodlust,* 82.

23. House Dark Haven, http://www.housedarkhaven.com/history.html (accessed June 25, 2008).

24. House Sahjaza, http://www.sahjaza.com (accessed June 25, 2008).

25. Ibid.

26. Inanna Arthen, "Real Vampires," *Fireheart,* no. 2, http://www.earthspirit,com/fireheart/fhvampire.html (accessed June 25, 2008).

27. Belanger, *Psychic Vampire Codex,* 15.

28. Guinn and Grieser, *Something in the Blood,* 49.

29. Campbell, *Cultic Milieu,* 15.

30. Belanger, *Psychic Vampire Codex,* 14.

31. Page, *Bloodlust,* 155; 201.

32. Guinn and Grieser, *Something in the Blood,* 48.

33. Belanger, *Psychic Vampire Codex,* 31.

34. Guinn and Grieser, *Something in the Blood,* 48.

35. Belanger, *Psychic Vampire Codex,* 18.

36. Guinn and Gieser, *Something in the Blood,* 42.

37. The Gnostics (from the Greek *gnosis,* meaning wisdom) were a heretical sect who believed that the world was evil and could only be escaped through occult knowledge.

38. Harold Bloom, *The American Religion* (New York: Simon and Schuster, 1992), 36.

39. Partridge, *Re-Enchantment of the West,* vol. 2, 148.

40. Pamela, "Vampire? Fake! The Story of Vincent Tremaine," *Journal of the Dark,* no. 1 (1994): 21–23.

41. Daemonox, personal communication with the author, August 4, 2008.

42. Belanger, *Psychic Vampire Codex,* 20.

43. Arthen, personal communication with the author, July 27, 2008.

44. Ibid., 149.

45. Voices of the Vampire Community public meeting transcript, April 27, 2008, http://www.veritasvosliberabit.com/vvc.html (accessed July 7, 2008).

46. Ramsland, *Piercing the Darkness,* 109.

47. Ibid., 104–8.

48. Father Sebastiaan, personal communication, 2008.

49. Russo, *Vampire Nation,* 18–19.

50. Ramsland, *Piercing the Darkness,* 103.

51. Frank Owen, *Clubland: The Fabulous Rise and Murderous Fall of Club Culture* (New York: St. Martin's Press, 2003), 3.

52. Ibid., 145.

53. Ibid., 306.

54. Father Sebastiaan, personal communication, 2008.

55. Mittelbach and Crewdson, *To Die For.*

56. Van Houten, *Vampyre Almanac,* 156.

57. Edwin G. Burrows and Mike Wallace, *Gotham: A History of New York City to 1898* (New York: Oxford University Press, 1999), 417 .

58. Russo, *Vampire Nation,* 24–25.

59. Belanger, *Psychic Vampire Codex,* 21.

60. Father Sebastiaan, personal communication, 2008.

61. Michelle Belanger, "But I Play One on TV," February 28, 2006, http://www.house-eclipse.org/hex/hex_plugins/content/content.php?content.5 (accessed June 28, 2008).

62. Nocturnum, *Embracing the Darkness,* 101.

63. Russo, *Vampire Nation,* 24–25.

64. This term also implies that these individuals are lifestylers and not real vampires.

65. Sahjaza.com, http://www.sahjaza.com/assets/php/main.php?sec=philosophy (accessed June 25, 2008).

66. Belanger, *Psychic Vampire Codex.*

67. Christine Wicker has written on the Open Source Order of the Golden Dawn, a magical group based in the San Francisco area. This group also uses the term "ping" to describe the apprehension of information received from the cosmos during ritual (Christine Wicker, *Not in Kansas Anymore: A Curious Tale of How Magic Is Transforming America* [New York: HarperCollins, 2005], 210).

68. Daemonox, personal communication.

69. Page, *Bloodlust,* 20.

70. Ibid., 205.

71. Ibid., 60.

72. Belanger, *Psychic Vampire Codex,* 67.

73. Mittelbach and Crewdson, *To Die For.*

74. Father Sebastiaan, personal communication, 2008.

75. Ramsland, *Science of Vampires,* 180.

76. SphynxcatVP, "Why We Use the Term Mundane," http://sphynxcatvp.nocturna.org/faq/most-mundane.html (accessed June 1, 2008).

77. Belanger, *Psychic Vampire Codex,* 48.

78. Oliver Krueger, "Methods and Theory for Studying Religion on the Internet," *Heidelberg Journal of Religions on the Internet* 1, no. 1 (2005), http:..www.online.uni-hd.de/ (accessed May 1, 2008).

79. Lupa, *A Field Guide to Otherkin* (Stafford: Megalithica Books, 2007), 168.

80. Ibid., 252.

81. Eyerman and Jamison, *Social Movements,* 119.

82. Wicker, *Not in Kansas Anymore,* 194.

83. Suscitatio Enterprises, LLC, "Vampirism and Energy Research Study," http://www.suscitatio.com (accessed June 1, 2008).

84. John Stoehr, "Vampire's Night Out," *Savannah Morning News,* August 30, 2005.

85. Anonymous, Vox Populi, *Savannah Morning News* (Electronic database, posted September 1, 2005, accessed July 9, 2008).

86. Angie Weathers, "Nauseating Vampire Story Had No Place in Newspaper," *Savannah Morning News* (Electronic database, posted September 4, 2005, accessed July 9, 2008).

87. Daemonox, personal communication.

88. Suscitatio Enterprises, LLC, "Vampirism and Energy Research Study," http://www.suscitatio.com (accessed June 1, 2008).

89. Russo, *Vampire Nation,* 73.

90. Ibid., 105.

91. Russo, *Vampire Nation,* 151–53.

92. Turner himself would probably have described conventions as "liminoid" rather than "liminal."

93. Nocturnum, *Embracing the Darkness,* 93.

94. Endless Night, http://www.endlessnight.com/ (accessed August 26, 2008).

95. Van Houten, *Vampyre Almanac,* 64.

96. Father Sebastiaan, personal communication, 2008.

97. Ibid.

98. The Court of Lazarus, http:www/courtoflazarus.org/ (accessed August 26, 2008).

99. Belanger, *Psychic Vampire Codex,* 31.

100. Michelle Belanger, *The Vampire Ritual Book* (2003), http://www.sacred-texts.com/goth/vrb/index.htm (accessed August 26, 2008).

101. Father Sebastiaan, personal communication, 2008.

102. Michelle Belanger and Chris Miller, "Religious Heritage (Or How We Cannot Escape Our Catholic Roots)," *Shadowdance Podcast,* October 15, 2007, 150–51.

103. House Eclipse, http://www.house-eclipse.org/, (accessed June 1, 2008).

104. Ordo Sekhemu, http://www.ordo-sekhemu.org/ (accessed June 25, 2008).

105. House Dark Haven, http://www.housedarkhaven.com/philosophy.html (accessed June 2, 2008).

106. House Quinotaur, http://www.house-quinotaur.org/ (accessed July 17, 2008).

107. Guinn and Grieser, *Something in the Blood,* 14.

108. Ibid., 19.

109. Sebastiaan, *Saguninomicon-V Edition,* 13.

110. Belanger, *Sacred Hunger,* 24.

111. Matt Cook, *London and the Culture of Homosexual, 1885–1914* (New York: Cambridge University Press, 2003), 32–33.

Chapter 6

1. Stuart, *Stage Blood,* 237.

2. Timothy Miller, "Religious Movements in the United States: An Informal Intro-duction," http://web.archive.org/web/20060827231029/religiousmovements.lib.virginia.edu/essays/miller2003.htm (accessed June 20, 2008). The Immigration and Nationality Act of 1965 abolished national-origin quotas. One result was an infusion of Asian immigrants and Asian religions that had an effect on American culture. It was in this environment that the rhetorical label "cult" began to gain usage in the United States

3. Suscitatio Enterprises, LLC, "Vampirism and Energy Research Study," http://www.suscitatio.com (accessed June 1, 2008).

4. Partridge *Re-Enchantment of the West,* vol. 2, 238.

5. Ibid.

6. Ellis, "Don Henrie."

7. Nocturnum, *Embracing the Darkness,* 122.

8. SphynxcatVP, "Notes for Interviewers," http//sphynxcatvp.nocturna.org/faq/most-interviewnotes.html (accessed June 20, 2008).

9. Belanger, *The Vampire Ritual Book.*

10. Belanger, *Vampires in Their Own Words,* 125–27.

11. Jonathan Z. Smith, "Religion, Religions, Religious" in *Critical Terms for Religious Studies,* ed. Mark C. Taylor (Chicago, University of Chicago Press, 1998), 281.

12. Clifford Geertz, *Islam Observed* (Chicago: University of Chicago Press, 1971), 96.

13. Smith, *Critical Terms for Religious Studies,* 281–82.

14. Randy Cassingham, "The 2002 True Stella Awards Winners," Stella Awards.com, http://www.stellaawards.com/2002.html (accessed June 20, 2008).

15. WiredSaftey, "Racially or Religiously Aggravated Offences," WiredSafety.org, http://www.wiredsafety.org/gb/stalking/racial_religious.html (accessed June 20, 2008).

16. Steward Payne, "Vampire Tells Court He Drank Blood with Friends," *The Telegraph,* October 15, 2003.

17. Stephen Khan, "Celebrity Cult of Vampires Can Turn into Real-Life Evil," *The Guardian,* October 26, 2003.

18. Roberto Cipriani and Laura Ferrarotti, *Sociology of Religion: An Historical Introduction* (Edison: Aldine Transaction, 2000), 1.

19. Temple of the Vampire, http://www.vampiretemple.com (accessed June 1, 2008).

20. Johnson, *Dhampir: Child of the Blood,* 68.

21. Belanger, *Psychic Vampire Codex,* 50.

22. The Vampire-Church, http://www.vampire-church.com/ (accessed October 11, 2008).

23. Guiley, *Vampires Among Us,* 23.

24. Guinn and Grieser, *Something in the Blood,* 35–42.

25. There does exist within Russian Orthodox theology an idea of "sin for the sake of salvation." The Russian Orthodox Church teaches that humanity is fallen and that sin is inevitable. Therefore, admitting one's sins is a necessary step toward redemption. See R. W. Blackmore, trans., *The Doctrine of the Russian Church* (New York: A Brown and Company, 1845), 60. It is possible that Gremlin had some familiarity with the Russian Orthodox view of sin. However, his account of using torture for soteriological purposes has no basis in either the history or the theology of the Russian Orthodox Church.

26. Jones, *The Embrace,* 120.

27. Stuart, *Stage Blood,* 183.

28. Ramsland, *Science of Vampires,* 187.

29. Guinn and Grieser, *Something in the Blood,* 11.

30. Page, *Bloodlust,* 23.

31. Riccardo, *Liquid Dreams of Vampires,* 202.

32. Martin Riccardo, personal communication with the author, June 19, 2008.

33. Eaves, *Modern Vampirism,* 3.

34. William James, *The Varieties of Religious Experience* (New York: Penguin Books, 1985), 28.

35. Ibid., 31.

36. Ibid., 487.

37. House Kheperu, http://www.kheperu.org/ (accessed June 20, 2008).

38. James, *Varieties of Religious Experience,* 512.

39. Andrew R. Fuller, *Psychology and Religion: Eight Points of View* (Lanham: Rowman and Littlefield, 1994), 86–87.

40. James, *Varieties of Religious Experience,* 512.

41. Fuller, *Psychology and Religion,* 86–87.

42. Melton, *Vampire Book,* 550.

43. Belanger, *The Vampire Ritual Book.*

44. Aquino, "The Order of the Vampyre."

45. Fuller, *Psychology and Religion,* 83–84.

46. Ibid, 162.

47. The Temple of Set, "General Information and Admissions Policies," http://www.xeper.org/pub/lib/xp_FS_lib.htm (accessed June 20, 2008).

48. Belanger, *Psychic Vampire Codex,* 273.

49. Sebastiaan, *Saguninomicon-V Edition,* 8.

50. Senf, "Daughters of Lilith," 211.

51. Guinn and Grieser, *Something in the Blood,* 52.

52. Sebastiaan, *Saguninomicon-V Edition,* 11.

53. Belanger, *Psychic Vampire Codex,* 115.

54. Emile Durkheim, *The Elementary Forms of Religious Life,* trans. Karen E. Fields (New York: The Free Press, 1995), 191–92.

55. Ibid., 116.

56. Belanger and Miller, "Religious Heritage."

57. Michelle Belanger and Chris Miller, "Kids, Don't Try This At Home," *Shadowdance Podcast,* January 22, 2008.

58. Ibid.

59. Our Lady of Grace Church and Shrine, http://ologchurchandshrine.org/shrine.asp (accessed June 20, 2008).

60. Gustavo Benavides, "Modernity," in *Critical Terms for Religious Studies,* ed. Mark C. Taylor (Chicago, University of Chicago Press, 1998), 190.

61. Melton, *Vampire Book,* 155.

62. Guiley, *Vampires Among Us,* 86.

63. Katherine Ramsland, *The Vampire Companion: The Official Guide to Anne Rice's The Vampire Chronicles* (New York: Ballantine Books, 1995), 301.

64. Guinn and Grieser, *Something in the Blood,* 29.

65. Guiley, *Vampires Among Us,* 72.

66. Cohen, *Science and the Founding Fathers,* 27–56.

67. Ibid.

68. Wade Clark Roof, *Spiritual Marketplace: Baby Boomers and the Remaking of American Religion* (Princeton: Princeton University Press, 1999), 195.

69. Guinn and Grieser, *Something in the Blood,* 40.

Chapter 7

1. David Keyworth. "The Socio-Religious Beliefs and Nature of the Contemporary Vampire Subculture," *Journal of Contemporary Religion* 17, no. 3 (2002): 356.

2. Belanger, *Sacred Hunger,* 116.

3. Kaplan and Kane, *Vampires Are,* 50.

4. Thorne, *Children of the Night,* 26–27.

5. Jill Morley, "Missing Girl," *New York Press,* April 29, 2001.

6. Guiley, *Vampires Among Us,* 104.

7. Bill Ellis, *Raising the Devil: Satanism, New Religions, and the Media* (Lexington: The University Press of Kentucky, 2000), 220.

8. Ibid., 221.

9. Guiley, *Vampires Among Us,* 103–111.

10. Russo, *Vampire Nation,* 55.

11. Ibid., 123–25.

12. Ellis, *Raising the Devil,* 207.

13. Robert D. Hicks, "The Police Model of Satanism Crime," in *The Satanism Scare,* ed. James T. Richardson, Joel Best, and David G. Bromley (New York: Aldine De Groyter, 1991), 183.

14. Ibid., 175.

15. Ibid., 183.

16. Guiley, *Vampires Among Us,* 91.

17. Peter H. Gilmore, "LaVey, Anton Szandor" in *Satanism Today: An Encyclopedia of Religion, Folklore, and Popular Culture,* ed. James R. Lewis (Santa Barbara: ABC-CLIO, 2001), 145.

18. Ibid., 181.

19. Dawn Perlmutter, "The Forensics of Sacrifice: A Symbolic Analysis of Ritualistic Crime" [Electronic version]. *Anthropetics,* 9, no. 2 (2004), http://www.anthropoetics.ucla.edu/ap0902/sacrifice.htm.

20. Schlegal, "Spiritual Sleuth Studies Violent Religions."

21. Katherine Ramsland, "Vampires as Victims," *The Vampire Killers: Murderers Who Were Inspired by a Lust for Blood,* TruTV.com, http://www.trutv.com/library/crime/serial_killers/weird/vampires/14.html (accessed July 17, 2008).

22. Katherine Ramsland, "A Most Vicious Vampire," *The Vampire Killers: Murderers Who Were Inspired by a Lust for Blood,* TruTV.com, http://www.trutv.com/library/crime/serial_killers/weird/vampires/11.html (accessed July 17, 2008).

23. Melton, *Vampire Book,* 318.

24. Ramsland, *Science of Vampires,* 109–10.

25. Ibid.

26. " 'Vampire' Murder Police Praised," BBC News.com International Version, May 31, 2003, http://news.bbc.co.uk/2/hi/uk_news/wales/north_west/2949530.stm (accessed July 19, 2008).

27. Ibid., 121–22.

28. BBC online news, "Satanists Killed Man on the Devil's Orders," http://news.bbc.co.uk/2/hi/europe/1767939.stm (accessed July 19, 2008).

29. Ibid., 121–22.

30. Russo, *Vampire Nation,* 58.

31. Lupa, *A Field Guide to Otherkin,* 251.

32. Jones, *The Embrace,* 307.

33. Ibid., 192.

34. Ibid., 381.

35. Ibid, 332–33.

36. Ibid., 383.

37. Ibid., 84.

38. Ibid., 331.

39. Ibid., 133.

40. Ibid., 369.

41. Day, *Vampire Legends,* 153.

42. Clifford L. Linedecker, *The Vampire Killers: A Horrifying True Story of Bloodshed and Murder* (New York: St. Martin's Press, 1998), 36.

43. Jones, *The Embrace,* 356.

44. Ibid., 305.

45. Ibid., 285.

46. Ibid., 300–1.

47. Ibid., 130.

48. Ibid., 249.

49. Simon, *The Necronomicon* (New York: Avon Books, 1980), xlix.

50. Melanie Yarrow, "Vampires, Astral Entities and Akhkharu," in *The Midnight Sun* 1, no. 8 (1996): 7.

51. Ron Popeski, "Members of 'Vampire Clan' Arrested in Louisiana," *Reuters,* (November 29, 1996).

52. Thorne, *Children of the Night,* 176.

53. Jones, *The Embrace,* 355.

54. Robert A. Orsi, *Between Heaven and Earth: The Religious Worlds People Make and the Scholars Who Study Them* (Princeton: Princeton University Press, 2005), 6–7.

55. Russo, *Vampire Nation,* 192.

56. "Angelina Jolie Played with Knives in Bed," OneIndia.com, http://entertainment .oneindia.in/hollywood/top-stories/scoop/2008/angelina-jolie-play-with-knives-190608.html (accessed July 18, 2008).

57. "Angenlina Jolie on the Blood Vial, Buying Gifts and Pregnant Sex: It's Great!" Huffingtonpost, http://www.huffingtonpost.com/2008/06/11/angelina-jolie-on-the -blo_n_106619.html (accessed July 18, 2008).

58. Page, *Bloodlust,* 194.

59. "Intervyew with the Vampyre," Citypages.com, January 17, 2006, http://blogs .citypages.com/blotter/2006/01/intervyew_with_the_vampyre.php (accessed July 18, 2008).

60. Nocturnum, *Embracing the Darkness,* 221.

61. DACA, "Darkness Against Child Abuse," http://www.magickalshadow.com/daca/ index2.html (accessed July 18, 2008).

Chapter 8

1. Anthony Giddens and Christopher Pierson, *Conversations with Anthony Giddens, Making Sense of Modernity* (Stanford: Stanford University Press, 1998), 18–19.

2. Peter Berger, "Identity As a Problem in the Socoiology of Knowledge," in *The Sociology of Knowledge,* ed. James E. Curtis and John W. Petras (New York: Praeger Publishers, 1970), 375.

3. Wicker, *Not in Kansas Anymore,* 12.

4. Rich Schull, *Autism Pre Rain Man: Pre Rain Man Autism* (New York: iUniverse, 2003), 5.

5. Ibid., 6.

6. Lupa, *A Field Guide to Otherkin,* 83.

7. The Associated Press, "Call it a Vampire Law," http://www.ijmc.com/archives/ 1999/August/04August1999.html (accessed August 26, 2008).

8. Ramsland, *Science of Vampires,* 200.

9. Lady CG, personal communication with the author, July 26, 2008.

10. Lady CG, "Raising a Crop O' Vampires (Or HELP! My Teenager Wants to Eat the Dog!)," http://www.sanguinarius.org/parents/CG_raising_vampyres.shtml (accessed August 1, 2008).

Bibliography

Abbot, Stacey. *Celluloid Vampires: Life after Death in the Modern World.* Austin: University of Texas Press, 2007.

Albanese, Catherine L. *A Republic of Mind and Spirit: A Cultural History of American Metaphysical Religion.* New Haven: Yale University Press, 2007.

The American Psychiatric Association. *The Diagnostic and Statistical Manual of Mental Disorders: DSM-IV-TR.* Arlington: American Psychiatric Association, 2000.

Anonymous. "From Dusk 'Til Dawn—Don't Give up the Day Job." *Midnight Sun* 1, no. 5 (1996).

Bane, Theresa. *Actual Factual: Dracula, a Compendium of Vampires.* Randleman: Ne Deo Press, 1997.

Barber, Paul. *Vampires, Burial, and Death.* New Haven: Yale University Press, 1988.

Barker, Chris, and Paul Willis. *Cultural Studies: Theory and Practice.* Los Angeles: Sage Publications, 2003.

Belanger, Michelle. "Living Vampires in Romania." *Midnight Sun* 1, no. 2 (1996).

———. *The Psychic Vampire Codex.* Boston: Weiser Books, 2004.

———. *Sacred Hunger.* Fort Wayne: Dark Moon Press, 2005.

———, ed. *Vampires in Their Own Words: An Anthology of Vampire Voices.* Woodbury: Llewellyn, 2007.

Bellah, Robert, Richard Madsen, William Sullivan, Ann Swidler, and Steven M. Tipton. *Habits of the Heart.* Berkeley: University of California Press, 1985.

Berger, Peter. "Identity as a Problem in the Sociology of Knowledge." In *The Sociology of Knowledge,* edited by James E. Curtis and John W. Petras, 373–86. New York: Praeger Publishers, 1970.

Blackstock, Sebastian Cade. "Suspension of Disbelief." *Journal of the Dark* no. 2 (Spring 1995): 26.

Blavatsky, Helena Petrovna. *Isis Unveiled.* Point Loma: Aryan Theosophical Press, 1919.

———. *Studies in Occultism, No II.* Boston: New England Theosophical Corporation, 1895.

Bloom, Harold. *The American Religion.* New York: Simon and Schuster, 1992.

Brooks, Douglas Renfrew. *The Secret of the Three Cities: An Introduction to Hindu Shakta Tantrism.* Chicago, University of Chicago Press, 1990.

Burrows, Edwin G., and Mike Wallace. *Gotham: A History of New York City to 1898.* New York: Oxford University Press, 1999.

Calmet, Dom Augustine. *The Phantom World; or, The Philosophy of Spirits, Apparitions.* Translated by Henry Christmas. London: Richard Bentley, 1850.

CG, Lady. *Practical Vampyrism for Modern Vampyres.* LuLu, 2005.

Cipriani, Roberto, and Laura Ferrarotti. *Sociology of Religion: An Historical Introduction.* Edison: Aldine Transaction, 2000.

Clark, Lynn Schofield. *From Angels to Aliens: Teenagers, the Media, and the Supernatural.* Oxford: Oxford University Press, 2003.

Clute, John, and John Grant. *The Encyclopedia of Fantasy.* London: St. Martin's Griffin, 1999.

Cohen, I. Bernard. *Science and the Founding Fathers.* New York: W.W. Norton and Company, 1995.

Cook, Matt. *London and the Culture of Homosexual, 1885–1914.* New York: Cambridge University Press, 2003.

Crow, Martha Rose. "Are Vampire Capitalists About to Descend on Crisis Wrought Myanmar?" *Atlantic Free Press,* May 9, 2008.

Curan, Bob. *Encyclopedia of The Undead: A Field Guide to Creatures That Cannot Rest in Peace.* Franklin Lakes: Career Press, 2006.

Day, William Patrick. *Vampire Legends in Contemporary American Culture.* Lexington: The University Press of Kentucky, 2002.

Dillon, Michelle, ed. *Handbook of the Sociology of Religion.* Cambridge: Cambridge University Press, 2003.

Dowd, Maureen. "Desperately Seeking Street Cred," *New York Times* (April 27, 2008), Opinion section.

Dresser, Norine. *American Vampires: Fans, Victims, Practitioners.* New York: Vintage Books, 1989.

Dundes, Alan, ed. *The Vampire: A Casebook.* Madison: The University of Wisconsin Press, 1998.

Durkheim, Emile. *The Elementary Forms of Religious Life.* Translated by Karen E. Fields. New York: The Free Press, 1995.

Eaves, Albert Osborne. *Modern Vampirism: Its Dangers and How to Avoid Them.* Harrogate: Talisman Publishing, 1904.

Eliade, Mircea. *Shamanism: Archaic Techniques of Ecstasy.* Princeton: Princeton University Press, 1964.

Ellis, Bill. *Raising the Devil: Satanism, New Religions, and the Media.* Lexington: The University Press of Kentucky, 2000.

Eyerman, Ron, and Andrew Jamison. *Social Movements: A Cognitive Approach.* University Park: Pennsylvania State University Press, 1991.

Fanger, Claire. "Mirror, Mask and Anti-Self: Forces of Literary Creation in Dion Fortune and W. B. Yeats." In *Esotericism, Art, and Imagination,* edited by Arthur Versluis et al., 161–84. East Lansing: Michigan State University Press, 2008.

Feuerstein, Georg. *Tantra: The Path of Ecstasy.* Boston: Shambala, 1998.

Florescu, Radu, and Raymond T. McNally. *Dracula: A Biography of Vlad the Impaler, 1431–1476.* New York: Hawthorn Books, 1973.

Flynn, John L. *Cinematic Vampires: The Living Dead of Film and Television.* Jefferson: McFarland and Company, Inc., 1992.

Fortune, Dion. *Psychic Self-Defense.* York Beach: Samuel Weiser, Inc., 1997.

Foucault, Michele, Martin, Luther H., and Hutton, Patrick, H. *Technologies of the Self: A Seminar with Michel Foucault.* Amherst: University of Massachusetts Press, 1988.

Frost, Brian J. *The Monster with a Thousand Faces: Guises of the Vampire in Myth and Literature.* Bowling Green: Bowling Green State University Popular Press, 1989.

Fuller, Andrew R. *Psychology and Religion: Eight Points of View.* Lanham: Rowman and Littlefield, 1994.

Geertz, Clifford. *Islam Observed.* Chicago: University of Chicago Press, 1971.

Gerard, Emily de Laszowska. "Transylvanian Superstitions." In *The Nineteenth Century: A Monthly Review, Vol. 18,* edited by James Knowles, 130–50. London: Kegan Paul, Trench, & Co., 1885.

Giddens, Anthony. *Modernity and Self-Identity: Self and Society in the Late Modern Age.* Stanford: Stanford University Press, 1991.

Giddens, Anthony, and Christopher Pierson. *Conversations with Anthony Giddens, Making Sense of Modernity.* Stanford: Stanford University Press, 1998.

Gilmore, Peter H. "LaVey, Anton Szandor." In *Satanism Today: An Encyclopedia of Religion, Folklore, and Popular Culture,* edited by James R. Lewis, 144–47. Santa Barbara: ABC-CLIO, 2001.

Greer, Mary K. *Women of the Golden Dawn: Rebels and Priestesses.* Rochester: Park Street Press, 1995.

Guiley, Rosemary Ellen. *The Complete Vampire Companion.* New York: Macmillan, 1994.

———. *Vampires Among Us.* New York: Pocket Books, 1991.

Guinn, Jeff, and Andy Grieser. *Something in the Blood: The Underground World of Today's Vampires.* Arlington: The Summit Publishing Group. 1996.

Gutman, Amy. *Identity in Democracy.* Princeton: Princeton University Press, 2003.

Hacking, Ian. "Making up People." In *Reconstructing Individuality: Autonomy, Individuality, and the Self in Western Thought,* edited by Thomas C. Heller, Morton Sosna, and Daved E Wellbey. Stanford: Stanford University Press, 1986.

Haining, Peter. *The Dracula Scrapbook.* London: Chancellor Press, 1992.

Hardman, Charlotte, and Graham Harvey, ed. *Paganism Today.* San Francisco: Thorsons, 1996.

Harvey, Graham. *Contemporary Paganism: Listening People, Speaking Earth.* New York: New York University Press, 1997.

Heelas, Paul, and Linda Woodhead. *The Spiritual Revolution: Why Religion Is Giving Way to Spirituality.* Malden: Blackwell Publishing, 2005.

Hines, Terence. *Pseudoscience and the Paranormal.* Amherst: Prometheus Books, 2003.

Hopkins, Jerry, and Danny Sugerman. *No One Here Gets Out Alive.* New York: Grand Central Publishing, 1995.

James, William. *The Principles of Psychology.* New York: Dover Publications, 1950.

———. *The Varieties of Religious Experience.* New York: Penguin Books, 1985.

Johnson, V. M. *Dhampir: Child of the Blood.* Fairfield: Mystic Rose Books, 1996.

Jones, Aphrodite. *The Embrace.* New York: Pocket Books, 1999.

Kamara. "Inside the Life of a Real Vampire." *Journal of the Dark* no. 7 (1996): 44–45.

Kaplan, Jeffrey, and Helene Loow. *The Cultic Milieu: Oppositional Subcultures in an Age of Globalization.* Oxford: AltaMira Press, 2002.

Kaplan, Stephen, and Carol Kane. *Vampires Are.* Palm Springs: ETC Publications, 1984.

Keyworth, David. "The Socio-Religious Beliefs and Nature of the Contemporary Vampire Subculture." *Journal of Contemporary Religion* 17, no. 3 (2002): 355–70.

Khan, Stephen. "Celebrity Cult of Vampires Can Turn Into Real-Life Evil." *The Guardian,* October 26, 2003.

Konstantinos. *Vampires: The Occult Truth.* St. Paul: Llewellyn, 1998.

Krueger, Oliver. "Methods and Theory for Studying Religion on the Internet." *Heidelberg Journal of Religions on the Internet* 1, no. 1 (2005): http://www.online.uni-hd.de/.

Laderman, Gary. *The Sacred Remains: American Attitudes Toward Death.* New Haven: Yale University Press, 1996.

Lasch, Christopher. "From the Culture of Narcissism." In *The Eighties: A Reader,* edited by Gilbert T. Sewall, 3–10. New York: Perseus Books, 1998.

LaVey, Anton Szandor. *The Satanic Bible.* New York: Avon Books, 1976.

Leadbeater, Charles W. *The Astral Plane: Its Scenery, Habits, and Phenomena.* New York: Cosimo, Inc., 1995.

Levi, Eliphaz. *Dogma et Ritual de la Haute Magie.* Translated by A. E. Waite. London: Rider and Company, 1896.

Linedecker, Clifford L. *The Vampire Killers: A Horrifying True Story of Bloodshed and Murder.* New York: St. Martin's Press, 1998.

Lotringer, Sylvere. *Overexposed: Treating Sexual Perversion in America.* New York: Pantheon, 1988.

Lupa. *A Field Guide to Otherkin.* Stafford: Megalithica Books, 2007.

Marovitz, Sanford E. "Poe's Reception of C. W. Webber's Gothic Western, 'Jack Long; or, The Shot in the Eye'," *Poe Studies* 4, no. 1 (1971): 11–13.

Martin, Luther H., Huck Gutman, and Patrick H. Hutton, ed. *Technologies of the Self: A Seminar with Michel Foucault.* Boston: University of Massachusetts Press, 1988.

McClelland, Bruce A. *Slayers and Their Vampires.* Ann Arbor: University of Michigan Press, 2006.

McDonald, Beth E. *The Vampire as a Numinous Experience: Spiritual Journeys with the Undead in British and American Literature.* Jefferson: McFarland and Company, 2004.

Melton, J. Gordon. *The Vampire Book: The Encyclopedia of the Undead.* Detroit: Visible Ink Press, 1999.

Mittelbach, Margaret, and Michael Crewdson. "To Die For: Painting the Town Red and the Capes and Nails Black." *New York Times,* November 24, 2000, Movies section.

Morley, Jill. "Missing Girl" *The New York Press,* April 29, 2001.

Morris, Glenn T. *Path Notes of an American Ninja Master.* Berkeley: North Atlantic Books, 1993.

Nocturnum, Corvis. *Embracing the Darkness: Understanding Dark Subcultures.* Fort Wayne: Dark Moon Press, 2005.

Noll, Richard. *Bizarre Diseases of the Mind.* New York: Berkley Books, 1990.

Nuzum, Eric. *The Dead Travel Fast: Stalking Vampires from Nosferatu to Count Chocula.* New York: Macmillan, 2007.

Olcott, Henry Steel. "The Vampire." In *The Theosophist: October 1890–April 1891,* edited by Henry Steel Olcott, 385–93. Whitefish: Kessinger Publishing, 2004.

Oliphant, Laurence. *Scientific Religion or Higher Possibilities of Life and Practice Through The Operation of Natural Forces.* London: William Blackwood and Sons, 1888.

Orsi, Robert A. *Between Heaven and Earth: The Religious Worlds People Make and the Scholars Who Study Them.* Princeton: Princeton University Press, 2005.

Overstreet, Deborah Wilson. *Not Your Mother's Vampire: Vampires in Young Adult Fiction.* Lanham: The Scarecrow Press, Inc., 2006.

Owen, Alex. *The Place of Enchantment: British Occultism and the Culture of the Modern.* Chicago: University of Chicago Press, 2004.

Owen, Frank. *Clubland: The Fabulous Rise and Murderous Fall of Club Culture.* New York: St. Martin's Press, 2003.

Page, Carol. *Bloodlust: Conversations with Real Vampires.* New York: Dell, 1991.

Palmer, David. *Qigong Fever: Body, Science, and Utopia in China.* New York: Columbia University Press, 2007.

Pamela. "Vampire? Fake! The Story of Vincent Tremaine." *Journal of the Dark* no. 1 (1994): 21–23.

Partridge, Christopher. *The Re-Enchantment of the West.* Vol. I. London: T&T Clark International, 2004.

Partridge, Christopher. *The Re-Enchantment of the West.* Vol. II. London: T&T Clark International, 2005.

———. "The Temple of the Vampire." In *New Religions: A Guide,* edited by Christopher Partridge, 353–54. New York: Oxford University Press, 2004.

Payne, Stewart. "Vampire Tells Court He Drank Blood with Friends," *The Telegraph,* October 15, 2003.

Perkowski, Jan L. *The Darkling: A Treatise on Slavic Vampirism.* Columbus: Slavica Publishers Inc., 1989.

Perlmutter, Dawn. "The Forensics of Sacrifice: A Symbolic Analysis of Ritualistic Crime" (Electronic version). *Anthropetics* 9, no. 2 (2004): http://www.anthropoetics.ucla.edu/ap0902/sacrifice.htm.

———. "The Sacrificial Aesthetic: Blood Rituals from Art to Murder." *Anthropetics* 5, no. 2 (2000): http://www.anthropoetics.ucla.edu/ap0902/sacrifice.htm.

———. "Vampire Culture." In *Religion and American Cultures: An Encyclopedia of Traditions, Diversity, and Popular Expressions,* edited by Gary Laderman, 279–83. Santa Barbara: ABC-CLIO, 2003.

Peterson, Mark Allen. "Consuming Youth: Vampires, Cyborgs, and the Culture of Consumption (review)." *Journal of American Folklore* 117, no. 464 (2004): 215–16.

Piérart, Z. J. *Review Spiritualiste.* Paris: Bureaux, 1861.

Popeski, Ron. "Members of 'Vampire Clan' Arrested in Louisiana." *Reuters,* November 29, 1996.

Radcliffe, Ann. *The Italian.* Oxford: Oxford University Press, 1981. First published 1796.

Ramsland, Katherine. *Piercing the Darkness: Undercover with Vampires in America Today.* New York: HarperPrism, 1998.

———. *The Science of Vampires.* New York: Berkley Boulevard Books, 2002.

———. *The Vampire Companion: The Official Guide to Anne Rice's The Vampire Chronicles.* New York: Ballantine Books, 1995.

Riccardo, Martin V. *Liquid Dreams of Vampires.* St. Paul: Llewellyn, 1996.

Rice, Anne. *Interview with the Vampire.* New York: Ballantine Books, 1976.

Richardson, James T., Joel Best, and David G. Bromley, ed. *The Satanism Scare.* New York: Aldine De Groyter, 1991.

Roof, Wade Clark. *Spiritual Marketplace: Baby Boomers and the Remaking of American Religion.* Princeton: Princeton University Press, 1999.

Russo, Arlene. *Vampire Nation* (uncorrected proof edition) Woodbury: Llewellyn, 2008.

The Sanguinarium. *The Scroll of Elorath.* Lulu, 2007.

Schlegel, Sharon. "Spiritual Sleuth Studies Violent Religions to Fight Crime." *Baptist Standard,* November 7, 2003.

Schull, Rich. *Autism Pre Rain Man: Pre Rain Man Autism.* New York: iUniverse, 2003.

Sebastiaan, Father. *The Sanguinomicon: Book III, Liber Calmae.* Limited 666 edition. New York: Rakasha Books, 2004.

———. *Sanguinomicon-V Edition.* Netherlands: The Sanguinarium, 2007.

Senf, Carol A. "Daughters of Lilith: Women Vampires in Popular Literature." In *The Blood is the Life: Vampires in Literature,* edited by Leonard G. Hildreth and Mary Pharr, 199–216. Bowling Green: Bowling Green State University Popular Press, 1999.

Shinobi, Frater. "Of the Undead/Vampyre Order." *Midnight Sun* 1, no. 5 (1996): 4.

———. "Vampire/Lycanthrope: As Above, So Below." *Midnight Sun* 1, no. 1 (1995): 6.

Silver-Isenstadt, Jean L. *Shameless: The Visionary Life of Mary Grove Nichols.* Baltimore: The Johns Hopkins University Press, 2002.

Simon. *The Necronomicon.* New York: Avon Books, 1980.

Steinberg, Neil. "Out of Time, Nearly: Feast of Fools." *Chicago Sun-Times,* August 15, 2007.

Stoehr, John. "Vampire's Night Out." *Savannah Morning News,* August 30, 2005.

Stoehr, Taylor. *Hawthorne's Mad Scientists: Pseudoscience and Social Science in Nineteenth Century Life and Letters.* Hamden: Archon Books, 1978.

Stoker, Bram. *Dracula.* New York: Scholastic Inc., 1999. First published 1897.

Stuart, Roxana. *Stage Blood: Vampires of the 19th Century Stage.* Bowling Green: Bowling Green State University Popular Press, 1994.

Summers, Montague. *The Vampire.* New York: Dorset Press, 1991.

———. *Werewolf.* Whitefish: Kessington Publishing, 2003.

Swidler, Ann. "Culture in Action: Symbols and Strategies." *American Sociological Review* 51 (1986): 27386.

Taylor, Mark C., ed. *Critical Terms for Religious Studies.* Chicago: University of Chicago Press, 1998.

Thompson, Clay. "Slaying Vampire Energy Is Easy—Just Unplug Idle Appliances." *The Arizona Republic* June 29, 2008.

Thorne, Tony. *Children of the Night: Of Vampires and Vampirism.* London: Indigo, 1999.

Van Houten, Sebastiaan. *Vampyre Almanac 2006.* New York: Rakasha Books, 2005.

Walter, Tony, and Helen Waterhouse. "A Very Private Belief: Reincarnation in Contemporary England." *Sociology of Religion* 60, no. 2 (1999): 187–97.

Webber, Charles W. *Yieger's Cabinet: Spiritual Vampirism: The History of Etherial Softdown and her New Friends of the "Inner Light."* Philadelphia: Lippincott, Grambo, and Co., 1853.

Weber, Max. *From Max Weber, Essays in Sociology,* edited by Hans H. Gerth and C. Wright Mills. New York: Oxford University Press, 1958.

Wicker, Christine. *Not in Kansas Anymore: A Curious Tale of How Magic Is Transforming America.* New York: HarperCollins, 2005.

Wilcox, Rhonda V., and David Lavery, ed. *Fighting the Forces: What's at Stake in Buffy the Vampire Slayer.* New York: Rowman and Littlefield Publishers, 2002.

Yarrow, Melanie. "Vampires, Astral Entities and Akhkharu." *The Midnight Sun* 1, no. 8 (1996): 7.

Index

About the Author

JOSEPH LAYCOCK is an independent scholar and recipient of a grant from the Pluralism Project.